D0745610

THE
BACON
BIBLE

PETER SHERMAN
with STEPHANIE BANYAS

photographs by CAROL LEE

Abrams, New York

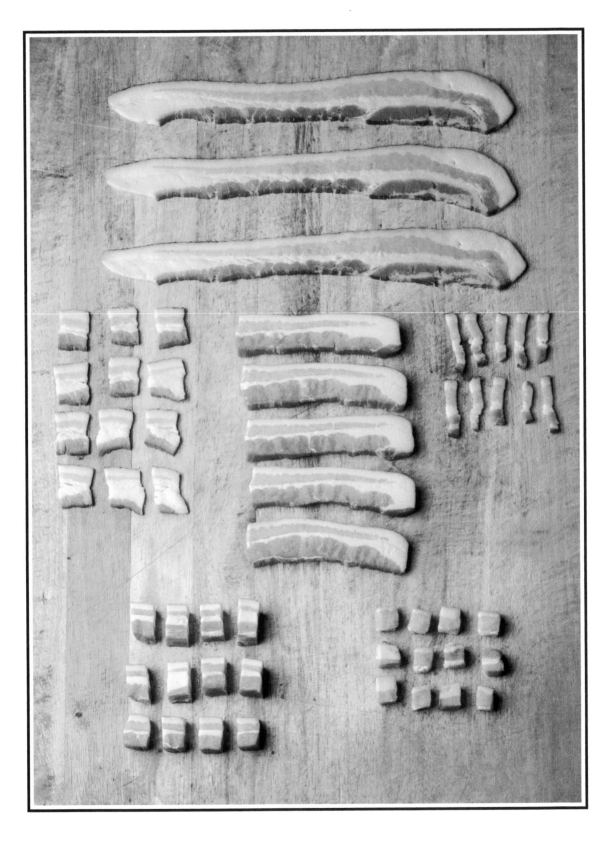

CONTENTS

INTRODUCTION

**IN IS IN, GASTRONOMICALLY SPEAKING.** Bacon, a savory workhorse ingredient that lends an underpinning of hauntingly rich and complex flavor to a dish, frequently without celebration or menu credit, is now finally having its heyday. Bacon Mania has officially taken over the entire country. It's a national obsession continuously being embraced by devotees in each new generation. What was once strictly a breakfast staple has now been injected into all food forms and multiple non-food retail outlets. Basically it sells everything it touches.

A few years ago, I had the crazy idea that bacon not only deserved to star in a few dishes; it deserved to star in a restaurant. And so BarBacon, my ode to one of America's greatest indulgences, was born. More than a few people were not too shy to tell me how nutty it sounded: A restaurant devoted to bacon was indeed crazy—and in New York City of all places. Rent alone was going to be at least $150 per square foot, so I was truly going to have to bring home the bacon.

Needless to say, I was nervous. I understood the classics. Hell, I worked my ass off and paid my dues in culinary school and up through the best of the French restaurants, culminating under Joël Robuchon. I learned what great food looks and tastes like and, perhaps more important, the painstaking effort it takes to make a truly amazing meal. Now, I was tasked to do the same, to create the same reaction, but instead of the whole of French cuisine to work from I had just one central ingredient: bacon.

Given my background working in restaurants of the highest caliber, my friends always found it peculiar that my biggest food craving was bacon, and not a well-marbled steak or freshly caught tuna. Nope, after a nightmare of a shift coming home at 4 AM starving, bacon has always been my go-to. It's been consistently delicious and unfailing in its ability to be exactly what I wanted when I wanted it. Now it's the food I crave when I wake up with my kids on weekends and want to make them something I love. It's the perfect food to me—no matter the time, the circumstance, or the weather.

I'm not sure why it took me so long to embrace it, but I have to share the gospel and enrich others as if I have been awoken to the intoxicating aroma of bacon seemingly for the first time. My vision for BarBacon was to enlighten people to this knowledge: that we make the very best bacon in the world and that you always lead with your best. No more bacon as an extra. As a side. Bacon is the star, the lead character. And that brings us to this book, *The Bacon Bible*. I needed to write this book because I realize that not everyone can visit New York or my restaurant, but that shouldn't mean that you should miss out on all of the fun and, most important, the great food. The great food that centers all around one ingredient, one incredibly delicious ingredient that, for far too long, was not given the starring role that it deserves. Bacon is ready for its close-up.

When I first opened the restaurant, bacon meant simply pork belly that had been cured and smoked. End of story. Well . . . that's actually not the end of this story. I realized early on that "bacon" was used to describe a number of dishes, some of which I wholly disagree with. While American bacon comes from pork belly, Canadian bacon comes from the loin, and European bacon from the shoulder; there is turkey bacon and lamb bacon and veggie bacon. If all of these are bacon, what defines bacon?

Defining what constitutes bacon is surprisingly difficult. Most of us would define bacon as cured smoked pork belly, but a quick trip to the grocery store proves otherwise, with shelves lined with a vast array of non-pork "bacon" options. Everything from turkey to lamb to beef has been cured and smoked and ultimately presented to the public as bacon. There is veggie bacon and vegan bacon, and for the most part, the public has accepted these inclusions. I am not so accepting. While I'm okay with including animals beyond pig, I can't bring myself to include variations with no actual animal present. So, for the purpose of this book, and perhaps life in general, I present this simple but clear definition: *Bacon: Smoked cured meat from a single cut of an animal.*

I debated expanding on this, but regressed because bacon is about simplicity and an homage to a now-ancient process that has sustained civilizations and withstood the test of time. In other words: If it ain't broke, don't fix it.

Today, bacon is a $4 billion dollar business and growing. As I write this book, we are in the midst of a bacon drought. The millions of pounds of bacon the meat packers freeze have all but run out. A serious concern, particularly for a chef that literally can't cook without it. But while the market corrects itself and the pundits claim bacon is trending again, as if it ever stopped, bacon will continue to evolve—not in its method of preparation, but in the flavors and variations on offer. Bacon has a place in almost every cuisine. I have tried Cajun and maple bacon, corn cob–smoked and apple cider–flavored, just to name a few. There are hundreds more variations. It is bacon's simplicity that allows for such an array of flavors; all it takes is some time, a smoker, and an imagination.

BarBacon's menu started by introducing better bacon to the classics we are all familiar with, like BLTs and wedge salads. These recipes were my foundation for growth, but they can't fill an entire menu, so bacon needed to evolve. It needed to be cooked in different ways and flavored with much more than just salt and smoke. I started exploring the potential of this workhorse ingredient: What if I played with new meats? What if I cured tuna and smoked that? What if I started with traditional pork bacon, but infused it with chipotle? Luckily, you'll find out.

This book is your bible. It will teach you everything you need to know about bacon. First, I'll teach you how to cure perfect, simple bacon from scratch, and then how to mix things up with some of my favorite seasonings, like soy and ginger, jerk, and maple, just to get your mouth watering. Once I've taught you how to make traditional pork bacon, I'll help you expand your repertoire with new meats. I'll take you through the steps to make Korean beef bacon bulgogi and a loaded tuna bacon New York–style bagel.

As much fun as it is to make your own bacon, you'll see that it takes time and a bit of patience. I'll get you off the hook by introducing you to a few of my favorite purveyors and will show you how to use their products beautifully. We'll go over every way you could possibly cook a simple piece of bacon.

Bacon always extended itself beyond breakfast for me, and this book teaches you how to think about bacon differently. It obviously belongs on the breakfast table, but sometimes it needs to be caramelized and layered in a bacon biscuit. I'll also show you how it's equally appropriate on the dinner table. You'll learn how to make the classics that I've spent years perfecting, like bacon cassoulet, Kentucky Fried Bacon Banh Mi, and Cobb salad, and recipes that needed just a bit of bacon kick—bacon baked beans, bacon macaroni and cheese, and Bacon Chili. Once I have gained your confidence, I will let you in my head. (Full disclosure: Things start to get weird.) We use classic forms of bacon and turn them on their heads, making dishes like bacon tempura and bacon dashi.

As appealing as bacon on bacon is, you may need to give your arteries a rest for a few pages. I guess you could say we're holding the bacon. Here I'll let you play with recipes I love to pair with bacon: sharp pickles, briny vinaigrettes, creamy slaws, you name it. These are all the perfect dishes to serve with your bacon masterpieces when friends come over. Some of them are entirely bacon free—uncharacteristic, I know. Some are sprinkled with bacon fat or infused with it. Homemade biscuits are amped up with leftover bacon fat, and countless other creations are brought to new heights with the addition of bacon and its renderings. A Bloody Mary to go with brunch? Fifthgear that, add the bacon infused vodka . . . Go whole-hog or go home!

Finally, we'll tackle dessert, adding just a hint of bacon's salty flavor to all of my favorite dishes. I love dessert and I know how important it is as the last impression you have of a

meal. Thankfully, bacon seamlessly takes to sweets: Smoked Chocolate Tart with Hazelnut Crust and Chocolate Glaze, Chocolate-Covered Bacon with pink peppercorns and smoked salt, Dulce de Leche Bars with Bacon-Pecan Shortbread Crust, and more. My French chef mentors, I'm sure, would never have taken me under their wing had they known I'd be using their pate a choux recipe for churros rolled in bacon sugar.

So here I am, living in the world of bacon and sharing it with you. I know what you're saying. You're saying it's been done, thinking about those other bacon cookbooks, rolling your eyes at the idea of yet another BLT. But we just trashed that BLT. This isn't an ordinary sandwich anymore, and in this book, bacon is not just a side to order for a little pleasure. This book acknowledges that bacon is not just a guilty pleasure; it is a requirement for your lifestyle. It is an indulgence, for sure, but a necessary one, and if you must indulge—and you *must*—you want to make sure you're getting the best. Bacon makes everything better, and good bacon can always become extraordinary.

Chef Peter Sherman
New York City

BARBACON PANTRY

A WELL-STOCKED PANTRY IS THE BEST WAY TO ENSURE YOU'LL HAVE EVERY-thing you need to cook from this book. These are the ingredients that I always have in my restaurant and at home, in addition to the common ingredients such as kosher salt, pepper, sugars, baking powder, and baking soda. The ingredients included below are those things that my cooking can't live without. Most can be found in grocery and specialty stores, and all of them can be found online.

All-purpose flour
King Arthur brand

Ancho chile powder

Bourbon

Canola oil

Chipotle chile powder

Chipotles in adobo puree
To make, empty the can of chipotle into a blender. Fill the can halfway with water, add to the blender, and blend until smooth. Scrape the puree into a bowl with a lid and store in the refrigerator for up to 1 month.

Clover honey

Dijon and whole-grain mustard
Grey Poupon brand

Extra-virgin olive oil

Frank's Red Hot sauce

Good-quality bittersweet, semisweet, and milk chocolate
Ghirardelli or Callebaut brand

Liquid smoke
Stubb's BBQ brand

Low-sodium soy sauce
Kikkoman brand

Maple syrup
pure dark amber

Molasses

Panko bread crumbs

Phosphates
These are used in a wide range of processed meat, poultry, and seafood. They're important because they help improve the retention of natural liquids, as well as brines and cures, in the animal muscle that would otherwise be lost in the cooking process. They basically assure that you'll end up with a juicy final product. I prefer Butchers BBQ brand.

Pink salt (also known as curing salt) aka Instacure #1

Pure almond extract

Pure vanilla extract

Sambal oelek

Sherry

Sriracha

Sweet chili sauce
Mae Ploy brand

Tabasco sauce

Toasted sesame oil

Vinegars
rice, apple cider, aged sherry, champagne, distilled white

Wood chips
Needed for smoking bacon. I recommend having an assortment of woods such as apple, mesquite, and cherry. Chips need to be soaked for at least 30 minutes before using. I always have a container of chips soaking in the restaurant and in my garage at home.

Worcestershire sauce

CHAPTER 1

BACON

**SUALLY BACON IS JUST SOMETHING ON THE GRO-**cery list. It's breakfast meat in a shrink-wrapped bag. It should be so much more than that, though. It's something you can (and should) be making from scratch because it's not only easy, but also delicious. This chapter is going to take you through some of my favorite homemade recipes. The process is surprisingly simple.

First step? Pork belly. Find a good one from a butcher you trust. Bacon is so simple that it's important you're getting good meat. You want the flavor to shine through and you want the meat to really be the star. **Second step?** Cure. Our classic recipe has salt, sugar, and a few spices. If you want to do a dry cure, you'll take these and rub them all over the meat and then stick it in the fridge for up to ten days. A wet cure is pretty similar with one big difference—water. I switch back and forth with my method, but usually use wet when I'm adding lots of flavors because they're often easier to combine that way. **Third step?** Smoking. This one is not optional if you're looking to make bacon. That classic smoky flavor you're used to only happens one way. If you want to skip it, you'll get something closer to Italian pancetta.

And believe it or not, that's that. Three steps. I think it's best to follow my classic recipe first. You'll make it once and wonder why you haven't been doing it forever. Once you've made my classic, you can also step up your bacon game even more by making changes to each of the three steps. To change up the meat, skip pork belly. Try lamb or turkey, even tuna. Switch up seasonings—add some chipotles in adobo or garlic and soy sauce. Want to play with the smoking step? Try different woods!

Start with these ideas. Make a few of my recipes. See which meats you like and get comfortable with the technique. Then make your own. See what you can do. Don't forget to send me samples.

THE TEN COMMANDMENTS
OF HOMEMADE PORK BACON

MAKING YOUR OWN BACON REALLY IS NOT DIFFICULT, AND THE PROCESS ALLOWS you to get creative with flavors and control the amount of smoke and seasoning. The recipes on the following pages will give you step-by-step instructions that take pork belly from the brine to the smoker to the frying pan. But first, some rules that will make the entire process even easier.

1 **CHOOSE THE RIGHT PORK BELLY:** Organic hogs (or hogs raised humanely without hormones or antibiotics) are the way to go. A full pork belly weighs 10 to 12 pounds (4.5 to 5.4 kg) and usually can be found at butcher shops or specially ordered at your grocery store. The base recipe below is for 5-pound (2.3-kg) half bellies, but if you want to make a smaller quantity, Whole Foods and other grocery stores sell pork belly by the pound. This may be easier to handle for some home smokers.

of the cure and smoke flavors.) Commercial smokehouses remove it using a slicing machine. At home, you'll have to work a bit harder. Start at one corner and use a sharp, slender knife to separate the skin from the meat and fat underneath it, angling the knife blade toward the skin. Better yet, ask your butcher to skin it for you.

NOTE: *Do not discard the pork skin. You will want to use it for Spice-Rubbed Fried Pork Rinds (aka Chicharrónes, page 138), or add it to beans or braised greens for more flavor.*

2 **REMOVE THE SKIN:** The bottom of a pork belly usually comes with skin (rind), which will be tougher than the rest of the belly. (It also blocks the absorption

3 **CREATE THE CURE:** Both of my basic cures (dry and wet) contain kosher salt, granulated sugar, and pink salt (curing salt, aka Instacure #1). You can achieve a wide, subtle range of flavors by varying the ingredients to include brown sugar or maple syrup instead of white sugar; other spices such as coriander, mustard seeds, or black peppercorns; and condiments such as Dijon mustard, chipotles in adobo, and sriracha to add a touch of heat. Wet cures include some kind of liquid, commonly water, but can also use a fruit juice such as peach nectar (see BBQ Bacon, page 30).

4 CURE THE PORK BELLY: Arrange the belly on a rimmed baking sheet. Rub the cure in on both sides as described in the recipe. Place the belly in a large, sturdy, resealable plastic bag in a foil pan or roasting pan on the bottom shelf of your refrigerator. (The pan will catch any potential leaks.) Cure the bacon for 10 days, turning it over each day. This is very important. As the cure dehydrates the bacon, liquid will gather in the bag. It's supposed to.

Remove the belly from the plastic bag inside a sink (there will be lots of liquid) and rinse well on both sides in a large colander with cold water. This removes excess salt. Next, blot the belly dry and place it, uncovered, on a wire rack set on a baking sheet on the bottom shelf of your refrigerator. Let dry for at least 4 hours or as long as overnight, turning once or twice. This helps form a pellicle—an exterior skin that feels papery and dry and just a touch tacky—for the smoke to adhere to. Without the pellicle, you won't get the bronzed surface that makes bacon look as good as it tastes.

5 CHOOSE YOUR WOOD: For smoking, use hickory, apple, or cherry, or other preferred hardwood (or blend of woods). Personally, I find mesquite too strong. Depending on your smoker, you'll use chunks, chips, sawdust, or pellets.

6 SMOKE THE BACON: Set up your smoker according to the manufacturer's instructions and preheat it to 200 to 225°F (93 to 107°C). If you're using a charcoal smoker, the temperature will fluctuate, so be mindful not to go over 250°F (120°C). If you're using an electric or gas smoker, you can set it right at 200 to 225°F (93 to 107°C).

To get the most smoke, soak wood chips in water for 30 minutes, then place them on the hot coals. The wood chips will start giving off smoke after 10 minutes or so. The smoking time will range between 2 and 3 hours; in most cases, you're looking for an internal temperature of 155°F (68°C).

NOTE: *Smoking to an internal temperature of 155°F (68°C) gives you traditional bacon* *that can be sliced thin and crisped in a pan to order, like the bacon you find in the grocery store. Some of my recipes require you to smoke the bacon to an internal temperature of 195°F (91°C), which is pulling temperature for pork. Once the belly is smoked to this temperature, it is too tender to slice thin; it is meant to be cut thick and grilled or crisped in a cast-iron pan.*

7 REST AND CHILL THE BACON: Let the bacon cool to room temperature on a wire rack over a baking sheet, then tightly wrap in plastic wrap and refrigerate for at least 4 hours, preferably overnight. (This sets the flavor and texture.) You can also press the bacon with 20 to 30 pounds (9 to 13.5 kg) of weight to ensure a perfectly intact, solid belly.

8 STORE YOUR BACON: Your pork belly—once cured, smoked, and rested and cooled overnight in the fridge—is now slab bacon, and ready to be sliced and cooked like any store-bought bacon. Tightly wrapped in plastic and then foil, it will keep in the refrigerator for up to 1 week and in the freezer for up to 6 months.

9 SLICE IT: One of the benefits of making your own bacon is that you can slice it as thick as you like. If you're used to soft, thin-sliced supermarket bacon, wait until you sink your teeth into a ¼- to ½-inch-thick (6- to 12-mm) slice.

10 COOK IT: I go into great detail on how to cook bacon properly on pages 44–45. Whether you want to cook off a few pieces quickly in a skillet or pounds on a sheet pan in a 350°F (175°C) oven, I've got you covered.

BARBACON HOMEMADE DRY CURE BACON

THIS IS THE RECIPE THAT STARTED IT ALL. SURE, MAKING YOUR own bacon is a labor of love and takes some time, but so do all great things. This is my "basic" recipe, and the sky's the limit when it comes to variations of flavors. I include a few of my favorite variations below to get your creative juices flowing, but feel free to allow the chef in you to come out. At BarBacon, I cure whole bellies that generally weigh between 10 to 12 pounds (4.5 to 5.4 kg) each. That's a lot of bacon and a lot of space needed in a refrigerator, so I've halved the quantities here, which should be much more manageable for the home cook.

1 (5-pound/2.3-kg) pork belly, skin removed and saved for another use (see page 17, step 2)

½ cup (90 g) Diamond Crystal kosher salt

½ cup (100 g) sugar

2 teaspoons pink curing salt (aka Instacure #1)

Soaked and drained apple, hickory, or cherry wood chips

Place the pork belly on a large rimmed sheet pan.

Combine the kosher salt, sugar, and pink salt in a medium bowl. Sprinkle the cure over the entire belly on both sides, rubbing in to make sure that the mixture penetrates the flesh. It will seem like a lot of salt, but that's okay. You are curing the meat, not seasoning it, and it needs all of that salt.

Seal the belly in a large zip-top bag and place in a pan just big enough to fit it (and store in your refrigerator).

Cure the belly in the refrigerator for 8 days, turning it over daily to redistribute the liquid that will accumulate.

Drain the pork belly in a colander or large basin and rinse well with cold water. Blot it dry with paper towels. Place the belly on a wire rack over a rimmed baking sheet in the refrigerator or in a cool place in front of a fan (the goal is to create good airflow), and let it dry until the surface feels dry and tacky, at least 4 hours, or overnight.

(continued)

Set up your smoker following the manufacturer's instructions and preheat it to between 200 and 225°F (93 and 107°C). Add the wood chips to the coals. Lay the pork belly directly on the grill grate opposite the coals (indirect heat). Smoke the pork belly until bronzed with wood smoke and firm, 2 to 3 hours. The internal temperature should reach 155°F (68°C). (Insert an instant-read thermometer probe through the side of the bacon at one end.)

Transfer the bacon to a clean wire rack over a baking sheet and let it cool to room temperature. Tightly wrap it in plastic wrap and refrigerate for at least 4 hours, ideally overnight.

To serve, thinly slice the bacon against the grain and cook in a skillet over medium-low heat until crisp. Bacon will last up to 1 week in the fridge; simply slice off pieces as needed.

NOTE: *I sometimes press the belly overnight after smoking to assure myself a solid intact belly with none of the fat separating. This is optional and purely for aesthetics.*

MAKES ABOUT 3½ POUNDS (1.6 KG)

BARBACON WET CURE (BRINED) BACON

MY WET CURE IS BASICALLY MY DRY CURE, BUT WITH WATER ADDED. Wet brines are good for when you have a less fatty piece of meat that needs some moisture, or when you need to evenly disperse flavor when cooking with ingredients like chipotles in adobo or fruit juice.

12 cups (2.8 L) cold water

½ cup (90 g) Diamond Crystal kosher salt

2 teaspoons pink curing salt (aka Instacure #1)

½ cup (100 g) sugar

1 (5-pound/2.3-kg) pork belly, skin removed and saved for another use (see page 17, step 2)

Soaked and drained apple, hickory, or cherry wood chips

In a large food-safe container with a tight-fitting lid, whisk together the water, kosher salt, pink salt, and sugar until it dissolves, about 5 minutes. Add the pork belly and make sure it stays submerged. I use a plastic container filled with cans to weigh it down.

Cure the belly in the refrigerator for 8 days.

Drain the pork belly in a colander or large basin and rinse well with cold water. Blot it dry with paper towels. Place the belly on a wire rack over a rimmed baking sheet in the refrigerator or in a cool place in front of a fan (the goal is to create good airflow), and let it dry until the surface feels dry and tacky, at least 4 hours, or overnight.

Set up your smoker following the manufacturer's instructions and preheat it to between 200 and 225°F (93 and 107°C). Add the wood chips to the coals. Lay the pork belly directly on the grill grate opposite the coals (indirect heat). Smoke the pork belly

until bronzed with wood smoke and firm, 2 to 3 hours. The internal temperature should reach 155°F (68°C). (Insert an instant-read thermometer probe through the side of the bacon at one end.)

Transfer the bacon to a clean wire rack over a baking sheet and let it cool to room temperature. Tightly wrap it in plastic wrap and refrigerate for at least 4 hours, ideally overnight.

To serve, thinly slice the bacon against the grain and cook in a skillet over medium-low heat until crisp. Bacon will last up to 1 week in the fridge; simply slice off pieces as needed.

MAKES ABOUT 3½ POUNDS (1.6 KG)

MAPLE BACON

THIS IS THE BACON I MAKE MOST OFTEN AT HOME, BECAUSE THE store-bought kind never tastes enough like maple. If you're going to call it maple bacon, it should taste like maple and mine does. The maple syrup makes this more of a wet cure. Try to find maple wood chips or chunks for smoking; if they're not available, apple or cherry wood are also good here.

~~~~~~

1 cup (180 g) Diamond Crystal kosher salt

1 cup (145 g) pure maple sugar

2 teaspoons pink curing salt (aka Instacure #1)

1 cup (240 ml) maple syrup

1 (5-pound/2.3-kg) pork belly, skin removed and saved for another use (see page 17, step 2)

Soaked and drained maple wood chips or chunks

Place the pork belly on a large rimmed sheet pan.

Combine the kosher salt, maple sugar, and pink salt in a medium bowl. Sprinkle the cure over the entire belly on both sides, rubbing in to make sure that the mixture penetrates the flesh. It will seem like a lot of salt, but that's okay. You are curing the meat, not seasoning it, and it needs all of that salt.

Put the belly in a large zip-top bag, pour in the maple syrup, seal tightly, and place in a pan just big enough to fit it (and store in your refrigerator).

Cure the belly in the refrigerator for 8 days, turning it over daily to redistribute the liquid that will accumulate.

Drain the pork belly in a colander or large basin and rinse well with cold water. Blot it dry with paper towels. Place the belly on a wire rack over a rimmed baking sheet in the refrigerator or in a cool place in front of a fan (the goal is to create good airflow), and let it dry until the surface feels dry and tacky, at least 4 hours, or overnight.

Set up your smoker following the manufacturer's instructions and preheat it to between 200 and 225°F (93 and 107°C). Add the wood chips or chunks to the coals. Lay the pork belly directly on the grill grate opposite the coals (indirect heat). Smoke the pork belly until bronzed with wood smoke and firm, 2 to 3 hours. The internal temperature should reach 155°F (68°C). (Insert an instant-read thermometer probe through the side of the bacon at one end.)

Transfer the bacon to a clean wire rack over a baking sheet and let it cool to room temperature. Tightly wrap it in plastic wrap and refrigerate for at least 4 hours, ideally overnight.

To serve, thinly slice the bacon against the grain and cook in a skillet over medium-low heat until crisp. Bacon will last up to 1 week in the fridge; simply slice off pieces as needed.

~~~~~~~~~~~~~~~~~~~~~~~~~~~

MAKES ABOUT 3½ POUNDS (1.6 KG)

GARLIC-SOY BACON

THIS IS MY PORK TERIYAKI BACON; IT HAS A RICH, SALTY, SWEET flavor. I use it for all my Asian-inspired recipes, including bacon fried rice (page 253), Bacon Ramen (page 166), and Tempura Bacon (page 133).

2 cups (475 ml) low-sodium soy sauce

¾ cup (180 ml) clover honey

1 head garlic, cloves separated, peeled and smashed

2 teaspoons pink curing salt (aka Instacure #1)

¼ cup (45 g) Diamond Crystal kosher salt

1 (5-pound/2.3-kg) pork belly, skin removed and saved for another use (see page 17, step 2)

Soaked and drained apple, hickory, or cherry wood chips

Combine the soy sauce, honey, garlic, pink salt, and kosher salt in a blender and blend until combined. Transfer the brine to a large food-safe container with a tight-fitting lid. Add the pork belly and make sure it stays submerged. I use a plastic container filled with cans to weigh it down.

Cure the belly in the refrigerator for 8 days.

Drain the pork belly in a colander or large basin and rinse well with cold water. Blot it dry with paper towels. Place the belly on a wire rack over a rimmed baking sheet in the refrigerator or in a cool place in front of a fan (the goal is to create good airflow), and let it dry until the surface feels papery and tacky, at least 4 hours, or overnight.

Set up your smoker following the manufacturer's instructions and preheat it to between 200 and 225°F (93 and 107°C). Add the wood chips or chunks to the coals. Lay the pork belly directly on the grill grate opposite the coals (indirect heat). Smoke the pork belly until bronzed with wood smoke and firm, 2 to 3 hours. The internal temperature should reach 155°F (68°C). (Insert an instant-read thermometer probe through the side of the bacon at one end.)

Transfer the bacon to a clean wire rack over a baking sheet and let it cool to room temperature. Tightly wrap it in plastic wrap and refrigerate for at least 4 hours, ideally overnight.

To serve, thinly slice the bacon against the grain and cook in a skillet over medium-low heat until crisp. Bacon will last up to 1 week in the fridge; simply slice off pieces as needed.

NOTE: *If you're using the Garlic-Soy Bacon in the Bacon Ramen (page 166), you want a super-tender piece of bacon that could be cut with a spoon. To achieve this texture, you need to smoke the pork belly to an internal temperature of 195°F (91°C), which is the same temperature that pulled pork is cooked to. This will give the meat a silky texture. Remove from the smoker and let it rest for at least 1 hour, or refrigerate until ready to cook and serve.*

MAKES ABOUT 3½ POUNDS (1.6 KG)

CHIPOTLE BACON

SMOKE ON SMOKE ON SMOKE, AND I LOVE IT. THIS IS GREAT SERVED alongside eggs on a BLT with avocado or, my favorite, rolled in soft tortillas for my chipotle bacon tacos (page 233).

1 cup (180 g) Diamond Crystal kosher salt

2 teaspoons pink curing salt (aka Instacure #1)

½ cup (100 g) sugar

1 (7-ounce/198-g) can chipotles in adobo, pureed

1 (5-pound/2.3-kg) pork belly, skin removed and saved for another use (see page 17, step 2)

¼ cup (55 g) Chipotle Rub (page 94)

Soaked and drained apple, hickory, or cherry wood chips or chunks, or pellets or sawdust (amount recommended by your smoker manufacturer)

Whisk together the kosher salt, pink salt, sugar, chipotles, and 12 cups (2.8 L) water in a large food-safe container with a tight-fitting lid. Add the pork belly and make sure it stays submerged. I use a plastic container filled with cans to weigh it down.

Cure the belly in the refrigerator for 8 days.

Drain the pork belly in a colander or large basin and rinse well with cold water. Blot it dry with paper towels.

Sprinkle the rub over the entire belly on both sides, rubbing in to make sure that the mixture penetrates the flesh.

Set up your smoker following the manufacturer's instructions and preheat it to between 200 and 225°F (93 and 107°C). Add the wood chips or chunks to the coals. Lay the pork belly directly on the grill grate opposite the coals (indirect heat). Smoke the pork belly until bronzed with wood smoke and firm, 2 to 3 hours. The internal temperature should reach 155°F (68°C). (Insert an instant-read thermometer probe through the side of the bacon at one end.)

Transfer the bacon to a clean wire rack over a baking sheet and let it cool to room temperature. Tightly wrap it in plastic wrap and refrigerate for at least 4 hours, ideally overnight.

To serve, thinly slice the bacon against the grain and cook in a skillet over medium-low heat until crisp. Bacon will last up to 1 week in the fridge; simply slice off pieces as needed.

NOTE: *We make this bacon specifically for the chipotle bacon tacos on page 233. The bacon needs to be fall-off-the-bone tender for that dish. To make the bacon pulled-pork tender, you need to smoke the belly to an internal temperature of 195°F (91°C).*

MAKES ABOUT 3½ POUNDS (1.6 KG)

JERK BACON

ONE OF THE OLDEST RECIPES I HAVE IS A JERK SPICE RECIPE. I GOT it from a woman I used to work with, and have cherished it ever since. It was obviously meant for chicken, but on pork belly it really is something special. Pork, like chicken, can take on a lot of flavor, but unlike chicken, the pork belly won't dry out. And, because you are smoking the meat at a low temperature, the spices in the dry rub won't burn like they would on chicken grilled over fire.

2 recipes Jerk Rub (page 95)

2 teaspoons pink curing salt (aka Instacure #1)

2 heads garlic, roasted

2 ribs celery, coarsely chopped

1 large Spanish onion, cut into 1-inch (2.5-cm) slices, grilled until very dark and burnt

½ cup (120 ml) fresh lime juice (from about 7 limes)

3 habanero peppers, stems removed

3 quarts (2.8 L) cold water

1 (5-pound/2.3-kg) pork belly, skin removed and saved for another use (see page 17, step 2)

Soaked and drained apple, hickory, or cherry wood chips or chunks, or pellets or sawdust (amount recommended by your smoker manufacturer)

Combine half of the rub with the pink salt, garlic, celery, onion, lime juice, habaneros, and 1 cup (240 ml) of the cold water in a blender or food processor and blend until smooth.

Transfer the mixture to a large food-safe container with a tight-fitting lid, add the remaining water, and mix to combine. Add the pork belly and make sure it stays submerged. I use a plastic container filled with cans to weigh it down.

Cure the belly in the refrigerator for 8 days.

Drain the pork belly in a colander or large basin and rinse well with cold water. Blot it dry with paper towels.

Sprinkle the rub over the entire belly on both sides, rubbing in to make sure that the mixture penetrates the flesh. (You will not need to use all of it to coat the belly, but it should be fully coated; put any leftover rub in a container with a tight-fitting lid and store in a dark, cool place, where it will keep for up to 6 months.)

Set up your smoker following the manufacturer's instructions and preheat it to between 200 and 225°F (93 and 107°C).

Add the wood chips or chunks to the coals. Lay the pork belly directly on the grill grate opposite the coals (indirect heat). Smoke the pork belly until bronzed with wood smoke and firm, for 2 to 3 hours. The internal temperature should reach 155°F (68°C). (Insert an instant-read thermometer probe through the side of the bacon at one end.)

Transfer the bacon to a clean wire rack over a baking sheet and let it cool to room temperature. Tightly wrap it in plastic wrap and refrigerate for at least 4 hours, ideally overnight.

To serve, thinly slice the bacon against the grain and cook in a skillet over medium-low heat until crisp. Bacon will last up to 1 week in the fridge; simply slice off pieces as needed.

NOTE: *If you are making this bacon for the jerk bacon tacos (page 234), smoke the belly to an internal temperature of 195°F (91°C).*

MAKES ABOUT 3½ POUNDS (1.6 KG)

BBQ BACON

THIS BACON APPLIES THE WET CURE METHOD. I ADJUSTED A BBQ injection I use often for pork butt to create this bacon curing brine. Peach is my go-to fruit for BBQ, but feel free to use apple or pineapple juice if you can't find peach. I have used both in this recipe and they work beautifully. You can also adjust the amount of chipotle depending on your preference. I like it spicy.

3 quarts (2.8 L) peach nectar

½ cup (100 g) sugar

1 cup (180 g) Diamond Crystal kosher salt

2 teaspoons pink curing salt (aka Instacure #1)

1 (7-ounce/198-g) can chipotles in adobo, pureed

1 (5-pound/2.3-kg) pork belly, skin removed and saved for another use (see page 17, step 2)

¼ cup (45 g) Magic Rub (page 94)

Soaked and drained apple, hickory, or cherry wood chips or chunks, or pellets or sawdust (amount recommended by your smoker manufacturer)

Whisk together the peach nectar, sugar, kosher salt, pink salt, and chipotles in a large food-safe container with a tight-fitting lid. Add the pork belly and make sure it stays submerged. I use a plastic container filled with cans to weigh it down.

Cure the belly in the refrigerator for 8 days.

Drain the pork belly in a colander or large basin and rinse well with cold water. Blot it dry with paper towels.

Sprinkle the rub over the entire belly on both sides, rubbing in to make sure that the mixture penetrates the flesh.

Set up your smoker following the manufacturer's instructions and preheat it to between 200 and 225°F (93 and 107°C). Add the wood chips or chunks to the coals. Lay the pork belly directly on the grill grate opposite the coals (indirect heat). Smoke the pork belly until bronzed with wood smoke and firm, 2 to 3 hours. The internal temperature should reach 155°F (68°C). (Insert an instant-read thermometer

probe through the side of the bacon at one end.)

Transfer the bacon to a clean wire rack over a baking sheet and let it cool to room temperature. Tightly wrap it in plastic wrap and refrigerate for at least 4 hours, ideally overnight.

To serve, thinly slice the bacon against the grain and cook in a skillet over medium-low heat until crisp. Bacon will last up to 1 week in the fridge; simply slice off pieces as needed.

NOTE: *If you are making this bacon for Burnt Ends (page 148), smoke the belly to an internal temperature of 195°F (91°C).*

MAKES ABOUT 3½ POUNDS (1.6 KG)

TURKEY BACON

THE TURKEY BACON YOU BUY AT THE STORE IS MEANT TO TASTE like pork bacon, but it doesn't, and, quite frankly, shouldn't. This turkey is bacon because of how it's prepared, cured, and smoked, not because of how it tastes—juicy, smoky, and a damn good stand-in if you find yourself needing to feed a family of Jews, like most of my family.

1 gallon (3.8 L) cold water

1 cup (180 g) Diamond Crystal kosher salt

2 teaspoons pink curing salt (aka Instacure #1)

1 cup (200 g) sugar

1 whole dried ancho chile, stem removed

1 tablespoon liquid smoke

1 (5- to 7-pound/2.3- to 3.2-kg) whole boneless turkey breast, skin on

3 tablespoons smoked paprika

2 tablespoons cracked black pepper

Soaked and drained hickory, apple, or cherry wood chips

Canola oil

Combine the cold water, kosher salt, pink salt, sugar, ancho chile, and liquid smoke in a large saucepan over high heat and bring to a boil. Remove from the heat and let cool to room temperature or cool over an ice bath.

Place the breast in a large plastic container with a lid, pour the cold brine over, and cure in the refrigerator for at least 12 hours, or up to 24 hours.

Remove the turkey from the brine, rinse with cold water, and pat it dry with paper towels. Put the turkey on a sheet pan and season both sides with the paprika and black pepper. Refrigerate, uncovered, for at least 1 hour, or up to 4 hours.

Set up your smoker following the manufacturer's instructions and preheat it to between 200 and 225°F (93 and 107°C). Add the wood chips or chunks to the coals. Lay the turkey directly on the grill grate opposite the coals (indirect heat). Smoke the turkey for 1 to 2 hours, to an internal temperature of 165°F (74°C). (Insert an instant-read thermometer probe into the thickest part of the breast.)

Transfer the turkey to a clean wire rack over a baking sheet and let it cool to room temperature. Tightly wrap it in plastic wrap and refrigerate for at least 4 hours, or up to 24 hours.

To serve, put the breast on a cutting board, and using a sharp chef's knife, slice crosswise into thin slices (see Note). Heat a few tablespoons oil in a sauté pan over high heat until it begins to shimmer and cook on both sides until golden brown, about 2 minutes per side. Bacon will last up to 1 week in the fridge, simply slice off pieces as needed.

NOTE: *At BarBacon, we use a meat slicer, which most home cooks do not have. If you do, use it to create deli-thin slices of turkey bacon. You can wrap the bacon in foil and heat in a 300°F (150°C) oven or serve cold.*

MAKES 4 TO 5½ POUNDS (1.8 TO 2.5 KG)

LAMB BACON

THIS IS A LABOR OF LOVE, BUT THE RESULTS ARE WORTH IT. LAMB bacon (made from lamb belly, which is also known as lamb breast) has a milder and sweeter flavor than pork, but this fatty and slightly gamey meat is perfect for smoking. Lamb bacon can be used exactly the same way as pork bacon. I love serving it with braised cabbage and potatoes for St. Patrick's Day, but it can be found every day on BarBacon's lunch menu as part of the lamb bacon reuben (page 221)—and it's kosher.

⅓ cup (60 g) Diamond Crystal kosher salt

⅓ cup (75 g) packed light brown sugar

2 teaspoons pink curing salt (aka Instacure #1)

2 teaspoons ground cinnamon

2 teaspoons dried herbs de Provence

1 teaspoon ground cayenne

1 teaspoon onion powder

1 teaspoon garlic powder

1 (4- to 5-pound/1.8- to 2.3-kg) boneless lamb breast, fat left on (have your butcher debone it)

Soaked and drained apple, hickory, or cherry wood chips or chunks, or pellets or sawdust (amount recommended by your smoker manufacturer)

Canola oil

Combine the kosher salt, brown sugar, pink salt, cinnamon, herbs de Provence, cayenne, onion powder, and garlic powder in a small bowl. Rub the lamb breast well on both sides with the mixture.

Place the meat on a sheet pan and wrap the top tightly with plastic wrap or put in a large plastic container with a lid and cure in the refrigerator for 7 days, turning it over daily to redistribute the liquid that will accumulate. After 7 days, rinse the lamb well with cold water and pat it dry with paper towels.

Line a clean baking sheet with parchment paper or foil, put the lamb breast on it, and refrigerate it for at least 8 hours, or up to 24 hours to dry out the surface.

Set up your smoker following the manufacturer's instructions and preheat it to between 200 and 225°F (93 and 107°C). Add wood chips or chunks to the coals. Lay the lamb directly on the grill grate opposite the coals (indirect heat). Smoke the lamb until bronzed with wood smoke and firm, 2 to 3 hours. The internal temperature should reach 155°F (68°C). (Insert an instant-read thermometer probe through the side of the lamb at one end.)

Transfer the lamb bacon to a clean wire rack over a baking sheet and let it cool to room temperature. Tightly wrap it in plastic wrap and refrigerate for at least 4 hours, or up to 24 hours.

To serve, put the lamb bacon on a cutting board, and using a sharp chef's knife, slice crosswise into thin slices (see Note). Heat a few tablespoons oil in a sauté pan over high heat until it begins to shimmer and cook on both sides until golden brown, about 2 minutes per side. Bacon will last up to 1 week in the fridge, simply slice off pieces as needed.

NOTE: *At BarBacon, we use a meat slicer, which most home cooks do not have. However, if you do, use it to create deli-thin slices of lamb bacon. You can wrap the thinly sliced meat in foil and heat in a 300°F (150°C) oven or serve cold.*

MAKES 3½ TO 4 POUNDS (1.6 TO 1.8 KG)

BEEF BACON

EVEN THOUGH COWS HAVE BELLIES—AND YOU CAN USE A CUT THAT is referred to as the navel—it is really hard to find for the home cook, so I use brisket. When smoking brisket, plan on shrinkage of about 30 percent. The pink salt and additional days of curing, in addition to the smoking, add a richness and concentrated beef flavor to the meat. It's what separates this brisket from your Texas-style or Jewish holiday–style brisket, which are typically braised in stock in the oven until fork-tender.

1 (7-pound/3.2-kg) beef brisket, fat cap on

1 cup (235 g) BB Rub (page 95)

2½ teaspoons pink curing salt (aka Instacure #1)

Soaked and drained hickory or mesquite wood chips

Place the beef brisket on a rimmed sheet pan large enough to hold the entire brisket.

Combine the rub and pink salt in a medium bowl. Sprinkle the cure over the entire brisket on both sides, rubbing in to make sure that the mixture penetrates the flesh.

Wrap the brisket tightly in plastic wrap and place in a pan just big enough to fit it (and store in your refrigerator).

Cure the brisket in the refrigerator for 10 days, turning it over daily to redistribute the liquid that will accumulate.

Drain the brisket in a colander or large basin and rinse well with cold water. Blot it dry with paper towels. Place the brisket on a clean wire rack over a rimmed baking sheet in the refrigerator or in a cool place in front of a fan (the goal is to create good airflow), and let it dry until the surface feels dry and tacky, at least 4 hours, or overnight.

Set up your smoker following the manufacturer's instructions and preheat it to between 200 and 225°F (93 and 107°C). Add wood chips or chunks to the coals. Lay the brisket directly on the grill grate opposite the coals (indirect heat). Smoke the brisket until bronzed with wood smoke and firm, 2 to 3 hours. The internal temperature should reach 155°F (68°C). (Insert an instant-read thermometer probe through the side of the brisket at one end.)

Transfer the beef bacon to a clean wire rack over a baking sheet and let it cool to room temperature. Tightly wrap it in plastic wrap and refrigerate for at least 4 hours, ideally overnight.

To serve, thinly slice the bacon against the grain and cook in a skillet over medium-low heat until crisp. Bacon will last up to 1 week in the fridge; simply slice off pieces as needed. Beef bacon is best when thinly sliced (see Note).

NOTE: *At BarBacon, we use a meat slicer, which most home cooks do not have. However, if you do, use it to create deli-thin slices of beef bacon. You can wrap the thinly sliced meat in foil and heat in a 300°F (150°C) oven or serve cold.*

MAKES ABOUT 5 POUNDS (2.3 KG)

TUNA BACON

THIS RECIPE CAME OUT OF NECESSITY: TO PRESERVE TUNA A FRIEND brought me that no one ever thought he would catch. Plus, I liked the idea of putting something other than smoked salmon on my bagel in the morning. There are two things you need to know before cooking this bacon. First, you are cold smoking this fish—applying smoke flavor but not looking to cook the fish at all—so be mindful of your smoker temperature. Second, the tuna you buy should be part of the loin that is closest to the head. Tuna is a fast, strong fish with a lot of muscle and very little fat. Any fat it has is closer to the head. Now, tuna does have a belly, but I don't use it for this bacon. I take my fillets, apply a little smoke, *et voilà*: tuna bacon!

2 quarts (2 L) Bacon Stock (page 43), cold

½ cup (120 ml) mirin

1 tablespoon low-sodium soy sauce

2 pounds (910 g) tuna loin, cut crosswise into slices 1 inch (2.5 cm) thick (about 6 steaks)

1 cup (110 g) Bacon Bits (page 49)

2 teaspoons coarsely ground black pepper

2 tablespoons canola oil

Soaked and drained hickory, apple, or cherry wood chips

Whisk together the cold stock, mirin, and soy sauce in a large bowl. Put the tuna steaks in a gallon-size zip-top bag, pour in the brine, press out all of the air, and seal tightly. Place the bag in a container to hold it in case it leaks and refrigerate for 48 hours.

Remove the tuna from the brine, rinse well in a colander with cold water, and pat dry with paper towels. Place on a baking sheet and refrigerate for at least 1 hour, or up to 4 hours, turning it over once.

Combine the bacon bits and pepper in a food processor and process until fine crumbs. Dump the mixture onto a large rimmed plate and spread to cover the surface.

Brush each steak lightly on the top, bottom, and sides with some of the oil. Coat the steaks on all sides with the bacon mixture, pressing down to ensure that the coating sticks. Transfer the steaks to a clean wire rack.

Set up your smoker following the manufacturer's instructions for cold smoking. Add the wood chips to the coals. Fill a shallow pan with ice and lay the wire rack with the tuna over the iced-filled pan. Place the pan directly on the grill grate opposite the coals (indirect heat). Smoke the tuna for 1 hour, replenishing the ice in the pan as needed so the smoker temperature never rises above 110°F (43°C).

Remove the tuna bacon and serve immediately or refrigerate covered in plastic wrap for up to 3 days.

MAKES ABOUT 2 POUNDS (910 G)

SMOKED PORCHETTA

THIS IS TECHNICALLY *NOT* PORCHETTA; IT IS PORK BELLY FLAVORED in the style of porchetta and prepared like bacon—but that would be too long of a recipe title. I use this alongside chicken in my Smoked Porchetta and Chicken Pot Pie (page 262), and I also love it thinly sliced and served on ciabatta bread with Pickled Fennel (page 283), sliced red onion, Bacon Mayonnaise (page 72), and hot cherry peppers.

12 garlic cloves, smashed

¼ cup (7 g) loosely packed fresh rosemary leaves, chopped

¼ cup (9 g) loosely packed fresh sage leaves, chopped

2 tablespoons fennel pollen or toasted fennel seeds

2 tablespoons coarsely ground black pepper

½ cup (90 g) Diamond Crystal kosher salt

2 teaspoons pink curing salt (aka Instacure #1)

½ cup (100 g) sugar

1 (5-pound/2.3-kg) pork belly, skin removed and saved for another use (see page 17, step 2)

Soaked and drained pecan wood chips or chunks (amount recommended by your smoker manufacturer)

Put the garlic, rosemary, sage, fennel pollen, and a splash of water in a food processor and process until a paste is formed. Scrape the mixture into a medium bowl and add the pepper, kosher salt, pink salt, and sugar and mix until combined.

Place the pork belly on a rimmed sheet pan large enough to hold the entire belly. Score the belly's top fat layer with a sharp knife. Rub the cure evenly over both sides, rubbing it in to make sure that the mixture penetrates the fat and flesh.

Seal the belly in a large zip-top bag and place in a pan just big enough to fit it (and store in your refrigerator).

Cure the belly in the refrigerator for 8 days, turning it over daily to redistribute the liquid that will accumulate.

Drain the pork belly in a colander or large basin and rinse well with cold water. Blot it dry with paper towels. Place the belly on a wire rack over a rimmed baking sheet in the refrigerator or in a cool place in front of a fan (the goal is to create good airflow), and let it dry until the surface feels papery and tacky, at least 4 hours, or overnight.

Set up your smoker following the manufacturer's instructions and preheat it to between 200 and 225°F (93 and 107°C). Add the wood chips or chunks to the coals. Lay the pork belly directly on the grill grate

opposite the coals (indirect heat). Smoke the pork belly until bronzed with wood smoke and firm, 2 to 3 hours. The internal temperature should reach 155°F (68°C). (Insert an instant-read thermometer probe through the side of the bacon at one end.)

Transfer the porchetta to a clean wire rack over a baking sheet and let it cool to room temperature. Tightly wrap it in plastic wrap and refrigerate for at least 4 hours, ideally overnight.

To serve, treat the porchetta like you would any slab bacon: Slice thin and crisp in the oven or a skillet over medium-low heat, or cook as a confit in bacon fat then cool and finish over the grill for tender bacon steaks, or for lardons in a salad. The porchetta will last up to 1 week in the fridge.

MAKES ABOUT 3½ POUNDS (1.6 KG)

PEAMEAL BACON
(AKA CANADIAN BACON)

THIS BACON COMES FROM PORK LOIN, WHICH IS A LEAN AND RATHER dry cut of meat that needs a brine to pump it up with lots of moisture and flavor. This bacon (which is cured but NOT smoked) is considered *the* real Canadian bacon thanks to the addition of pure maple syrup and cornmeal on the outside, which gives it a distinct texture and appearance, as opposed to what Americans consider Canadian bacon (the thinly sliced meat served with eggs Benedict).

¼ cup (45 g) Diamond Crystal kosher salt

1 tablespoon pink curing salt (aka Instacure #1)

¼ cup (60 ml) pure Grade B maple syrup

2 fresh bay leaves

3 sprigs fresh thyme

1 lemon, quartered

2 tablespoons yellow mustard seeds

3 garlic cloves, smashed

8 whole cloves

2 teaspoons black peppercorns

1 (3-pound/1.4-kg) center-cut pork loin, trimmed of all excess fat

1½ cups (180 g) coarse yellow cornmeal

Canola oil

Unsalted butter

Combine 4 cups (960 ml) water, the kosher salt, pink salt, maple syrup, bay leaves, thyme, lemon, mustard seeds, garlic, cloves, and peppercorns in a medium pot and bring to a simmer, stirring to dissolve the salts. Remove from the heat and let cool completely.

Put the loin in a large zip-top bag, pour in the brine, seal well, and place in a large bowl.

Cure in the refrigerator for 72 hours, turning the bag once every 24 hours.

Drain the loin in a colander or large basin and rinse well with cold water. Blot it dry with paper towels. Place the loin on a wire rack over a rimmed baking sheet in the refrigerator or in a cool place in front of a fan (the goal is to create good airflow), and let it dry until the surface feels papery and tacky, at least 4 hours, or overnight.

Put the cornmeal on a large plate and roll the loin in the cornmeal to coat evenly. Wrap tightly in plastic wrap until ready to eat.

To serve, heat 2 tablespoons oil and 2 tablespoons butter in a large cast-iron skillet or non-stick pan over medium-high heat until the butter melts and the mixture starts to shimmer. Slice the bacon crosswise into slices ¼ inch (6 mm) thick and sauté until cooked through and golden brown on both sides, about 2 minutes per side. Bacon will last up to 1 week in the fridge, simply slice off pieces as needed.

MAKES ABOUT 3 POUNDS (1.4 KG)

BACON CONFIT

THINK OF THIS AS A LOW-TEMPERATURE DEEP-FRY. COOKING MEAT, in this case bacon, slowly in its own fat (what the French call *confit*) may sound intimidating, but it is actually quite easy and much faster than the classic duck confit. The result is a slab of bacon that is fork-tender and slices of meat that literally melt in your mouth. In a subtle way, it is almost like BBQ, where low temperature is applied to thick, fatty meat for long periods of time to tenderize the meat and make it more palatable. Confited bacon produces two unbelievable products: the most tender fall-apart bacon you can imagine and bacon stock. Cut super thick as it must be, this bacon can be grilled as is, breaded for Kentucky Fried Bacon (page 42), or glazed in any number of ways for any number of cuisines. Use with caution; it is very addictive.

3 pounds (1.4 kg) slab bacon, skin removed

4 cups (960 ml) rendered bacon fat, melted (see page 50)

Preheat the oven to 220°F (105°C). Put the bacon in a small baking dish and pour the fat over the bacon, making sure that it is totally submerged. Cover with aluminum foil and bake in the oven until the bacon is tender when poked with a knife, about 1½ hours. The internal temperature of the bacon should reach 200°F (93°C).

Carefully remove the bacon from the fat and let cool to room temperature, about 30 minutes. Wrap the bacon in plastic wrap and refrigerate until cold, at least 4 hours. The fat and any pan drippings can be cooled to room temperature, covered and refrigerated, and used again. Bacon stock will pool at the bottom of the jar you stored the fat in. Bacon confit can be stored, tightly wrapped in plastic wrap then foil, for up to 1 week in the refrigerator.

MAKES ABOUT 2¼ POUNDS (1 KG)

KENTUCKY FRIED BACON

YOU CAN EAT CONFITED BACON AS IS, SERVED ON A SALAD, OR IN between bread for a sandwich that rivals brisket, but being one that can't leave well enough alone, I bread the slices, then deep-fry them for my Kentucky Fried Bacon Tacos (page 238) and topped with pickled vegetables for my banh mi (page 217).

2 pounds (910 g) Bacon Confit (page 41), wrapped in foil and chilled for at least 4 hours

1 cup (125 g) all-purpose flour

3 large eggs

2 cups (160 g) panko bread crumbs

Hot sauce

Salt and freshly ground black pepper

2 cups (480 ml) vegetable oil

Slice the bacon, crosswise, into slices 1 inch (2.5 cm) thick. Put the flour, eggs, and panko in three separate shallow baking dishes or bowls. Whisk the eggs until smooth, add a few dashes of hot sauce, and season with salt and pepper.

Heat the oil in a deep medium-size sauté pan over medium heat until it begins to shimmer or registers 350°F (175°C) on an instant-read thermometer.

Dredge the bacon slices in flour and tap off any excess, then dip in the egg and let excess drip off, then dredge in the bread crumbs, pressing lightly to make sure they stick.

Fry the bacon, in batches, until golden brown on both sides, about 3 minutes total. Drain on paper towels. Cooked bacon can be kept, tightly covered, in the refrigerator for up to 3 days. Reheat on a baking sheet in a preheated 350°F (175°C) oven until heated through and crispy, about 10 minutes.

MAKES 8 TO 10 SLICES

BACON STOCK

WHEN YOU'RE TRIMMING AND COOKING THOUSANDS OF POUNDS OF bacon every week and want to keep waste and food costs down, you get creative. One way to use the scraps is to make rich, smoky broth that can become a delicious bacon ramen soup (page 166), the base of a sausage gravy served over biscuits (page 327), or the base of a brine for Tuna Bacon (page 37). At home, I recommend using any bacon you have hanging out in the fridge or buying slab bacon.

2 tablespoons canola oil

1 pound (455 g) slab bacon, cut into 2-inch (5-cm) pieces

1 large Spanish onion, chopped

1 large carrot, chopped

1 large rib celery, chopped

6 sprigs fresh thyme

1 bay leaf

12 black peppercorns

Heat the oil in a large stockpot over medium heat. Add the bacon and cook, stirring a few times, until golden brown, about 10 minutes.

Add the onion, carrot, and celery to the pot and cook until soft, about 5 minutes.

Add 9 cups (2.1 L) water, the thyme, bay leaf, and peppercorns to the pot and bring to a boil over high heat. Reduce the heat to low and simmer, partially covered, for 2 hours. Remove from the heat, cover, and let steep for 30 minutes.

Strain the stock through a chinois into a large bowl. Cover and refrigerate until cold and the fat has risen to the top and solidified, about 4 hours. Skim the fat off the stock and discard. Use the stock immediately or cover and store in the refrigerator for up to 3 days, or freeze for up to 1 month.

MAKES 2 QUARTS (2 L)

HOW TO COOK BACON

IN MY OPINION, THERE IS ONLY ONE CORRECT WAY TO COOK BACON AND THAT IS on a sheet pan in an oven. However, there are those rare occasions when only a few slices of bacon are needed, and then I pull out the frying pan and cook it on top of the stove. Read on for guidance on how to master these techniques.

PAN-FRIED BACON

Traditionalists like to cook their bacon strips in a frying pan. Maybe they enjoy the sounds and aromas released during this process, or they like to cook their eggs in the resulting bacon-greased pan, or maybe it's just the way they have always seen bacon cooked. I use this method when I just need a few slices quickly.

Start with a cold frying pan and add just a few teaspoons of canola oil to get the cooking process going. Heat over medium-low heat. If you add bacon to an already hot pan, you run the risk of scorching it. I recommend using a flat pan, preferably cast iron.

Take the bacon out of the fridge about 5 minutes before frying. This will bring the

fat back to its natural state, making it more suitable for frying.

Place enough bacon in the pan to fill it up, but not so much so that it overlaps. If it overlaps, there will be sections that aren't cooked. If there is too much space in the pan, not enough bacon grease will be released and the bacon can burn.

Cook the bacon on both sides until golden brown and crispy, about 6 minutes total for thin-sliced bacon, and 8 to 10 minutes for thick-sliced bacon. Take the bacon out of the pan and immediately place on a plate with paper towels to absorb the excess grease. Immediately pour the rendered fat from the pan into your "grease jar," cover, and refrigerate.

PROS: Good for cooking a few pieces quickly, and you get the pleasure of watching the bacon transform to crisp perfection. The aroma and sounds during cooking build anticipation for the glorious meal about to occur.

You also season your pan with bacon flavor, as bits of bacon will collect and stick to the pan as you cook this way. Those bits (which we chefs refer to as *sucs*) are concentrated bacon flavor that will season whatever you cook in the pan next.

CONS: Uneven cooking and splattered grease everywhere.

OVEN-ROASTED BACON

People like me who not only cook bacon every single day, but also like it perfectly straight, perfectly crisp, every time, bake it in the oven. It is also the method that should be used when cooking bacon for a crowd. When you own a restaurant that is making more than a thousand pounds of bacon a week, cooking on the range just isn't efficient—you'd be standing in front of the stove all day and night.

Preheat the oven to 350°F (175°C). Arrange the bacon on a rimmed sheet pan so that it just slightly overlaps; you can also arrange it on slotted broiler tray (or something similar) set on top of a sheet pan, but I typically only do this when I am glazing my bacon and want it really crisp.

Bake the bacon for 10 to 15 minutes for thinly sliced bacon, or 15 to 20 minutes for thick-cut bacon.

Remove from the oven and serve. Carefully pour the fat into your "grease jar," cover, and refrigerate. This is a much cleaner fat than the fat from pan-frying, as it has never reached a temperature that would burn it.

PROS: You don't have to worry about being burned by sputtering grease from the pan. With this method, bacon comes out evenly cooked, every time.

CONS: I sure as heck can't think of any!

HONEY MUSTARD–GLAZED BACON

THIS BACON IS GREAT SERVED AS AN HORS D'OEUVRE WITH A cocktail, on a sandwich with lettuce and tomato, or alongside sauerkraut and mashed potatoes. Sweet honey and slightly spicy Dijon mustard pair beautifully with bacon.

1 pound (455 g)
thick-sliced bacon

1 recipe Honey Mustard Glaze
(page 86)

Preheat the oven to 350°F (175°C). Lay the bacon on wire racks over rimmed sheet pans and bake for 10 to 15 minutes, until the bacon has rendered some fat and is starting to color on the edges.

Remove the bacon from the oven and pour the rendered fat through a sieve and save for another use.

Apply a thick coating of the honey mustard glaze to one side of each slice of bacon and return the baking sheet to the oven for 5 minutes. Remove from the oven, apply a second coating of glaze to each slice of bacon, and bake for an additional 5 minutes.

Let rest for 30 minutes or serve immediately.

SERVES 4 TO 6

THE PERFECT LARDONS

LARDONS **IS JUST A FANCY WORD FOR SLAB BACON THAT IS SLICED** into matchsticks. Lardons were originally used to add fat and richness to lean cuts of meat before roasting or braising. Cut into thin matchsticks (there's some debate among chefs as to the appropriate dimensions, but about ¼ inch (6 mm) thick by 1 inch (2.5 cm) long seems to be the way to go, for me), the lardons could be inserted right into the meat itself. Appropriately enough, this process is called *larding*! Because they are more fat than meat, lardons are slightly chewier than cooked sliced bacon. They are excellent in salads, the most classic being the *frisée-lardon*, and to add flavor and texture to frittatas, soups, and braises.

1 tablespoon canola oil

4 slices thick-cut bacon, cut crosswise into strips ¼ inch (6 mm) thick by 1 inch (2.5 cm) long

Combine the oil and bacon in a large sauté pan over medium heat and cook, stirring occasionally, until golden brown and slightly crispy, about 8 minutes.

Remove the bacon with a slotted spoon to a plate lined with paper towels. Pour the rendered fat into your "grease" jar and refrigerate.

Use immediately in dishes such as Spinach Salad (page 191) or Sweet Potato Hash (page 328), or store tightly covered in the refrigerator for up to 1 week. Reheat in a dry sauté pan over medium heat.

MAKES ABOUT 48 PIECES

BACON BITS

WITH ALL THE LEFTOVER SCRAPS OF BACON WE HAVE HANGING around in the BB kitchen, using them for bacon bits seems only natural. They definitely beat the ones you find in the jar at your local grocery store. Use them to top salads and casseroles, mix into scrambled eggs, or just keep them around as a snack whenever you need a quick pop of salty, smoky goodness.

1 pound (455 g) sliced bacon

Preheat the oven to 350°F (175°C). Line two rimmed baking sheets with aluminum foil, and lay the bacon slices on the foil. Bake for 18 to 20 minutes, until the bacon is cooked and crispy.

Remove from the oven and transfer the bacon with tongs to a plate lined with paper towels. Try to remove as much of the fat as possible, as the dryer the bacon is, the better it will freeze. Let cool completely. Transfer to a food processor and pulse until broken into tiny bits. Alternatively, finely chop the bacon using a chef's knife.

Transfer the bacon bits to a jar or freezer bag. Store in the freezer and use whenever you need them. Reheat in a dry skillet on top of the stove over medium heat.

MAKES ABOUT 1½ CUPS (160 G)

HOW TO RENDER AND COOK WITH BACON FAT

WHILE IT'S COMMON KNOWLEDGE THAT BACON MAKES EVERYTHING BETTER, home cooks often throw out the most valuable part of that tasty breakfast staple: the fat. A little spoonful of bacon fat can bring a meaty, smoky flavor to anything, from eggs to greens to baked goods. So before you ditch the drippings, read these tips!

HOW TO PROPERLY RENDER AND STORE FAT

When it comes to adding flavor and richness to your cooking, flakiness to your baking (think biscuits, tortillas, and piecrust), and smokiness and mouthfeel to your liquor and cream, there's nothing better than bacon fat. And guess what? If you are really going to cook from this book (and I hope that you are), you are going to have lots of rendered fat to store in your refrigerator. You'll be getting the fat from thin slices of bacon, thick slices, lardons, and chopped pieces. There is, however, a way to render fat from bacon just for the sake of rendering the fat. But before you pull out that skillet or sheet pan, here are a few rules to follow to get the most fat out of that bacon and store it properly for future use.

Chop your bacon—slab if possible, but chopped thick-sliced bacon works too—into small dice. The goal is to expose as much of the surface area of the bacon as you can to get more fat out using lower heat. This prevents the bacon or fat from cooking too quickly and burning.

Add a few teaspoons of neutral oil (I like canola) to the pan to get it going, then fry slowly over medium heat in a heavy skillet (cast iron, if possible), stirring occasionally to keep the pieces from sticking. The bacon is done when it's golden brown and has shrunk about 50 percent in volume and the pan has a nice thick layer of grease in it.

Remove the pieces of bacon using a slotted spoon and drain them on a layer of paper towels until you're ready to use. You can use immediately as a garnish for baked potatoes, salads, popcorn, or ice cream, or store in plastic bags in the freezer for future use (see Bacon Bits, page 49).

Strain the fat through a fine-mesh sieve into your "grease jar." Don't use plastic—if the fat is still hot, it could melt the container; plastic can also impart a flavor to the stored grease. I use a pint-size glass jar with a wide mouth. The wide opening is convenient for spooning out dollops of fat.

NOTE: *As the bacon cooks, it will inevitably leave behind bits and pieces of meat. You don't want those in your bacon grease, because when you cook with it later, they'll burn and impart a bitter flavor to your food. Removing the solids by straining the fat means it'll last for just about forever in your fridge.*

HOW TO DISCARD FAT

At some point, you have to throw out the fat. You can't use the same batch over and over forever, because the fat was cooked with foods that are capable of producing bacteria if left to sit around long enough, and it can take on the flavor of whatever you are cooking. After the fat has been rendered, we recommend using it only once, and then discarding the used portion. So what is the proper way to toss it?

Bacon grease hardens when it cools. The easiest cleanup is to allow the fat to harden and then use a paper towel or rubber spatula to knock it into the trash.

Important: Never pour hot bacon fat down the drain, even if you have a garbage disposal! As it cools, it will harden and clog the pipes. Running water isn't enough to dislodge this grease. Bacon fat, like the fat of other animals, can turn rancid, and it is not a smell you want emanating from your kitchen sink. You also shouldn't use any type of meat or meat product in compost because the meat could contain pathogens that the compost may not be hot enough to kill. This can attract predatory animals, which can pose a danger to small children and house pets.

HOW MUCH FAT WILL A POUND OF BACON RENDER?

It depends on if it's properly cooked and how fatty the cut is. General estimates are:

1 pound (455 g) thin-sliced bacon yields about ⅓ cup (75 ml) fat

1 pound (455 g) thick-sliced bacon yields about ½ cup (120 ml) fat

HOW TO COOK AND BAKE WITH RENDERED BACON FAT

Bacon is salty—salt is part of the curing process. So when cooking with the fat, adjust the amount of salt you add to the dish accordingly. Remember, you can always add more salt. It is hard to fix a dish that is oversalted.

Okay, so you cooked all this bacon, rendered the fat, and stored it properly in the refrigerator. Now what? Well, I'm glad you asked. Here is how I use it:

BACON CONFIT (PAGE 41)
Cooking bacon in its own fat is so decadent that it should be illegal, but it's not. Cooking it low and slow tenderizes the meat. This low-temperature deep-fry is similar to BBQ, where low temperature is applied to thick, fatty meat for long periods of time until fork-tender.

INFUSED LIQUORS (PAGE 100)
Liquor has an unbelievable ability to pull flavor from fat. I knew I wanted bacon-flavored drinks at the bar when we opened BarBacon. We make our own bacon vodka, bacon bourbon, and bacon rum (see page 98 for Cocktails). It's super easy and results in a surprisingly intense bacon flavor for such little effort.

BAKING
Bacon fat adds a smoky flavor, flaky texture, and a unique mouthfeel to chocolate chip cookies (page 342), pie dough (page 354), whipped cream (page 353), and biscuits (page 327). I find that adding it in place of a few tablespoons of oil and/or butter adds just the right amount of smoke and salt. You definitely do not want to use all bacon fat in your baking; it would be too overwhelming. Also, when using bacon fat for pie doughs or biscuits, make sure that it is very cold, so that you can cut it into the flour just like you would with lard, shortening, or butter.

MY FAVORITE SMOKEHOUSE
OR PREPARED BACONS

WHEN I AM NOT COOKING WITH MY OWN HOMEMADE BACON, I AM LIKELY USING bacon from one of my favorite smokehouses listed below. The best part is that many of them can be purchased in grocery stores and all are available online for ordering. This is by no means a comprehensive list or even a best list. It's a starting point with some of the best bacons—with a good mix of flavors beyond just wood-smoked. I leave it to you to determine your favorites, but I've included my tasting notes to help guide you.

Before buying, keep in mind that there are two types of bacon: the traditional kind we all grew up with that has pink salt (sodium nitrite) in the cure; and the no-nitrite version. No-nitrite bacon tends to have more of a pork flavor rather than a bacon flavor . . . yes, there is a difference. Pork chops don't taste like bacon. Only bacon tastes like bacon.

BURGERS' SMOKEHOUSE

APPLEWOOD SMOKED BACON: Dry-rubbed with a recipe of salt, cane sugar, and spice, then naturally smoked with applewood until golden brown. A truly nice bacon with a great fat-to-meat ratio and saltiness, with a mild smokiness. The best part of Burgers' is that all their bacon is thick cut; the more traditional varieties are even available in a super-thick-cut option.

PEPPER COATED ORIGINAL COUNTRY BACON: Nice pepper flavor that does not overwhelm the bacon. Good fat-to-meat ratio and saltiness.

SLICED COUNTRY JOWL: Hand-cured and hickory-smoked, we loved this alternative bacon. The strips are smaller than traditional belly strips, but when cooked, they fry up like bacon potato chips with a great porky bacon flavor.

FATHER'S COUNTRY HAMS

FATHER'S APPLE CINNAMON BACON: Hickory-smoked bacon coated with an apple-cinnamon rub. This is a nice breakfast bacon alternative with the fruit and spice notes coming through clearly.

FATHER'S MAPLE COUNTRY BACON: Flavored with pure maple sugar made from maple sap that is extracted from wild maple trees. It has a great maple flavor that dominates the flavor profile. You can't cook this bacon to a crispy texture because the sugars will burn; if you are looking for crispy bacon, this is not it.

NODINE'S SMOKEHOUSE

APPLEWOOD BACON: Smoked with apple pomace from the cider mill and hickory hardwood. This is a terrific bacon that has a less salty flavor than most artisanal-style bacons, along with a really nice balance of fat to meat and a mild smoke flavor.

GARLIC BACON: Has a great balanced salt and smoke flavor, and, as advertised, there is a definite garlic flavor present in every bite.

MAPLE BACON: Pure maple syrup flavors ring through, but not so much that they disguise the bacon. This one can be cooked in an oven to the point of achieving crispiness without burning, which is uncommon for high-sugar cured bacons.

PEPPER BACON: For the pepper lovers! This bacon is covered in coarsely ground black pepper, and has all the great flavor of the hardwood bacons but with black pepper added.

BUFFALO GAL

WILD BOAR BACON: Delicious bacon; very mild, and not overly gamey in flavor. It's thick cut, so it cooks up chewy, not crispy, but with sweet undertones from a high-sugar cure.

SWABIAN HALL PORK BACON: Nice thick-cut bacon with high fat content that cooks up chewy, not crisp. I would classify this more as bacon candy that you would eat on its own rather than adding to sandwiches or composed dishes. It has rich lingering sweet notes of maple and sugar instead of a porky or even salty aftertaste.

NUESKE'S

APPLEWOOD SMOKED BACON: Smoked for a full twenty-four hours over applewood embers. This is one of the most award-winning bacons in the country, and there is good reason why.

WILD CHERRYWOOD SMOKED BACON: Naturally cured and smoked for twenty-four hours over embers of fresh-cut cherrywood logs. Smoky with a subtle sweetness.

BENTON'S

HICKORY SMOKED COUNTRY BACON: Easily the smokiest bacon I have ever tried. It's almost unpalatable on its own, but nothing is better for flavoring stocks, sauces, liquor, or whatever is in need of a smoky bacon takeover.

CHAPTER 2

BACON SAUSAGES

**T BREAKFAST, WE'RE ALWAYS FORCED TO** choose between bacon and sausage. I hate picking between the two, so I did something about it and made a bacon sausage. Instead of using regular or plain ground meat, I use a combination of plain ground meat (pork or lamb or both) with finely cut bacon. It adds just enough fat to make the sausages come together—and, obviously, makes them way more delicious. It also adds just a little texture and smoke.

We make a few kinds of bacon sausages at the restaurant, and I'm always creating new ones, experimenting with herbs and spices. One of the first ones I came up with was our bacon bratwurst, which I form into patties, grill on both sides until perfectly charred, then serve on a soft pretzel bun with sauerkraut and honey mustard–glazed bacon (page 46). It's tailgate meets breakfast with just enough of the bacon coming through that you know you're eating something special. Even easier is our breakfast sausage, which is made with fresh sage, or our fall version, with maple syrup and apple added. I fry this one up in patties, so you don't even need to think about stuffing those pesky casings. The sausages freeze really well and will keep for up to six months. I always have some ready to go in the freezer just in case I have a late-night or early-morning sausage craving. They're perfect alongside a stack of pancakes or tucked into a split bacon biscuit (page 327).

HOW TO STUFF SAUSAGES

MAKING YOUR OWN SAUSAGE LINKS—RATHER THAN PATTIES—REQUIRES A FEW extra tools. Don't get carried away with expensive oversize products unless you intend to start selling them retail. To make my recipes, you will just need the items listed below. Luckily, all are available in kitchen supply stores and online.

WHAT YOU'LL NEED

MEAT GRINDER: You can use your stand mixer (I prefer a KitchenAid) with the meat grinder attachment, or you can purchase a manual grinder.

SAUSAGE STUFFER: Again, you can use your stand mixer with the sausage stuffer attachment, or you can purchase a manual stuffer.

CASINGS: If you are going to make links instead of patties, you will need casings. There are several kinds of casings on the market, but I prefer natural hog (of course). If you can't find those, my second choice would be sheep casing. They are the best for the money. The natural casings "snap" when you bite into them and also help to give a beautiful color to the sausage.

~~~~~~~~~~~~~~~~~~~~~~~~~~~~~~~~~~~~

Take out some of the casings. You need 15 to 18 feet (4.6 to 5.5 m) for a 5-pound/2.3-kg batch of link. Put the casings in a medium bowl and set it in the sink. Rinse the casings under cool running water: Hold one end of each piece of casing open under the tap and flush it out by gently running cool water through it. (Once you fill part of the casing, use your hands to push the water through to the other end.) Fill the bowl with fresh, cool water and let the casings soak for 10 minutes.

Attach a ⅝- or ¾-inch (1.6- or 2-cm) sausage-stuffing tube to the front of your grinder or to a sausage stuffer. (If using a grinder with a stuffing attachment, be sure to remove the grinding plate and blade first.) Splash cool water onto the tube to moisten it. Open an end of one piece of casing and pull it over the end of the tube. Push the rest of the casing onto the tube accordion-style, leaving 3 to 4 inches (7.5 to 10 cm) hanging off the end.

Fill the hopper with the sausage mixture and feed it through just until it reaches the end of the stuffing tube. Check with your finger to feel if the meat is flush with the opening. Tie the end of the attached casing into a knot, and slide it up over the tube until the knot hits the tip of the tube.

Feed the meat mixture through the tube to fill the casing, pressing your thumb and forefinger against the tip of the tube to control the rate and tightness of the filling. Go slowly, don't overstuff (but do stuff firmly), and watch for air holes. When there are only 3 to 4 inches (7.5 to 10 cm) of empty casing left, stop the feeder, slip the casing off the tube, and tie it in a knot about ½ inch (12 mm) from the end of the sausage filling—this extra space will fill in as you make links.

Put the sausage on a flat surface and use a skewer or toothpick to prick any air holes that have formed during stuffing.

To make links, lay one sausage at a time on a clean work surface, with the front end of the sausage (the end where you began filling) in front of you and the rest of the sausage lying to the right. Measure 5 inches (12 cm) from left to right and pinch the casing at that spot between your thumb and forefinger. Twist the unlinked portion away from you four or five turns to bind off the link on the left. Measure another 5 inches and pinch and twist away from you to form another link. Repeat until you reach the end of the casing, always twisting in the same direction. Prick any remaining air holes.

Lay the links, uncovered, on a rack set over a rimmed baking sheet. Dry in the refrigerator for 24 hours to allow the flavors to meld and to give the casings a good bite when cooked. Drying will also reduce the amount of moisture in the meat, too much of which can steam and lead to bursting.

HOW TO COOK SAUSAGES

FOR PATTIES:

Heat 2 teaspoons canola oil in a large, preferably cast-iron skillet over medium heat. Cook, turning as needed, until browned and cooked through, about 10 minutes total.

FOR LINKS:

TO GRILL: Heat a grill to high or a grill pan over high heat. Brush the links with canola oil and grill until golden brown and cooked through on both sides, about 12 minutes total.

TO PAN-FRY: Heat a few tablespoons of canola oil in a large sauté pan (I prefer cast iron or nonstick) over medium-high heat until it begins to shimmer. Cook the sausage until golden brown on both sides, about 10 minutes.

TO COOK IN THE OVEN: Preheat the oven to 350°F (175°C). Place the sausage in a shallow baking dish and bake until golden brown, turning once, about 15 minutes.

HOW TO STORE SAUSAGES

Patties and links should be individually wrapped in plastic, then in foil before storing. Uncooked, raw sausage will keep, tightly wrapped in plastic wrap then wrapped inside of aluminum foil, in the refrigerator for 2 days and in the freezer for up to 2 months.

Wrapping the sausages tightly in plastic first, then in aluminum foil will help prevent freezer burn and protect the sausage's flavor.

TO DEFROST: When you are ready to cook with the sausage, remove from the freezer and defrost in the refrigerator. Follow these rules:

1. Do not remove the wrapping.
2. Place the sausage on a plate in the bottom of the fridge.
3. Leave in the refrigerator until fully defrosted.

Very important: You should never defrost sausages at room temperature. Defrosted sausage should not be re-frozen until it has been thoroughly cooked.

BACON AND MUSTARD SAUSAGE

OUR LINE OF BACON SAUSAGES STARTED WITH THE OBJECTIVE OF creating sausages that needed nothing else. No sauce or accompaniment; just slice, eat, and enjoy. This bacon mustard sausage was one of my first successes. The Dijon and garlic give it a nice kick, and the whole-grain mustard, bacon, and caraway seeds provide texture. My favorite way to serve this sausage is with sauerkraut and spicy Dijon mustard. We link this sausage at the restaurant and then smoke it in a 225°F (107°C) smoker just to add a touch more smokiness. Smoking it is not necessary, though, as the bacon in the grind gives you a hint of smoke as well.

12 ounces (340 g) thin-sliced bacon

4 pounds (1.8 kg) ground pork (80/20)

2½ tablespoons kosher salt

2 teaspoons phosphates (see page 13)

4 garlic cloves, finely chopped

2 teaspoons finely chopped fresh rosemary leaves

1 teaspoon caraway seeds

2 tablespoons sugar

¼ cup (60 ml) Dijon mustard

¼ cup (60 ml) whole-grain mustard

1¼ cups (300 ml) cold water

Hog casings, if using (see page 56)

Put the bacon on a plate and freeze for 15 minutes before slicing to make it easier to cut. Transfer to a cutting board, stack several pieces on top of each other, and slice crosswise into pieces ¼ inch (6 mm) thick.

Put the bacon, pork, salt, phosphates, garlic, rosemary, caraway, sugar, and both mustards in an extra-large bowl and mix with your hands until combined. Add the cold water and carefully incorporate so you don't spill any water out of the bowl.

If you are planning to make patties and not links, divide the mixture into 16 equal portions (5 ounces/140 g each), then form into patties. (Alternatively, the meat mixture can be frozen to be made into patties later: Shape and roll mixture into two logs about 6 inches [15 cm] long each. Wrap in plastic wrap and foil and freeze. To use, thaw and slice into patties with a knife, then cook following the instructions on page 57. Or if you like, you can shape into patties, and layer them individually onto a parchment-lined baking sheet and freeze. Then remove and add to a gallon-size zip-top freezer bag.)

If you plan to stuff your sausage, see the instructions on page 56.

Cook the sausage patties or links according to the instructions on page 57.

MAKES ABOUT 5 POUNDS (2.3 KG); 16 (5-OUNCE/140-G) LINKS OR PATTIES

BACON BRATWURST

AT BARBACON WE MAKE THIS SAUSAGE FOR OUR BACON BRATWURST
Burger (page 202) . . . it's perfectly grilled and served on a soft salty pretzel bun
piled high with sauerkraut and honey mustard–glazed bacon (page 46).

1 pound (455 g)
thin-sliced bacon

4 pounds (1.8 kg) ground
pork (80/20)

1½ tablespoons kosher salt

2 teaspoons phosphates
(see page 13)

1 teaspoon ground
white pepper

1 teaspoon ground ginger

1 teaspoon grated nutmeg

2 large eggs

1 cup (240 ml) heavy cream

Hog casings, if using
(see page 56)

Put the bacon on a plate and freeze for 15 minutes before slicing to make it easier to cut. Transfer to a cutting board, stack several pieces on top of each other, and slice crosswise into pieces ¼ inch (6 mm) thick.

Put the bacon, pork, salt, phosphates, white pepper, ginger, nutmeg, eggs, and cream in an extra-large bowl and mix with your hands until combined.

If you are planning to make patties and not links, divide the mixture into 16 equal portions (5 ounces/140 g each), then form into patties. (Alternatively, the meat mixture can be frozen to be made into patties later: Shape and roll mixture into two logs about 6 inches

[15 cm] long each. Wrap in plastic wrap and foil and freeze. To use, thaw and slice into patties with a knife, then cook following the instructions on page 57. Or if you like, you can shape into patties, and layer them individually onto a parchment-lined baking sheet and freeze. Then remove and add to a gallon-size zip-top freezer bag.)

If you plan to stuff your sausage, see the instructions on page 56.

Cook the sausage patties or links according to the instructions on page 57.

**MAKES 5 POUNDS (2.3 KG);
16 (5-OUNCE/140-G) LINKS
OR PATTIES**

BACON-CHEDDAR-JALAPEÑO SAUSAGE

THIS WAS SORT OF A RIFF ON A STUFFED JALAPEÑO, A FAVORITE BAR snack of mine. It is important to use a good-quality cheese in this recipe; the sharper and more pronounced the cheese, the better this sausage will taste.

12 ounces (340 g) thin-sliced bacon

4 pounds (1.8 kg) ground pork (80/20)

3 tablespoons kosher salt

2½ teaspoons phosphates (see page 13)

¼ cup (60 ml) light corn syrup

2½ teaspoons dextrose sugar

1½ teaspoons freshly ground black pepper

½ teaspoon mustard powder

½ teaspoon garlic powder

¼ teaspoon ground ginger

6 jalapeños, seeded and finely diced

1 pound (455 g) extra-sharp cheddar cheese, coarsely grated

1 cup (240 ml) cold water

Hog casings, if using (see page 56)

Put the bacon on a plate and freeze for 15 minutes before slicing to make it easier to cut. Transfer to a cutting board, stack several pieces on top of each other, and slice crosswise into pieces ¼ inch (6 mm) thick.

Put the bacon, pork, salt, phosphates, corn syrup, dextrose, pepper, mustard powder, garlic powder, ginger, jalapeños, and cheese in an extra-large bowl and mix with your hands until combined. Add the cold water and carefully incorporate so you don't spill any water out of the bowl.

If you are planning to make patties and not links, divide the mixture into 16 equal portions (5 ounces/140 g each), then form into patties. (Alternatively, the meat mixture can be frozen to be made into patties later: Shape and roll mixture into two logs about 6 inches [15 cm] long each. Wrap in plastic wrap and foil and freeze. To use, thaw and slice into patties with a knife, then cook following the instructions on page 57. Or if you like, you can shape into patties, and layer them individually onto a parchment-lined baking sheet and freeze. Then remove and add to a gallon-size zip-top freezer bag.)

If you plan to stuff your sausage, see the instructions on page 56.

Cook the sausage patties or links according to the instructions on page 57.

**MAKES 5 POUNDS (2.3 KG);
16 (5-OUNCE/140-G) LINKS
OR PATTIES**

MAPLE BACON AND APPLE BREAKFAST SAUSAGE

THIS SAUSAGE MAKES AN APPEARANCE ON OUR FALL BRUNCH MENU when apples are aplenty and at their peak in New York State. I love using Rome or Honeycrisp apples—something slightly sweet and slightly tart, and that will hold its shape in the sausage—and a quality-grade New York State maple syrup for this sausage. Serve alongside sunny-side-up eggs.

12 ounces (340 g) thin-sliced bacon

4 pounds (1.8 kg) ground pork (80/20)

2½ tablespoons kosher salt

2 teaspoons phosphates (see page 13)

4 cups (5.7 ounces/160 g) peeled and diced Rome or Honeycrisp apples (about 2 large apples)

3 garlic cloves, finely chopped

1 (2-inch/5-cm) piece fresh ginger, peeled and finely grated

2 tablespoons finely chopped fresh sage leaves

¾ cup (180 ml) pure maple syrup, preferably Grade B

1 cup (240 ml) cold water

Hog casings, if using (see page 56)

Put the bacon on a plate and freeze for 15 minutes before slicing to make it easier to cut. Transfer to a cutting board, stack several pieces on top of each other, and slice crosswise into pieces ¼ inch (6 mm) thick.

Put the bacon, pork, salt, phosphates, apples, garlic, ginger, sage, and maple syrup in an extra-large bowl and mix with your hands until combined. Add the cold water and carefully incorporate so you don't spill any water out of the bowl.

If you are planning to make patties and not links, divide the mixture into 16 equal portions (5 ounces/140 g each), then form into patties. (Alternatively, the meat mixture can be frozen to be made into patties later: Shape and roll mixture into two logs about 6 inches [15 cm] long each. Wrap in plastic wrap and foil and freeze. To use, thaw and slice into patties with a knife, then cook following the instructions on page 57. Or if you like, you can shape into patties, and layer them individually onto a parchment-lined baking sheet and freeze. Then remove and add to a gallon-size zip-top freezer bag.)

If you plan to stuff your sausage, see the instructions on page 56.

Cook the sausage patties or links according to the instructions on page 57.

MAKES 5 POUNDS (2.3 KG); 16 (5-OUNCE/140-G) LINKS OR PATTIES

BACON-CHIPOTLE CHORIZO

I AM A LITTLE OBSESSED WITH CANNED CHIPOTLE CHILES—WHICH are smoked jalapeños in a vinegary adobo sauce. Traditional Mexican chorizo has a lot of smoked paprika, which gives it its deep red color. I prefer using the chipotle, which adds the same color and smokiness but a good kick of heat too that, in my opinion, store-bought chorizo is lacking.

12 ounces (340 g) thin-sliced bacon

4 pounds (1.8 kg) ground pork (80/20)

¼ cup (60 ml) plus 1 tablespoon pureed chipotles in adobo

3 garlic cloves, finely chopped

2 teaspoons finely chopped fresh thyme leaves

¼ cup (10 g) finely chopped fresh cilantro leaves

3 tablespoons kosher salt

1 tablespoon phosphates (see page 13)

2 teaspoons freshly ground black pepper

1 teaspoon dried oregano

½ teaspoon ground cloves

½ teaspoon ground allspice

1¾ cups (420 ml) cold water

Hog casings, if using (see page 56)

Put the bacon on a plate and freeze for 15 minutes before slicing to make it easier to cut. Transfer to a cutting board, stack several pieces on top of each other, and slice crosswise into pieces ¼ inch (6 mm) thick.

Put the bacon, pork, chipotles, garlic, thyme, cilantro, salt, phosphates, black pepper, oregano, cloves, and allspice in an extra-large bowl and mix with your hands until combined. Add the cold water and carefully incorporate so you don't spill any water out of the bowl.

If you are planning to make patties and not links, divide the mixture into 16 equal portions (5 ounces/140 g each), then form into patties. (Alternatively, the meat mixture can be frozen to be made into patties later: Shape and roll mixture into two logs about 6 inches [15 cm] long each. Wrap in plastic wrap and foil and freeze. To use, thaw and slice into patties with a knife, then cook following the instructions on page 57. Or if you like, you can shape into patties, and layer them individually onto a parchment-lined baking sheet and freeze. Then remove and add to a gallon-size zip-top freezer bag.)

If you plan to stuff your sausage, see the instructions on page 56.

Cook the sausage patties or links according to the instructions on page 57.

MAKES 5 POUNDS (2.3 KG); 16 (5-OUNCE/140-G) LINKS OR PATTIES

CHERRY PEPPER SAUSAGE

ONE OF MY FAVORITE ACCOMPANIMENTS TO SAUSAGE IS HOT CHERRY peppers, but I never check to see if I have them until I'm ready to eat—and no, they are never there when I need them. I made this sausage so I didn't have to remember to keep them in stock. The spice and acid from the peppers cut through the fattiness of the bacon and pork, making this a true one-stop meal. Nothing more is needed.

12 ounces (340 g) thin-sliced bacon

4 pounds (1.8 kg) ground pork (80/20)

¾ cup (170 g) chopped hot pickled cherry peppers

5 garlic cloves, finely chopped

2½ tablespoons sugar

2 tablespoons smoked paprika

1½ tablespoons kosher salt

2½ teaspoons phosphates (see page 13)

2 teaspoons coarsely ground black pepper

1 teaspoon finely chopped fresh rosemary leaves

½ teaspoon finely chopped fresh thyme leaves

1½ cups (360 ml) cold water

Hog casings, if using (see page 56)

Put the bacon on a plate and freeze for 15 minutes before slicing to make it easier to cut. Transfer to a cutting board, stack several pieces on top of each other, and slice crosswise into pieces ¼ inch (6 mm) thick.

Put the bacon, pork, cherry peppers, garlic, sugar, paprika, salt, phosphates, black pepper, rosemary, and thyme in an extra-large bowl and mix with your hands until combined. Add the cold water and carefully incorporate so you don't spill any water out of the bowl.

If you are planning to make patties and not links, divide the mixture into 16 equal portions (5 ounces/140 g each), then form into patties. (Alternatively, the meat mixture can be frozen to be made into patties later: Shape and roll mixture into two logs about 6 inches [15 cm] long each. Wrap in plastic wrap and foil and freeze. To use, thaw and slice into patties with a knife, then cook following the instructions on page 57. Or if you like, you can shape into patties, and layer them individually onto a parchment-lined baking sheet and freeze. Then remove and add to a gallon-size zip-top freezer bag.)

If you plan to stuff your sausage, see the instructions on page 56.

Cook the sausage patties or links according to the instructions on page 57.

MAKES 5 POUNDS (2.3 KG); 16 (5-OUNCE/140-G) LINKS OR PATTIES

BACON AND LAMB MERGUEZ

THIS IS MY TAKE ON THE SPICY MOROCCAN LAMB SAUSAGE, MERGUEZ, which is usually made with lamb and beef or beef fat. No surprise, I substitute pork and bacon here. The addition of pork makes this sausage a bit juicier, and the bacon and smoked paprika add additional smoke. It's one of my favorite sausages of all time. Merguez is not smoked, but nothing about this sausage is traditional. Serve with grilled pita, Thyme Tzatziki (page 76), and Bread and Butter Pickles (page 276).

4 cups (960 ml) dry red wine, such as Merlot

Ice

12 ounces (340 g) thin-sliced bacon

4 pounds (1.8 kg) ground lamb shoulder (80/20)

3 garlic cloves, finely chopped

4 teaspoons Diamond Crystal kosher salt

2 teaspoons phosphates (see page 13)

1 tablespoon smoked paprika

1 tablespoon finely chopped fresh oregano leaves

1 teaspoon freshly ground black pepper

½ teaspoon red chile flakes

5 ounces (140 g) finely diced roasted red pepper (about 1 large roasted red pepper)

Hog casings, if using (see page 56)

In a medium-size pot over high heat, boil the wine until reduced by half, then let cool completely over an ice bath.

Put the bacon on a plate and freeze for 15 minutes before slicing to make it easier to cut. Transfer to a cutting board, stack several pieces on top of each other, and slice crosswise into pieces ¼ inch (6 mm) thick.

Put the bacon, lamb, garlic, salt, phosphates, paprika, oregano, black pepper, chile flakes, roasted pepper, and cooled reduced wine in an extra-large bowl and mix with your hands until combined.

If you are planning to make patties and not links, divide the mixture into 16 equal portions (5 ounces/140 g each), then form into patties. (Alternatively, the meat mixture can be frozen to be made into patties later: Shape and roll mixture into two logs about 6 inches [15 cm] long each. Wrap in plastic wrap and foil and freeze. To use, thaw and slice into patties with a knife, then cook following the instructions on page 57. Or if you like, you can shape into patties, and layer them individually onto a parchment-lined baking sheet and freeze. Then remove and add to a gallon-size zip-top freezer bag.)

If you plan to stuff your sausage, see the instructions on page 56.

Cook the sausage patties or links according to the instructions on page 57.

MAKES 5 POUNDS (2.3 KG); 16 (5-OUNCE/140-G) LINKS OR PATTIES

CHAPTER 3

SAUCES & RUBS

ACON ADAPTS TO THE THINGS AROUND IT. It lives just as harmoniously with mild vegetables as it does in a rich port wine marinara. The sauces in this chapter are from different cultures and have different spice levels. There are ones meant to complement the bacon on the plate and others where the sauce is cooked right into the bacon. Making your own sauce is also a great way to use up some of that leftover bacon fat I keep telling you to save. Use it in mayonnaise instead of canola oil or as the fat to cook your onions for a BBQ sauce or marinara.

BACON MAYONNAISE

DON'T BE INTIMIDATED. MAKING HOMEMADE MAYONNAISE IS ACTU- ally really easy and is so much more flavorful than the jarred kind (not that I don't love Hellmann's). The secret to this recipe is making sure to emulsify with the olive oil first, then whisk in the bacon fat; otherwise, the mayonnaise will break, or separate. There are so many variations you can try—horseradish, chipotle, and maple are my favorites.

½ cup (120 ml) rendered bacon fat (see page 50)

1 large egg yolk

2 tablespoons Dijon mustard

2 teaspoons white wine vinegar

1 teaspoon warm water

¼ teaspoon kosher salt

⅔ cup (160 ml) extra-virgin olive oil

In a small saucepan, heat the bacon fat over low heat and cook until just melted. Remove from the heat and let cool to room temperature, about 5 minutes.

Place a medium bowl (stainless steel is preferable) on a dish towel to keep the bowl from moving. Add the egg yolk, mustard, vinegar, warm water, and the salt and whisk until pale and foamy. While whisking constantly, add the olive oil slowly, drop by drop, until the mixture begins to thicken and emulsify.

Once you have created an emulsification, you can begin to add the oil a bit faster. Once the oil has been added, add the bacon fat in a slow, steady stream, whisking until completely emulsified. The mayonnaise will keep, tightly covered in the refrigerator, for up to 5 days.

MAKES 1¼ CUPS (300 ML)

HORSERADISH BACON MAYONNAISE

1 recipe Bacon Mayonnaise

¼ cup (55 g) prepared horseradish, drained

Whisk together the bacon mayonnaise and horseradish in a bowl. Cover and refrigerate for at least 30 minutes before serving.

CHIPOTLE BACON MAYONNAISE

1 recipe Bacon Mayonnaise

2 tablespoons pureed chipotles in adobo

Whisk together the bacon mayonnaise and chipotles in a bowl. Cover and refrigerate for at least 30 minutes before serving.

MAPLE BACON MAYONNAISE

1 recipe Bacon Mayonnaise

2 tablespoons pure maple syrup

Pinch of freshly ground black pepper

Whisk together the bacon mayonnaise, maple syrup, and pepper in a bowl. Cover and refrigerate for at least 30 minutes before serving.

MAPLE-BACON MAYONNAISE

ADDING A TOUCH OF SWEETNESS, A TOUCH OF SMOKE, AND ADDI-tional fat to mayonnaise makes it a delicious spread for a BLT, turkey sandwich, or as a dip for crispy French fries. Try this version when you don't feel like making my Bacon Mayonnaise (page 72) from scratch.

1 cup (240 ml) store-bought mayonnaise

½ cup (120 ml) pure maple syrup

2 tablespoons rendered bacon fat (see page 50), melted and slightly cooled

Pinch of freshly ground black pepper

In a small bowl, whisk together the mayonnaise, maple syrup, bacon fat, and pepper. Cover and refrigerate for at least 30 minutes before serving to allow the flavors

to meld. The mayonnaise will keep, tightly covered in the refrigerator, for up to 1 week.

**MAKES ABOUT
1½ CUPS (360 ML)**

CHIPOTLE-LIME MAYONNAISE

AN EASY WAY TO ADD EXTRA FLAVOR TO SANDWICHES OR CREATE simple sauces for grilled meats and seafoods is to add a few extra ingredients to prepared mayonnaise. I love the combination of smoky chipotle and tangy lime in this version. It's delicious slathered on a BLT or drizzled over Chipotle Bacon Tacos with Toasted Cumin Slaw (page 233).

1 cup (240 ml) store-bought mayonnaise

2 tablespoons pureed chipotles in adobo

Juice of 1 small lime

In a small bowl, whisk together the mayonnaise, chipotles, and lime juice. Cover and refrigerate for at least 30 minutes, or up to 24 hours to

allow the flavors to meld. The mayonnaise will keep, tightly covered in the refrigerator, for up to 2 weeks.

**MAKES ABOUT
1 CUP (240 ML)**

RÉMOULADE SAUCE

THIS NEW ORLEANS–STYLE RÉMOULADE IS PIQUANT THANKS TO A good dose of hot sauce, and is most often served with fried food and grilled seafood. It is also good slathered on a BLT or burger or as a dipping sauce for Kentucky Fried Bacon (page 42) or Tempura Bacon (page 133).

2⅓ cups (555 ml) store-bought mayonnaise

½ cup (120 ml) plus 2 table-spoons Dijon mustard

1 generous teaspoon Tabasco sauce

1 generous teaspoon Worcestershire sauce

4 small garlic cloves, finely chopped

¼ cup (35 g) finely chopped red onion

2 tablespoons capers, drained

Kosher salt and freshly ground black pepper

Whisk together the mayon-naise, mustard, Tabasco sauce, Worcestershire sauce, and garlic in a medium bowl until smooth. Fold in the onion and capers and season with salt and pepper to taste.

Cover and refrigerate for at least 30 minutes to allow the flavors to meld. The sauce will keep, tightly covered in the refrigerator, for up to 5 days.

MAKES ABOUT 3 CUPS (710 ML)

THYME TZATZIKI

CLASSICALLY, THIS GREEK SAUCE IS MADE WITH LOTS OF FRESH dill. But dill always makes me think of ranch dressing, which this is not. Thyme is a hearty herb that stands up well to the smokiness and fat of bacon and pairs really well with the tomato confit that I always serve in tandem with this sauce.

2 cups (480 ml) plain
Greek yogurt

½ small cucumber, peeled,
seeded, and finely diced

2 tablespoons finely diced
red onion

2 garlic cloves, finely chopped

1 tablespoon freshly squeezed
lemon juice

1½ teaspoons finely chopped
fresh thyme leaves

Kosher salt

In a bowl, combine the yogurt, cucumber, onion, garlic, lemon juice, thyme, and salt to taste and stir. Cover and refrigerate for at least 30 minutes or up to 8 hours to allow the flavors to meld. The tzatziki will keep, tightly covered in the refrigerator, for up to 3 days.

**MAKES ABOUT
2½ CUPS (600 ML)**

TARRAGON BUTTERMILK DRESSING

I THINK OF THIS AS A BÉARNAISE SAUCE, WITHOUT THE BUTTER but all of the flavor. I love using it as a dip for vegetables, a dressing for salads, or an easy sauce for grilled chicken and fish.

2 large shallots, chopped

1 cup (240 ml) champagne vinegar or white wine vinegar

1 cup (240 ml) dry white wine (such as a chardonnay)

3 tablespoons chopped fresh tarragon leaves

1½ cups (360 ml) store-bought mayonnaise

¼ cup (60 ml) shaken buttermilk

¼ teaspoon kosher salt

In a medium nonreactive saucepan, combine the shallots, vinegar, wine, and 2 tablespoons of the tarragon, bring to a boil, and cook until the mixture is reduced to ½ cup (120 ml), about 15 minutes. Let cool slightly.

In a food processor, combine the mayonnaise, buttermilk, and shallot reduction and process until smooth. Add the remaining tarragon and the salt and pulse a few times just to incorporate.

Transfer to a container with a tight-fitting lid and refrigerate for at least 30 minutes to allow the flavors to meld. The dressing will keep, tightly covered in the refrigerator, for up to 3 days.

MAKES ABOUT 2¼ CUPS (540 ML)

BACON–BLUE CHEESE RANCH

WHAT DO YOU GET WHEN YOU MIX RANCH DRESSING WITH BLUE cheese dressing and add bacon? Bacon–Blue Cheese Ranch. Our most popular dressing at BarBacon is great drizzled on the Wedge Salad (page 183), served alongside a platter of chicken wings, or used as a base for potato salad or coleslaw.

1 cup (240 ml) sour cream

½ cup (120 ml) store-bought mayonnaise

¼ cup (60 ml) buttermilk

2 tablespoons red wine vinegar

1 teaspoon Worcestershire sauce

3 garlic cloves, chopped

4 ounces (115 g) blue cheese (such as Maytag or Cabrales), crumbled

3 tablespoons finely chopped fresh dill

4 ounces (115 g) thin-sliced bacon, cooked until crisp (see page 44) and chopped

¼ teaspoon freshly ground black pepper

In a blender, combine the sour cream, mayonnaise, buttermilk, vinegar, Worcestershire sauce, garlic, half of the cheese, the dill, bacon, and pepper and blend until smooth.

Pour the mixture into a bowl and fold in the remaining cheese. Cover tightly and refrigerate for at least 30 minutes. The dressing will keep, tightly covered in the refrigerator, for up to 3 days.

MAKES ABOUT 2 CUPS (480 ML)

CAESAR DRESSING

MY CAESAR DRESSING IS PRETTY TRUE TO THE ORIGINAL: LOTS OF anchovy and garlic and the raw egg yolks that give this classic dressing its richness and create that creamy emulsion. I use it, obviously, as the dressing for a Caesar salad or any mixed green salad, but it is also great served on a BLT or burger.

1 large egg yolk

4 large garlic cloves, smashed

4 anchovy fillets, patted dry (optional)

3 tablespoons Dijon mustard

Finely grated zest of 1 lemon

¼ cup (60 ml) fresh lemon juice (from about 2 lemons)

1 tablespoon aged sherry vinegar

½ teaspoon kosher salt, or more to taste

¼ teaspoon freshly ground black pepper, or more to taste

1 cup (240 ml) vegetable oil, or ½ cup (120 ml) pure olive oil and ½ cup (120 ml) canola oil

⅓ cup (30 g) grated Parmesan cheese

In a blender, combine the egg yolk, garlic, anchovies (if using), mustard, lemon zest, lemon juice, vinegar, salt, and pepper and blend until smooth.

With the motor running, slowly add the oil and continue blending until emulsified. Add the cheese and pulse a few times until just blended. Taste and add more salt and pepper if needed. The dressing will keep, tightly covered in the refrigerator, for up to 3 days.

MAKES ABOUT 2 CUPS (480 ML)

SPECIAL SAUCE

MCDONALD'S HAS THEIRS AND SO DOES BARBACON. I LOVE THIS pink-hued sauce slathered on burgers, brisket, and BLTs, or even as a dip for crudité.

½ cup (120 ml) store-bought mayonnaise

¼ cup (60 ml) ketchup

12 Bread and Butter Pickles (page 276), drained and finely chopped

1 teaspoon Magic Rub (page 94)

In a medium bowl, mix together the mayonnaise, ketchup, pickles, and rub. Cover and refrigerate for at least 30 minutes, or up to 24 hours to allow the flavors to meld. The sauce will keep, tightly covered in the refrigerator, for up to 3 days.

MAKES ABOUT 1 CUP (240 ML)

WHITE WINE GRAINY MUSTARD SAUCE

WE MAKE THIS SAUCE SPECIFICALLY FOR OUR BURGER. THE WHITE wine and grainy mustard give an everyday burger a high-class taste without having to buy foie gras or truffle butter. The sauce is killer, so don't feel like you should relegate it only to burgers. We put that shit on everything.

1 cup (240 ml) dry white wine

1 shallot, finely diced

2 cups (480 ml) heavy cream

3 tablespoons whole-grain mustard

1 tablespoon Dijon mustard

½ teaspoon kosher salt

⅛ teaspoon freshly ground black pepper

Combine the wine and shallot in a medium nonreactive saucepan and cook over high heat until reduced to about 3 tablespoons. Add the cream. Bring to a boil, lower the heat to low, and cook until reduced by half.

Remove the pan from the heat and whisk in both mustards, the salt, and the pepper. Transfer to a bowl and let cool. The sauce will keep, tightly covered in the refrigerator, for up to 3 days.

MAKES ABOUT 1½ CUPS (360 ML)

BARBACON BBQ SAUCE

OKAY, SO THE SECRET IS OUT...I GET SOME HELP FROM THE GROCERY
store when making my "homemade" BBQ sauce. So what? It is delicious and no
one has to know—until now, that is. My personal favorite is Sweet Baby Ray's, but
feel free to substitute your favorite brand. Starting with a good base is essential,
and then the sky's the limit when it comes to additions.

2 tablespoons canola oil

1 onion, finely diced

5 garlic cloves, chopped

2 cups (480 ml) Bacon Stock
(page 43), or 2 cups (480 ml)
water plus 1 piece of bacon

¼ cup (60 ml) molasses

2 tablespoons Habanero Sauce
(page 89 or store-bought)

1 tablespoon
Worcestershire sauce

2 cups (480 ml) store-bought
BBQ sauce

Heat the oil over high heat
in a medium saucepan until
it begins to shimmer. Add
the onion and cook until soft,
about 4 minutes. Add the
garlic and cook for 1 minute
longer.

Add the stock (or water and
bacon, if using), bring to a boil,
and cook until reduced by half,
about 5 minutes.

Add the molasses, habanero
sauce, Worcestershire sauce,
and BBQ sauce and bring
to a boil. Lower the heat
to low and simmer, stirring
occasionally, for 15 minutes.
Remove from the heat and let
cool for 15 minutes. Transfer
to a blender and blend until
smooth. The sauce will keep,
tightly covered in the refrigerator, for up to 3 days.

MAKES 4 CUPS (960 ML)

CHIPOTLE-PEACH BBQ SAUCE

FRUIT AND FRUIT-FLAVORED SAUCES GO INCREDIBLY WELL WITH the fatty, salty taste of bacon. It is, in my opinion, the ultimate sweet-savory pairing. Peaches are paired often with ham in the South, but it's also one of my favorites with bacon. Every summer I serve a rib special with this sauce and a smoked peach John Daly (a delightful combination of lemonade, peach ice tea, and bacon vodka). If you aren't into peaches, you can definitely substitute pineapple, apricot, or mango nectar instead.

4 cups (960 ml) peach nectar

4 cups (960 ml) BarBacon BBQ Sauce (opposite) or your favorite store-bought BBQ sauce

¼ cup (60 ml) pureed chipotles in adobo

In a large saucepan, bring the nectar to a boil over high heat, then lower the heat to medium and cook, stirring occasionally, until thickened and reduced to about 1½ cups (360 ml), about 30 minutes.

Add the BBQ sauce and chipotles and cook until just heated through, about 5 minutes. Use immediately, or cool to room temperature and transfer to a container with a tight-fitting lid. The sauce will keep, tightly covered in the refrigerator, for up to 7 days, or freeze for up to 1 month.

MAKES 5 CUPS (1.2 L)

BRISKET SAUCE

THE NAME GIVES IT AWAY, BUT THIS SAUCE IS DELICIOUS ON BRISKET. Don't let that stop you from serving it alongside steaks, pork roast, and burgers, too.

1 cup (240 ml) BarBacon BBQ Sauce (page 82) or your favorite store-bought BBQ sauce

½ cup (120 ml) Bacon Stock (page 43), or ½ cup water cooked with 4 chopped slices bacon (see Note)

⅓ cup (75 ml) molasses

3 tablespoons apple cider vinegar

1 tablespoon Worcestershire sauce

1 tablespoon beef base, or 1 beef bouillon cube

In a medium saucepan over high heat, combine the BBQ sauce, stock, molasses, vinegar, Worcestershire sauce, and beef base and cook, whisking occasionally, until just heated through, about 5 minutes.

Remove from the heat and use immediately, or let cool to room temperature and store in a container with a tight-fitting lid. The sauce will keep, tightly covered in the refrigerator, for up to 3 days.

NOTE: *If not using premade bacon stock, in a small saucepan, combine the water and bacon and bring to a boil over high heat. Remove from the heat, cover, and let steep for at least 30 minutes, or up to 2 hours. Strain and reserve the bacon to make Bacon Bits (page 49), if desired.*

MAKES 2 CUPS (480 ML)

BBQ GLAZE

I USE THIS GLAZE FOR ALL OF MY BBQ. IT GIVES IT THAT NICE TACKY, sticky-sweet coating that all good BBQ should have. There is a lot of sugar in this recipe—and it will burn—so don't apply the glaze until the last ten minutes of cooking.

1 pound (455 g) light brown sugar

1 cup (240 ml) apple cider vinegar

In a medium saucepan over high heat, combine the sugar and vinegar and bring to a boil. Whisk until the sugar has melted and the mixture thickens slightly, about 5 minutes.

Transfer to a container with a tight-fitting lid. The glaze will keep, tightly covered in the refrigerator, for up to 1 week.

MAKES ABOUT 2 CUPS (480 ML)

SOY GLAZE

I USE THIS GLAZE ON THICK-CUT BACON CONFIT (PAGE 41) FOR MY version of a banh mi. It also pairs well with most meats, like tenderloins, chops, or short ribs, glazed on the grill. This is a thin glaze, so it needs to be applied several times while the meat is on the grill.

1 cup (240 ml) low-sodium soy sauce

1 cup (240 ml) dry sherry

⅔ cup (160 ml) pure maple syrup

2 tablespoons anise seeds

1 teaspoon red chile flakes

Combine the soy sauce, sherry, maple syrup, anise seeds, and chile flakes in a medium saucepan over high heat. Bring to a boil, then remove from the heat and let cool to room temperature.

Transfer to a container with a tight-fitting lid. The glaze will keep, tightly covered in the refrigerator, for up to 1 week.

MAKES ALMOST 3 CUPS (710 ML)

VIETNAMESE GLAZE

THIS IS THE GLAZE FOR BARBACON'S FAMOUS BRUSSELS SPROUTS. The longer this glaze sits, the better the flavor . . . Give it a good shake or stir before using.

¼ cup (60 ml) low-sodium soy sauce

¼ cup (60 ml) rice vinegar

3 tablespoons fresh lime juice

3 tablespoons fresh orange juice

2 teaspoons sriracha

1 (1-inch/2. 5-cm) piece fresh ginger, peeled and finely grated

3 garlic cloves, finely chopped

3 tablespoons vegetable oil

1 tablespoon toasted sesame oil

In a blender, combine the soy sauce, vinegar, lime juice, orange juice, sriracha, ginger, garlic, and both oils and blend until smooth.

Transfer to a container with a tight-fitting lid. The glaze will keep, tightly covered in the refrigerator, for up to 2 days.

MAKES ABOUT 1¼ CUPS (300 ML)

HONEY MUSTARD GLAZE

THERE IS NOTHING FANCY HERE, JUST A GOOD HONEY MUSTARD sauce that gets its kick from cayenne and black pepper. Use it in the honey mustard bacon on page 46 or slathered on a BLT, the Bacon Bratwurst Burger (page 202), or just a simple ham sandwich.

1 cup (240 ml) clover honey

¾ cup (170 g) Dijon mustard

1 teaspoon freshly ground black pepper

½ teaspoon garlic powder

¼ teaspoon ground cayenne

In a medium bowl, whisk together the honey, mustard, black pepper, garlic powder, and cayenne. Cover and let sit at room temperature for at least 30 minutes before using to allow the flavors to meld.

The glaze will keep tightly covered in the refrigerator for up to 2 days.

MAKES 1¾ CUPS (420 ML)

NUOC MAM CHAM

I COULD DRINK THIS AND BATHE IT IN EVERY DAY. LIKE MOST ASIAN condiments, this one is incredibly flavorful, but simple to make. Use it as a dipping sauce for dumplings or as the sweet-and-spicy vinegar for quick-pickling vegetables, which are great served on the side of any bacon dish to cut through the richness.

2 cups (400 g) sugar

2½ cups (600 ml) rice vinegar

1 (2-inch/5-cm) piece fresh ginger, peeled and finely grated

1 (2-inch/5-cm) piece carrot, peeled and finely grated

2 teaspoons sambal oelek, or more if you like spicy

Combine the sugar, vinegar, ginger, and carrot in a medium saucepan over high heat, bring to a boil, and cook until the sugar has dissolved, about 2 minutes. Remove from the heat and whisk in the sambal.

Transfer to a bowl and let cool to room temperature. Cover and refrigerate for at least 1 hour to allow the flavors to meld. The sauce will keep, tightly covered in the refrigerator, for up to 5 days.

MAKES 2 CUPS (480 ML)

NUOC CHAM

NUOC CHAM IS A COMMON VIETNAMESE DIPPING SAUCE. IT'S SWEET, sour, salty, savory, and spicy all at once. It does wonders to balance the fattiness of fried pork belly, and with some additional fresh vegetables culinary harmony is quickly achieved.

1 tablespoon palm sugar

2 garlic cloves

½ teaspoon kosher salt

1 Thai chile, minced

⅓ cup (75 ml) fresh lime juice

3 tablespoons fish sauce

In a food processor, blend the palm sugar, garlic, and salt until smooth. Add the chile and pulse to combine.

Transfer the mixture to a medium bowl, add the lime juice and fish sauce, and whisk together. The sauce will keep, tightly covered in the refrigerator, for up to 2 weeks.

**MAKES ABOUT
½ CUP (120 ML)**

THAI CHILE HONEY

ADDING SOME HEAT TO YOUR EVERYDAY HONEY TURNS IT INTO A really delicious condiment that is great drizzled over biscuits and fried chicken. Here, I use Thai chiles, which add a potent, lingering heat even through the sweetness of the honey. If you can't find Thai chiles, serrano chiles will work well, too. At BarBacon, we use this as a dip for our Kentucky Fried Bacon Bites (page 142).

1 cup (240 ml) clover honey

3 Pickled Thai Chiles (page 282), thinly sliced; or 2 pickled serrano chiles (pickled same way as the Thai chiles), drained and minced

In a small bowl, combine the honey and Thai chiles. Let the honey sit at room temperature for at least 30 minutes to allow the flavors to meld. Transfer to a container with a tight-fitting lid and store in the refrigerator for up to 3 days.

MAKES 1 CUP (240 ML)

PICKLED JALAPEÑO CHIMICHURRI

THE PICKLED JALAPEÑO SALAD WE MAKE AT BARBACON CAN BE TOO spicy for many people. I love it, though, and wasn't willing to reduce the heat level. Instead, my compromise was this sauce, in which the heat is tamed by olive oil and cilantro. It's addictive, and mild enough for most palates. I serve it over grilled skirt steak, mixed into mayonnaise and slathered on a BLT or club sandwich, or added to a vinaigrette and spooned over seafood.

2 cups (500 g) Pickled Jalapeño Salad (page 285)

2 cups (60 g) packed fresh cilantro leaves

¼ cup (60 ml) extra-virgin olive oil

In a blender or food processor, combine the jalapeño salad and cilantro and blend. With the blender running, slowly add the oil and blend until everything is incorporated and the pieces are uniform in size.

Pour the mixture into a plastic container with a tight-fitting lid and refrigerate for up to 1 week. The bright green color will fade after 12 hours, but the sauce will still be good to eat.

MAKES ABOUT 3 CUPS (720 ML)

HABANERO SAUCE

MAKING YOUR OWN HOT SAUCE IS FUN BECAUSE YOU CAN CONTROL
the ingredients—all natural—and the amount of heat. Habaneros are incredibly
hot and need to be handled with care: Be sure to wear gloves! This sauce is very
spicy, but the carrot and agave give it a nice sweetness that also brings out the
fruity flavor of the chile.

1 small carrot, peeled
and chopped

½ small white onion, chopped

4 ounces (115 g) orange
habanero chiles (about 10),
stems removed

2 garlic cloves, smashed

1 cup (240 ml) apple
cider vinegar

2 teaspoons kosher salt,
or more to taste

1 cup (240 ml) cold water

1 tablespoon agave nectar or
clover honey, or more to taste

Combine the carrot, onion, habaneros, garlic, vinegar, salt, and cold water in a medium saucepan and bring to a boil over high heat. Lower the heat to low, partially cover the pan, and cook until the carrot and habaneros are tender when pierced with a paring knife or skewer, about 10 minutes. Remove from the heat and let cool for 5 minutes.

Transfer the mixture to a blender, add the agave, and blend until smooth. Taste for seasoning, adding more salt if needed. If it's too spicy, add more agave, 1 teaspoon at a time, until you reach the desired flavor. Pour into a container with a tight-fitting lid and refrigerate for at least 1 hour before using. The sauce will keep, tightly covered in the refrigerator, for up to 2 weeks.

**MAKES ABOUT
2 CUPS (480 ML)**

AVOCADO SALSA VERDE

THIS PUREED GUACAMOLE-LIKE DIP IS BEST WHEN SERVED WITH chicharrónes (page 138) or tortilla chips, or even slathered on tacos and BLTs.

8 ounces (225 g) tomatillos (6 to 8), husks removed, scrubbed, and quartered

1 small white onion, coarsely chopped

2 garlic cloves, smashed

1 jalapeño, chopped

2 tablespoons canola oil

Kosher salt and freshly ground black pepper

2 ripe Hass avocados, peeled, pitted, and chopped

1 cup (40 g) chopped cilantro leaves

Juice of 2 or 3 limes

Pinch of ground cumin (optional)

Preheat the oven to 400°F (205°C). In a large bowl, toss the tomatillos, onion, garlic, and jalapeño in the oil and season with salt and pepper. Transfer to a baking sheet in a single layer and cook, stirring once, until slightly charred and softened, about 25 minutes. Let cool for 10 minutes.

Scrape the tomatillo mixture into a food processor. Add the avocados, cilantro, lime juice, and cumin (if using), and process until smooth. Season with salt and pepper to taste, pulse a few more times, and transfer to a bowl. The salsa verde can be made up to 8 hours in advance and stored, tightly covered in the refrigerator, for up to 2 days. Bring to room temperature before serving.

MAKES ABOUT 4 CUPS (960 ML)

CHICKEN TACO SAUCE

SOUR CREAM ADDS RICHNESS AND CREAMINESS WHILE ALSO BAL-ancing the heat of the chipotle and cayenne in this sauce. I love it on chicken (obviously), but also on pork or fried seafood dishes as well.

2 cups (480 ml) sour cream

½ cup (120 ml) store-bought mayonnaise

Finely grated zest of 1 lime

¼ cup (60 ml) fresh lime juice

1 teaspoon chipotle powder

1 teaspoon ground cumin

½ teaspoon ground cayenne

1 teaspoon kosher salt

2 tablespoons chopped fresh cilantro leaves

In a medium bowl, whisk together the sour cream, mayonnaise, lime zest, lime juice, chipotle, cumin, cayenne, salt, and cilantro. Cover and refrigerate for at least 1 hour to allow the flavors to meld. The sauce will keep, tightly covered in the refrigerator, for up to 3 days.

MAKES ABOUT 2¾ CUPS (660 ML)

BAJA SAUCE

I ORIGINALLY CREATED THIS SAUCE FOR MY BAJA FISH TACOS (PAGE 237) when BarBacon first opened, but it really goes with anything fried.

1¼ cups (300 ml) sour cream

¾ cup (180 ml) store-bought mayonnaise

3 generous tablespoons sriracha sauce

¾ teaspoon garlic powder

Kosher salt and freshly ground black pepper

In a medium bowl, whisk together the sour cream, mayonnaise, sriracha, and garlic powder. Season with salt and pepper to taste. Cover and refrigerate for at least 1 hour to allow the flavors to meld. The sauce will keep, tightly covered in the refrigerator, for up to 1 week.

MAKES 2 CUPS (480 ML)

PORT WINE–BACON MARINARA

YOUR ITALIAN GRANDMOTHER PROBABLY DOESN'T USE BACON IN her marinara, but I am not Italian and I am not your grandmother. Bacon adds a smoky, salty flavor to this classic red sauce that pairs perfectly with my bacon meatballs (page 124), as a base for fried calamari, ladled over pasta, or anything that you would normally eat with tomato sauce.

1 tablespoon olive oil

4 ounces (110 g) slab bacon

3 garlic cloves, thinly sliced

2 tablespoons tomato paste

⅛ teaspoon red chile flakes

1 cup (240 ml) port wine

1 cup (240 ml) Bacon Stock (page 43) or chicken stock

2 pounds (910 g) canned plum tomatoes, and their juices (28-ounce/794-g can plus 14-ounce/397-g can), tomatoes crushed with your hands

8 whole fresh basil leaves

Heat the oil in large saucepan over low heat until it begins to shimmer. Add the bacon and cook until golden brown on both sides, about 8 minutes total. Remove the bacon to a plate. Add the garlic to the pan and cook until soft and lightly golden brown, about 3 minutes.

Add the tomato paste and chile flakes and cook, stirring constantly, until the tomato paste begins to darken in color, about 2 minutes. Add the wine, increase the heat to high, and cook until completely reduced, about 5 minutes.

Add the stock, tomatoes, and the cooked bacon to the pot and bring to a boil. Add the basil. Lower the heat to low and cook, stirring occasionally, until the sauce has thickened, about 30 minutes.

Remove and discard the bacon and basil. Puree the sauce with a hand blender, or process, in batches, in a food processor until smooth. Use immediately or let cool to room temperature and store in a container with a tight-fitting lid. The sauce will keep, tightly covered in the refrigerator, for up to 3 days or in the freezer for up to 1 month.

MAKES 4 CUPS (960 ML)

BACON-MUSHROOM GRAVY

I LOVE THE SMOKINESS THE BACON LENDS TO THIS MUSHROOM gravy. There are a few ingredients that may be hard to find in your local grocery store, so feel free to substitute where needed. I like the flavor of rosemary with this sauce but if that is not your favorite herb, fresh thyme or flat-leaf parsley works nicely, too. This sauce is good enough to just eat on its own but at BB, I serve it with pork schnitzel (page 265).

4 tablespoons canola oil

1 pound (455 g) cremini mushrooms, wiped clean and quartered

Kosher salt and freshly ground black pepper

1 large Spanish onion, halved and thinly sliced

1 cup (240 ml) dry white wine

2 teaspoons dried porcini powder, or dried mushrooms ground to a powder in a blender

4 cups (960 ml) Pork Stock (page 158) or chicken stock

1½ cups (360 ml) Bacon Stock (page 43) or chicken stock

2 sprigs fresh rosemary, or 2 teaspoons finely chopped fresh thyme leaves, or 2 tablespoons chopped fresh parsley leaves

1 teaspoon cornstarch mixed with 1 tablespoon cold water

2 tablespoons whole-grain mustard

Heat 3 tablespoons of the oil in a large, deep sauté pan over high heat until it begins to shimmer. Add the cremini mushrooms and cook, stirring a few times, until golden brown and their liquid has evaporated, about 8 minutes. Season with 1 teaspoon salt and ¼ teaspoon pepper and cook for 2 minutes longer. Remove the mushrooms to a plate.

Add the remaining 1 tablespoon oil to the pan, add the onion, and cook, stirring occasionally, until lightly golden brown and caramelized, about 8 minutes. Return the mushrooms to the pan and add the wine and porcini powder and cook until the wine has completely reduced.

Add the pork stock and cook until reduced by half. Add the bacon stock and rosemary and cook until reduced by half and slightly thickened, about 15 minutes longer. Whisk in the cornstarch slurry and bring to a boil. Cook until thickened slightly, about 1 minute. Remove from the heat, remove and discard the rosemary stems, and whisk in the mustard. Season with salt and pepper to taste.

Serve hot or let cool completely and refrigerate, tightly covered, for up to 3 days.

MAKES 5 CUPS (1.2 L)

CHIPOTLE RUB

IT'S ONLY NATURAL THAT WHAT IS TYPICALLY REFERRED TO AS "the bacon of the spice world"—chipotle (which is a smoked and dried jalapeño)—would pair nicely with the smokiness of bacon. I use the two together a lot, and for good reason . . . it is a delicious combination. Use this rub to make your own Chipotle Bacon (page 27) or sprinkle on store-bought bacon before cooking. You should also try it on pork, beef, or chicken.

¾ cup (165 g) packed light brown sugar

⅓ cup (60 g) Diamond Crystal kosher salt

¼ cup (50 g) granulated sugar

2 tablespoons lemon pepper

2 tablespoons chipotle powder

1½ tablespoons garlic powder

1½ tablespoons onion powder

In a small bowl, stir together all the ingredients until combined. Transfer to a container with a tight-fitting lid and store in a cool, dark place for up to 6 months.

**MAKES ABOUT
2¼ CUPS (650 G)**

MAGIC RUB

MAGIC RUB IS MY GO-TO BBQ RUB FOR ANYTHING PORK RELATED. I also use it in my special sauce recipe (page 80). This spice gives me the flavor of BBQ without actually cooking anything. I wasn't the first to call it "magic." It is a common rub name among pit masters in the BBQ circuit.

¾ cup (75 g) smoked paprika

¾ cup (150 g) sugar

½ cup (50 g) garlic powder

½ cup (90 g) Diamond Crystal kosher salt

⅓ cup (30 g) ground cumin

¼ cup (25 g) mustard powder

¼ cup (25 g) chipotle powder

¼ cup (25 g) ancho chile powder

2 tablespoons ground black pepper

2 tablespoons ground cayenne

In a large bowl, stir together all the ingredients until combined. Transfer to a container with a tight-fitting lid and store in a cool, dry place for up to 6 months.

**MAKES ABOUT
4 CUPS (945 G)**

JERK RUB

THIS BLEND OF SWEET AND SAVORY SPICES GETS A KICK IN MY VERsion from red chile flakes, but feel free to use dried ground Scotch bonnet or habanero chile instead for a more traditional jerk flavor. I love using this rub on chicken, fish, and, of course, bacon.

5 tablespoons (60 g) sugar

3 tablespoons onion powder

3 tablespoons dried thyme

2 tablespoons ground allspice

2 tablespoons freshly ground black pepper

2 tablespoons red chile flakes

1 tablespoon kosher salt

2 teaspoons grated nutmeg

2 teaspoons ground cloves

In a small bowl, stir together all the ingredients until combined. Transfer to a container with a tight-fitting lid and store in a cool, dark place for up to 6 months.

MAKES ABOUT 1¼ CUPS (285 G)

BB RUB

THIS IS AN ALL-PURPOSE RUB THAT'S GREAT ON ALL THINGS, BUT ESPEcially burgers, steaks, and roasts. I recommend making a big batch, because once you try it, you tend to put it on everything: beef, pork, chicken, venison. I literally never eat burgers without it anymore. The rub will keep in your pantry for up to six months.

1 cup (200 g) granulated sugar

⅓ cup (65 g) light brown sugar

⅓ cup (60 g) Diamond Crystal kosher salt

¼ cup (40 g) garlic powder

⅓ cup (75 g) Lawry's seasoned salt

⅓ cup (75 g) celery salt

¼ cup (55 g) onion salt

¼ cup (25 g) smoked paprika

3 tablespoons chipotle powder

1 tablespoon freshly ground black pepper

½ teaspoon lemon pepper

½ teaspoon ground dried thyme

½ teaspoon ground sage

½ teaspoon mustard powder

In a medium bowl, stir together all the ingredients until combined. Transfer to a container with a tight-fitting lid and store in a cool, dark place for up to 6 months.

MAKES 3 CUPS (720 G)

BARBACON BLOODY MARY SEASONING

MIX THIS INTO TOMATO JUICE FOR THE BASE OF A BLOODY MARY
(page 107) or use it as a seasoning for seafood and chicken.

¼ cup (55 g) plus 1 tablespoon celery salt

¼ cup (50 g) sugar

1 tablespoon plus 1 teaspoon lemon pepper

1 tablespoon plus 1 teaspoon onion powder

1 tablespoon plus 1 teaspoon garlic powder

1 tablespoon plus 1 teaspoon smoked paprika

1 tablespoon ground cayenne

In a small bowl, stir together all the ingredients until combined. Transfer to a container with a tight-fitting lid and store in a cool, dark place for up to 6 months.

**MAKES ABOUT
¾ CUP (175 G)**

FISH DREDGE

I LIKE FRIED FISH WITH A HARD, CRUNCHY SHELL; THE TEXTURE
contrast between the flaky fish and the crunchy crust is what makes the dish for
me. Cornmeal provides that shell far better than bread crumbs. It's also a one-step
process—just dump the fish in the dredge and fry. There's no need to dirty multiple
bowls with flour, egg, and bread crumbs.

2½ cups (450 g) fine yellow cornmeal

1 tablespoon garlic powder

1 tablespoon Old Bay seasoning

2 teaspoons lemon pepper

1 teaspoon freshly ground black pepper

In a medium bowl, stir together all the ingredients until combined. Transfer to a container with a tight-fitting lid and store in a cool, dark place for up to 6 months.

**MAKES ABOUT
2¾ CUPS (460 G)**

POULTRY RUB

LIKE THE NAME STATES, IT'S PERFECT ON ANY POULTRY, WHICH, AS
you know, includes turkey and duck, too!

¼ cup (50 g) sugar

2 tablespoons kosher salt

1½ tablespoons
smoked paprika

2 teaspoons dried thyme

1 teaspoon freshly ground
black pepper

¼ teaspoon ground
white pepper

¼ teaspoon onion powder

¼ teaspoon garlic powder

In a small bowl, stir together all the ingredients until combined. Transfer to a container with a tight-fitting lid and store in a cool, dark place for up to 6 months.

**MAKES ABOUT
½ CUP (120 G)**

PORK BRINE

I ALWAYS BRINE ANY LARGE MUSCLE OF PORK, SUCH AS SHOULDER
or belly, before cooking it. Brining seasons the whole piece of meat inside and out, and, most importantly, ensures a juicy and tender finished product. Use this for other meats, like chicken or turkey, before they are smoked.

1 teaspoon black peppercorns

1 teaspoon coriander seeds

1 teaspoon mustard seeds

4 cups (960 ml) cold water

⅓ cup (65 g) sugar

¼ cup (45 g) Diamond Crystal
kosher salt

8 sprigs fresh thyme

3 bay leaves

In a small sauté pan over low heat, combine the peppercorns, coriander, and mustard seeds and toast, stirring occasionally, until just fragrant, about 5 minutes. Let cool for 5 minutes, transfer to a mortar and pestle, and coarsely crush.

In a large saucepan, combine the cold water, sugar, salt, thyme, bay leaves, and toasted spices and bring to a boil over high heat. Cook until the sugar and salt are completely dissolved.

Let cool to room temperature and refrigerate before using. Or, transfer to a bowl over an ice bath, and whisk until cool. The brine will keep, tightly covered in the refrigerator, for up to 3 days.

MAKES 4 CUPS (960 ML)

CHAPTER 4

COCKTAILS

**VERYBODY PUTS BACON IN BREAKFAST.**
Plenty of people put bacon in lunch. Some people put bacon in dinner. A few people put bacon in dessert. I put bacon in cocktails.

I know it's not traditional, but I'm here to break you out of your bacon rut, and what better way to get the juices flowing than with a little bacon vodka? It was one of the first drinks I came up with when I wanted to work with bacon and cocktails, because it seemed like a great way to both showcase the bacon and blend it with other flavors. Once you use bacon vodka in your Bloody Mary, you'll never be able to drink a plain one again. Want something a little sweeter? Try infusing bourbon or dark rum with bacon flavor. It doubles down on the lovely smokiness and balances out an Old Fashioned or a Dark and Stormy like you wouldn't believe.

If adding bacon directly to your drink is a little too far, start with something that pairs with bacon instead. A drink is the perfect way to balance out a meal with acidity and sweetness—both of which can be used to balance out the beautiful fat of bacon. Add one more thing, a little bit of heat, and you have my Habanero Margarita (page 111), created to go with our Taco Tuesday. There is no better pairing to our chipotle bacon tacos (page 233).

Once you get going, you'll realize that drinks are another fun way to work with bacon, whether there's bacon in the drink itself or whether you're making the drink as a surprising complement to your favorite bacon dish. Better yet—both!

BACON-INFUSED LIQUOR

IN THE SAME WAY THAT I KNEW I NEEDED A BLT ON THE MENU, I also knew that I needed something that combined bacon with cocktails. Infusing hard liquor with bacon fat adds a richness and smokiness that is perfect in a cocktail, or even for drinking straight up or on the rocks. Vodka, bourbon, and dark rum work best, and obviously you don't need to use top shelf for this. These infused liquors are the base for most of the specialty cocktails at BarBacon.

1 L vodka, bourbon, or dark rum

1 cup (240 ml) rendered bacon fat (see page 50)

Pour the liquor into a heat-proof container with a lid and set aside. Keep the bottle and the screw top. You will need them later.

In a small saucepan, bring the bacon fat to a simmer over low heat. Remove from the heat and add it to the vodka. Stir well to combine. Cover and refrigerate overnight. Remove the top layer of fat and store the fat in a container with a tight-fitting lid to use later in the baking chapter. (Bourbon and dark rum rendered fat work especially well in desserts.)

Strain the liquor through a sieve lined with cheesecloth into a large bowl, then using a funnel, return the infused vodka back to its original bottle. Store in the freezer or in a cool, dark place until ready to use.

MAKES 4 CUPS (960 ML)

MIDNIGHT IN MOLASSES

WHAT DO YOU GET WHEN YOU MIX ELDERFLOWER LIQUEUR, WITH its honey, floral flavor, with smoky bacon and molasses and crisp sparkling wine? You get this cocktail, and trust me when I say it is delicious. This is one of the best-selling cocktails at the restaurant.

Ice cubes

1½ ounces bacon-infused bourbon (page 100)

¾ ounce St. Germain

½ ounce Shani Syrup (page 112)

¼ ounce molasses

Chilled sparkling wine or champagne

Crisp cooked bacon strip (see page 44)

Fresh mint sprigs

Fill a white wine glass with ice. Add the bourbon, St. Germain, syrup, and molasses and stir briskly to combine. Top off with sparkling wine. Garnish with the bacon and mint.

MAKES 1 COCKTAIL

BARBACON OLD FASHIONED

THE ORIGINAL OLD FASHIONED CONTAINED JUST WHISKEY, SUGAR, bitters, and water. No offense, but BarBacon's version is so much better and more complex, with a triple dose of smoke from the bourbon, maple syrup, and bacon. Don't believe me? Try it for yourself.

2 ounces (60 ml) bacon-infused bourbon (page 100)

½ ounce maple syrup

4 dashes orange bitters

4 dashes aromatic bitters

Ice cubes

Crisp cooked bacon strip (see page 44)

Fresh rosemary sprig

Orange slice

Combine the bourbon, maple syrup, orange bitters, and aromatic bitters in a cocktail shaker and stir for a few seconds. Fill a glass with ice and pour the mixture over. Garnish with the bacon, rosemary, and orange slice.

MAKES 1 COCKTAIL

BLOODY BACON BLOODY

THE BLOODY MARY IS THE QUINTESSENTIAL BREAKFAST OR BRUNCH cocktail, and with tomato juice and bacon it is also a nutritious one (well, in my opinion). This obviously is great to drink with egg dishes, but this savory cocktail goes well with sandwiches and tacos, too.

4 cups (960 ml) freshly pressed store-bought tomato juice

¾ cup (180 ml) bacon-infused vodka (page 100)

2 tablespoons prepared horseradish

1 tablespoon hot sauce, such as Tabasco

1 teaspoon celery salt

1 teaspoon freshly ground black pepper

2 teaspoons Worcestershire sauce

Juice of 1 lemon

Ice cubes (optional)

Crisp cooked bacon (see page 44)

Pitted green olives

Dill pickle spears

Lemon slices

Mix together the tomato juice, vodka, horseradish, hot sauce, celery salt, pepper, Worcestershire sauce, and lemon juice in a pitcher. Cover and refrigerate for at least 1 hour, or up to 48 hours.

Pour into tall glasses, over ice (if desired), and garnish each glass with a strip of bacon, green olives, a pickle spear, and a slice of lemon.

MAKES 4 TO 6 COCKTAILS

HOG STORM

THIS IS MY VERSION OF THE DARK AND STORMY, BUT WITH A BIT OF smoke courtesy of bacon, of course. If you don't have bacon-infused rum on hand, no worries, just use regular dark rum. My preference is Gosling's.

2 ounces (60 ml) bacon-infused dark rum (page 100)

1 ounce ginger liqueur, such as Canton

1 ounce Simple Syrup (page 112)

½ ounce fresh lime juice

Ice cubes

4 ounces (120 ml) cold ginger beer

Candied ginger

Crisp cooked bacon strips (see page 44)

Orange slice

Combine the rum, ginger liqueur, syrup, lime juice, and 2 ice cubes in a shaker and shake for 10 seconds. Strain into a Mason jar filled with ice and top up with the ginger beer. Garnish with the candied ginger, bacon, and orange slice.

MAKES 1 COCKTAIL

HABANERO MARGARITA

MARGARITAS GO WELL WITH BACON: THAT ACIDIC BITE FROM THE fresh lime juice and tequila helps cut right through the bacon fat. If you aren't into spicy, you can skip the habanero in the syrup, or just use a milder chile such as a jalapeño or serrano.

Ice cubes

2 ounces (60 ml) mezcal

1½ ounces Habanero Syrup (recipe follows)

1 ounce triple sec

2 tablespoons kosher salt

Crisp cooked bacon strip (see page 44; optional)

2 lime wedges

Fill a cocktail shaker with ice. Add the mezcal, syrup, and triple sec and shake or stir for 10 seconds.

Spread the salt on a small plate. Moisten the rim of a glass with one of the lime wedges; dip the rim in the salt and twist to coat. Pour or strain the mixture into the glass. Garnish with the bacon (if using) and lime wedge.

MAKES 1 COCKTAIL

HABANERO SYRUP

1 cup (200 g) sugar

⅓ cup (75 ml) fresh lime juice

½ navel orange, not peeled, halved

2 habanero chiles, stemmed and halved

In a small saucepan over high heat, combine the sugar, lime juice, orange, and habaneros and bring to a boil. Cook until the sugar has dissolved and the mixture thickens slightly, about 5 minutes. Cover, remove from the heat, and let steep for 30 minutes.

Transfer the mixture to a blender and blend until smooth. Strain the syrup through a sieve into a container with a tight-fitting lid and refrigerate until chilled, at least 1 hour. The syrup will keep, tightly covered in the refrigerator, for up to 1 month.

**MAKES ABOUT
1½ CUPS (360 ML)**

SHANI LA LA

SHANI IS MY WIFE, BUT LONG BEFORE THAT, SHE MOVED INTO MY apartment with me in New York, and I sent her a package addressed to: Princess Shani La La. The rest is history. The big oaky flavor of bourbon is tamed by the citrusy sweetness of the Shani Syrup, and the champagne adds sparkle and effervescence, which reminds me of Shani's personality.

Ice cubes

1½ ounces bacon-infused bourbon (page 100)

1½ ounces Shani Syrup (recipe follows)

Chilled champagne

Fresh mint sprig

Fill a cocktail shaker with ice and add the bourbon and syrup. Put the lid on and shake for 10 seconds. Strain the mixture into a champagne coupe, top with champagne, and garnish with the mint.

MAKES 1 COCKTAIL

SHANI SYRUP

THIS WAS CREATED FOR THE SHANI LA LA, BUT IT'S ALSO A NICE addition to other cocktails and iced tea.

1 cup (240 ml) fresh lime juice

¾ cup (150 g) sugar

1 (2-inch/5-cm) piece fresh ginger, peeled and chopped

In a small nonreactive saucepan, combine the lime juice, sugar, and ginger. Bring to a boil over high heat and cook, whisking a few times, until the sugar has completely dissolved. Remove from the heat and let cool to room temperature.

Transfer the syrup to a blender and blend until smooth, then strain into a container with a tight-fitting lid and refrigerate until cold, about 1 hour. The syrup will keep, tightly covered in the refrigerator, for up to 1 month.

MAKES ABOUT 1¼ CUPS (300 ML)

BACON WHITE RUSSIAN

WHITE RUSSIANS ARE USUALLY MADE WITH HEAVY CREAM, BUT with the slightly fatty taste of the bacon, milk will do just fine. To make a Bacon Black Russian, don't add the milk; instead, double the amount of bacon vodka you use.

Ice cubes

2 ounces (60 ml) whole milk

1 ounce Kahlúa

1 ounce bacon-infused vodka (page 100)

Orange peel

Fill a cocktail shaker with ice. Add the milk, Kahlúa, and vodka, put the lid on, and shake for 10 seconds. Strain the cocktail into a chilled glass filled with ice and garnish with the orange peel.

MAKES 1 COCKTAIL

CHAPTER 5

SNACKS & SIDES

OR MANY CHEFS, APPETIZERS ARE THEIR favorite course. Maximum flavor in a small portion format. They are flavor bombs, teasers for the rest of your meal. Bacon thrives in this environment, bringing an underpinning of intensely smoky and salty flavor to each dish. It's full of rich bite and crunch. Appetizers are purposefully indulgent, passed around in small portions so nobody feels too guilty. It's the fat you want to eat.

Luckily for me, bacon pairs so easily with everything. It adds a natural smoky depth to the chili I top my nachos with. It adds a crisp and salty layer to shrimp that I grill. It changes traditional appetizers and pumps them up, adding that final touch you need to make a dish memorable. Appetizers are where I work with wild flavors before escalating those into full-size portions.

I pull inspiration from the seasons—what's fresh and around me. The recipes in this chapter show creativity combined with my devotion to finding what's in season, such as Brussels sprouts (page 130) during the fall and winter months and new potatoes (page 151) in the springtime.

MAPLE-BACON NUTS

I LOVE EATING CANDIED NUTS AS A SNACK, ADDING THEM TO SAL-ads or pancake batters, and sprinkling them on a bowl of ice cream. I love them even more when bacon is added to cut a bit of that sugary sweetness, and even *more* when dried cranberries are thrown in for a touch of tartness. Dried cherries work really well, too.

1 tablespoon canola oil

6 ounces (170 g) slab bacon, cut into lardons (see page 48)

2 tablespoons unsalted butter

1 teaspoon pumpkin pie spice

1 teaspoon finely grated orange zest

3 tablespoons pure maple syrup

¼ teaspoon kosher salt

2 cups (200 g) pecan halves

½ cup (60 g) dried cranberries

Line a baking sheet with parchment paper or aluminum foil and spray lightly with nonstick spray or grease with a bit of butter.

In a large sauté pan, combine the oil and bacon and cook over medium heat until golden brown and crispy and the fat has rendered, about 8 minutes. Remove to a plate with a slotted spoon. Pour all but 1 tablespoon of the rendered bacon fat from the pan into a small bowl and save for another use (see page 50).

Add the butter to the pan with the bacon fat and cook until melted. Add the pumpkin pie spice, orange zest, and 2 tablespoons water and cook for 30 seconds. Add the maple syrup and salt and cook until the syrup begins to simmer, about 1 minute. Add the pecans and cook, stirring occasionally, until lightly toasted and the glaze has evenly coated the nuts, about 5 minutes. Return the bacon to the pan, along with the cranberries, and cook for 1 minute longer.

Transfer the mixture to the prepared baking sheet and separate the nuts immediately using two forks. Let cool completely. (Do not try to touch with your hands or eat. The maple syrup is very hot.) Store the cooled nuts in a container with a tight-fitting lid at room temperature for up to 2 days.

**MAKES ABOUT
3 CUPS (360 G)**

CANDIED BACON

THIS RECIPE DOUBLES AND TRIPLES EASILY—AND YOU'LL PROBABLY want to do that once you try the candied bacon. The sky's the limit when it comes to toppings, too. Add a touch of savory to the equation with a sprinkling of fennel seeds for a licorice flavor, crushed pink peppercorns for a fruity floral taste, black pepper for a pure pepper kick, or cayenne for a touch of heat.

12 thin slices bacon

⅓ cup (75 g) packed light brown sugar

Spice of your choice (optional)

Preheat the oven to 350°F (175°C). Line a baking sheet with aluminum foil or parchment paper and set aside.

In a large bowl, toss the bacon and brown sugar together gently to coat each slice in the sugar. Lay the bacon in an even layer on the baking sheet, leaving a bit of room in between the slices. If desired, sprinkle any spice evenly over the top. Bake until golden brown and crispy, about 15 minutes. Remove to a platter and let cool slightly before serving. The bacon will continue to get crispier as it cools. Best eaten the day it is made.

MAKES 12

LOADED POTATO SPRING ROLLS
with Garlic Sour Cream

EVERYONE'S FAVORITE VEGGIE SIDE DISH AND BAR DISH ROLLED into a crispy roll. This recipe was created a few years ago when I was trying to come up with bar snacks for Super Bowl Sunday. I don't remember much about that game, but I do remember that these sold out in about an hour. Crispy exterior, creamy, cheesy interior bursting with green onion and bacon flavor. The only thing left to say is: Can I get a beer with that?

FOR THE GARLIC SOUR CREAM

1 cup (240 ml) sour cream

3 garlic cloves, smashed and chopped to a paste with ¼ teaspoon kosher salt

¼ teaspoon freshly ground black pepper

2 tablespoons minced fresh chives, for garnish

FOR THE POTATO SKIN FILLING

1 pound (455 g) Idaho potatoes (about 3 medium), peeled and cut into large dice

Cold water

Kosher salt

10 thin slices bacon

1 large egg, lightly beaten

¼ cup (60 ml) sour cream

2 tablespoons all-purpose flour

2 green onions (dark green and pale green parts only), thinly sliced

1 cup (4 ounces/115 g) coarsely shredded cheddar cheese

Freshly ground black pepper

FOR THE SPRING ROLLS

16 spring roll wrappers (made with wheat), covered with a damp cloth

Egg wash (1 large egg, lightly beaten with 1 tablespoon water)

6 cups (1.4 L) canola oil for deep-frying

Kosher salt

Make the garlic sour cream: In a small bowl, combine the sour cream and garlic, season with the pepper, and stir. Cover and refrigerate for at least 30 minutes, or up to 24 hours to allow the flavors to meld.

Make the filling: Put the potatoes in a medium pot, cover with cold water by 2 inches (5 cm), and add 1 tablespoon salt. Bring to a boil over high heat and cook until the potatoes are fork-tender, about 15 minutes.

Drain well, return the potatoes to the pot, and let any excess water evaporate for 1 minute over low heat. Spoon the potatoes in batches into a ricer and rice into a large bowl.

While the potatoes are cooking, cook the bacon according to the directions on page 44 until the fat has rendered and the bacon is golden brown and crispy. Remove the bacon to a plate lined with paper towels, let cool slightly, then coarsely chop. Transfer the fat to a heatproof cup or bowl.

While the potatoes are still warm, add the reserved

rendered bacon fat, the egg, sour cream, and flour and mix well until combined. Fold in the green onions and cheese and season with salt and pepper. Let cool to room temperature. The filling can be made 1 day in advance and stored tightly covered in the refrigerator. Let come to room temperature before using.

Make the spring rolls: Transfer the filling to a pastry bag with a large plain tip. Orient the wrappers like diamonds on a clean, dry surface and add a heaping tablespoon of the filling to the center of each

wrapper, then brush the sides with the egg wash. Fold the bottom corner over the filling. Fold the left corner over the filling. Fold the right corner over the filling. Brush the rest of the spring roll wrapper with more of the egg wash, then tuck in the sides of the upper corner of the spring roll wrapper. This is to avoid overhang. Roll the spring roll upward, tightly, until the final remaining corner is wrapped and secured.

Heat the oil in a large Dutch oven until it reaches 350°F (175°C) on a deep-fry

thermometer and line a baking sheet with several layers of paper towels.

Fry the spring rolls in batches of 4 until golden brown and the filling is heated through, about 5 minutes. Remove with a spider or slotted spoon to the prepared baking sheet and season with a bit of salt.

To serve, transfer the sour cream to a clean bowl and garnish with the chives. Serve alongside the spring rolls.

MAKES 16

BACON GRITS ARANCINI

IT IS HARD TO BELIEVE THAT ANYONE WOULD EVER HAVE GRITS left over, but if you do, just follow the recipe from the second step down. We serve these with everything from sausage gravy (page 327) to Piperade (page 287), and you can make the argument that grits are great with everything.

4 cups (960 ml) whole milk

1¼ cups (215 g) instant grits

Kosher salt and freshly ground black pepper

½ cup (50 g) grated Parmigiano-Reggiano cheese

2 tablespoons sriracha

2 tablespoons unsalted butter

6 ounces (170 g) goat cheese, cut into small pieces

12 thin slices bacon, cooked until crisp (see page 44) and coarsely chopped

3 green onions (dark green and pale green parts only), thinly sliced

1 (1-pound/455-g) block white cheddar cheese, cut into 24 equal squares

6 cups (1.4 L) canola oil

3 cups (375 g) all-purpose flour

4 large eggs

3 cups (240 g) panko bread crumbs

In a large saucepan, bring the milk to a simmer over medium heat. Slowly whisk in the grits and continue whisking until the mixture is thickened and smooth, about 5 minutes.

Whisk in 1 teaspoon salt, ¼ teaspoon pepper, the Parmesan, sriracha, butter, and goat cheese until smooth. Remove from the heat, then fold in the bacon and green onions. Scrape the mixture onto a baking sheet lined with aluminum foil or parchment paper and let cool to room temperature. Cover and refrigerate until very cold, at least 8 hours, or up to 48 hours.

Scoop a scant ¼ cup (60 ml) of the grits into one hand, forming it into a flat disk. Place a cube of cheddar cheese into the center of the disk and, using your hands, gently form the grits into a ball around the cheese. Place the arancini onto the baking sheet and chill in the refrigerator for 15 minutes.

Heat the oil in a deep-fryer or a Dutch oven until it reaches 350°F (175°C) and line a baking sheet with several layers of paper towels.

Place the flour, eggs, and panko in three separate shallow dishes and season each lightly with salt and pepper. Working in batches, dredge the arancini in flour, shaking off any excess; dip into egg, then transfer to the panko, covering the arancini completely and pressing lightly to adhere.

Fry the arancini until golden brown and crispy, about 2 minutes. Remove with a slotted spoon to the prepared baking sheet. Serve hot or at room temperature.

MAKES ABOUT 24

BACON MEATBALLS

with Port Wine–Bacon Marinara Sauce

THESE ARE SOME OF THE BEST MEATBALLS THAT YOU WILL EVER eat. Chock full of savory goodness courtesy of the usual suspects: onion, garlic, red chile flakes, and Parmesan cheese and a not-so-usual ingredient—bacon. I serve them at the restaurant simply in a bowl of port wine marinara sauce; not exactly your grandma's recipe. You can use them for a meatball sandwich smothered with provolone or on a bed of perfectly cooked spaghetti.

2 tablespoons vegetable oil

1 small onion, finely diced

3 garlic cloves, finely chopped

Pinch of red chile flakes

1 pound (455 g) ground chuck (80/20)

6 thin slices bacon, finely diced

2 large eggs, lightly beaten

¾ cup (70 g) grated Parmesan cheese

¾ cup (60 g) panko bread crumbs

¼ cup (13 g) finely chopped fresh flat-leaf parsley leaves

1 teaspoon kosher salt

¼ teaspoon ground black pepper

Canola oil

1 recipe Port Wine–Bacon Marinara (page 92)

Heat the oil in a medium sauté pan, add the onion, and cook until soft, about 4 minutes. Add the garlic and chile flakes and cook for 30 seconds longer. Remove from the heat and let cool for 5 minutes.

In a large bowl, combine the onion mixture, beef, bacon, eggs, Parmesan, panko, and parsley and gently mix until just combined; season with the salt and pepper. Cover and refrigerate for at least 1 hour, or up to 24 hours to allow the flavors to meld.

Line a sheet pan with several layers of paper towels and set aside. Form the meat mixture into meatballs about the size of Ping-Pong balls. Heat about ½ inch (12 mm) of oil in a skillet over medium heat until it begins to shimmer. Fry the meatballs until they are browned on all sides, about 10 minutes. (They will continue to cook through in the sauce.) Using a slotted spoon, transfer the meatballs to the prepared baking sheet.

In a large, deep sauté pan, bring the sauce to a simmer over medium heat. Carefully place the meatballs in the sauce, cover, and cook for 15 minutes. Uncover, turn the meatballs, and cook for 10 minutes longer, until tender and cooked through and sauce has reduced slightly. Serve immediately or let cool to room temperature and store, tightly covered in the refrigerator, for up to 3 days, or in the freezer for up to 3 months.

**SERVES 4 TO 6;
MAKES 20 TO 22**

BACON HUMMUS

HUMMUS IS SO POPULAR THAT YOU WILL FIND IT JUST ABOUT everywhere these days. What you may not find, however, is hummus made with bacon fat—and garnished with bacon, too. For this recipe, I replace olive oil with bacon fat, which gives an extra level of richness as well as smokiness. I then amplify that with the addition of chipotle powder and smoked paprika.

1 tablespoon canola oil

8 thin slices bacon

2 garlic cloves, chopped

1 teaspoon ground cumin

1 teaspoon chipotle powder

½ teaspoon smoked paprika

1 teaspoon kosher salt

1 (15½-ounce/439-g) can chickpeas, drained, rinsed, and drained again

¼ cup (60 ml) cold water

¼ cup (60 ml) tahini

2½ teaspoons honey

2 green onions (dark green and pale green parts only), thinly sliced

1 teaspoon toasted sesame seeds

Heat the oil over medium heat in a large sauté pan. Add the bacon in a single layer and cook until golden brown and crispy on both sides, about 8 minutes. Transfer the bacon to a plate lined with paper towels. Let cool, then coarsely chop.

Return the pan to the heat (you should have about ½ cup/120 ml fat in the pan), add the garlic, and cook for 30 seconds. Stir in the cumin, chipotle, paprika, and salt and cook for 20 seconds longer. Remove from the heat.

Put the chickpeas in a food processor and pulse to coarsely chop. Add the bacon fat–garlic mixture, cold water, tahini, and honey and pulse until just combined (do not make it too smooth). Scrape the mixture into a bowl and garnish with the crispy bacon, green onion, and sesame seeds. The hummus will keep (not garnished), tightly covered in the refrigerator, for up to 3 days. Serve with vegetables, fresh pita, or pita chips.

MAKES ABOUT 2 CUPS (455 G)

BACON AND POTATO RACLETTE

RACLETTE IS BOTH A SEMI-FIRM COW'S MILK CHEESE AND A DISH that hails from France and Switzerland. The raclette cheese is heated until melted (use your broiler or a raclette grill) then scraped onto a diner's plate and served with pickled vegetables, boiled potatoes, and cured meat. I like to push the envelope and cook my potatoes in butter and bacon fat, not water, for an extra level of richness. My cured meat of choice is bacon, of course.

1 tablespoon canola oil

8 ounces (225 g) slab bacon, cut into lardons (see page 48)

1 tablespoon unsalted butter

12 Brussels sprouts, trimmed cut in half

8 ounces (225 g) Confited Potatoes (page 151)

1 pound (455 g) raclette cheese

1 (14-ounce/400-g) jar cornichons, drained

In a large sauté pan, heat the oil and bacon over medium heat and cook until golden brown and crispy, about 8 minutes. Remove the bacon with a slotted spoon to a plate lined with paper towels.

Return the pan to the heat, add the butter to the rendered fat, and cook until it begins to shimmer. Add the Brussels sprouts, cut-side down, and cook until golden brown, about 5 minutes. Turn over and continue cooking until just cooked through, about 5 minutes longer. Transfer the sprouts to the plate with the bacon. Set aside.

Add the potatoes to the pan, cut-side down, and cook until golden brown, about 5 minutes. Turn over and cook until just warmed through, about 2 minutes longer.

Preheat the broiler. Slice the raclette into ⅛-inch (3-mm) slices and lay them flat across a large cast-iron pan or a baking sheet lined with foil. Place the pan under the broiler and cook until very soft and golden brown on top, 2 to 4 minutes, depending on the heat of your broiler.

Arrange the potatoes, bacon, and Brussels sprouts on a platter, and slide the cheese on top. Serve with the cornichons on the side.

SERVES 4 TO 6

VIETNAMESE-GLAZED BRUSSELS SPROUTS
with Greek Yogurt and Honey

LIKE KALE, BRUSSELS SPROUTS SEEM TO BE ON NEARLY EVERY MENU, and at BarBacon they are consistently one of the most popular dishes. These leafy green veggies taste best when cooked over high heat until caramelized and crispy, and luckily they have an affinity for smoked meat . . . like bacon! Not one to let well enough alone, I also toss them in a spicy glaze flavored with soy sauce, rice vinegar, ginger, garlic, and sriracha.

2 tablespoons vegetable oil

6 thick slices bacon, cut into lardons (see page 48)

2 tablespoons unsalted butter

1 pint (about 1 pound/455 g) Brussels sprouts, trimmed and sliced in half, top to bottom

Kosher salt and freshly ground black pepper

½ cup (120 ml) Vietnamese Glaze (page 85)

½ cup (120 ml) plain Greek yogurt

2 tablespoons clover honey

Heat the oil in a large sauté pan over medium heat, add the bacon, and spread out in the pan. Cook until the bacon is golden brown and crispy, about 10 minutes. Using a slotted spoon, remove the bacon to a plate lined with paper towels. Remove all but 3 tablespoons of the fat from the pan and save or let cool and discard.

Increase the heat to high, add the butter and Brussels sprouts, season with salt and pepper, and cook until the sprouts begin to turn golden brown, about 8 minutes. The outer leaves will burn, while the cut sides will turn perfectly golden brown. The centers should be slightly al dente.

Add the glaze, reduce the heat to medium, cover the pan, and cook for 5 minutes. Remove the lid and continue cooking until the glaze has thickened and the sprouts are crisp tender, about 5 minutes longer. Add the bacon and cook for 1 minute longer. Remove the Brussels sprouts from the heat and transfer to a platter. Garnish with the yogurt and drizzle with the honey. Serve immediately.

SERVES 4

TEMPURA BACON

LORD KNOWS THAT BACON NEEDS VERY LITTLE TO MAKE IT delicious, but every now and then it's fun to gild the lily. I present to you: deep-fried bacon. The secret to perfectly crisp and light tempura is making sure that the liquid you use (in this case water and vodka) in the batter is ice cold. Serve this with chipotle-lime mayonnaise (page 74) or Nuoc Mam Cham (page 87) for dipping. Even better, serve it with both.

⅔ cup (80 g) all-purpose flour

⅔ cup (60 g) cornstarch

2½ tablespoons baking powder

½ teaspoon kosher salt

1 cup (240 ml) ice-cold vodka

1 cup (240 ml) ice-cold water

6 cups (1.4 L) canola oil

1 pound (455 g) thin-sliced bacon, preferably Garlic-Soy Bacon (page 26)

In a large bowl, sift the flour, cornstarch, and baking powder together. Add the salt, cold vodka, and cold water and whisk until the batter is smooth. Let the batter rest at room temperature for 10 minutes to allow the flour to absorb the water.

Heat the oil in a deep-fryer or a Dutch oven over medium heat until it reaches 350°F (175°C).

On a baking sheet lined with paper towels, lay the bacon slices out in single layer and blot the tops of them with more paper towels to remove any excess moisture. Using tongs, dip each slice of bacon in the batter and fry, 3 or 4 slices at a time (do not overcrowd the pan), until the batter is golden brown and crisp and the bacon is cooked through, about 4 minutes. Drain the bacon on paper towels and let cool 5 minutes before serving.

SERVES 4 TO 6

LOADED TATER TOTS
with BBQ Bacon, BBQ Sauce, and Cheese

I'VE MADE MY OWN TATER TOTS BEFORE, AND IT'S NOT WORTH THE effort. A little help from frozen tater tots makes this recipe even better. Less work, just as satisfying. For the toppings, you can make your own BBQ Bacon or simply dust some store-bought bacon with Magic Rub (page 94). This recipe works really well with Bacon-Chipotle Chorizo (page 64) instead of the bacon too!

1 (2-pound/907-g) package frozen tater tots

1 pound (455 g) BBQ Bacon (page 30) or plain slab bacon, cut into lardons (see page 48)

¾ cup (180 ml) BarBacon BBQ Sauce (page 82)

¾ cup (180 ml) sour cream

4 cups (16 ounces/460 g) shredded cheddar cheese

5 pickled jalapeños, thinly sliced (optional)

2 green onions (dark green and pale green parts only), thinly sliced

Preheat the oven to 450°F (230°C) and line a large baking sheet with parchment paper. Put the tots in a single layer on the baking sheet and bake until golden brown and crispy, about 20 minutes, turning once halfway through.

While the tots are baking, put the bacon in a small sauté pan over medium heat and cook until golden brown and the fat has rendered, about 8 minutes. Drain the rendered fat from the pan and to the pan add ½ cup (120 ml) of the BBQ sauce and cook, stirring occasionally, until the bacon is glazed with the sauce, about 10 minutes longer. Remove from the heat and set aside.

In a small bowl, combine the sour cream and the remaining ¼ cup (60 ml) BBQ sauce and whisk until smooth. Set aside.

Remove the tater tots from the oven and sprinkle the cheese evenly over the top. Return to the oven and bake until the cheese has melted, about 5 minutes. Using a wide metal spatula, transfer the tots to a large platter. Top with the bacon, jalapeños (if using), and green onion. Drizzle with the sour cream and serve.

SERVES 4 TO 6

BACON CHORIZO FUNDIDO

THIS IS MORE OR LESS A CHEESE DIP WITH SOME AMPED-UP BACON extras. The cheese really acts as a binder for the bacon chorizo sausage, and yes, more pork product (chicharrónes, or fried pork skins) are added to scoop it all up. If you don't have chicharrónes on hand, plain old tortilla or pita chips will work, too.

2 tablespoons canola oil

6 ounces (170 g) thin-sliced bacon

6 ounces (170 g) Bacon-Chipotle Chorizo (page 64), removed from casings, or any fresh store-bought chorizo

1 small Spanish onion, finely diced

¼ cup (30 g) all-purpose flour

4 cups (960 ml) whole milk, plus more if needed

6 ounces (170 g) white American cheese slices

6 ounces (170 g) white cheddar cheese, shredded

6 ounces (170 g) smoked gouda cheese, shredded

¼ teaspoon smoked paprika

Pinch of ground cayenne

¼ cup (40 g) sliced pickled jalapeños

¼ cup (10 g) fresh cilantro leaves, for garnish

Spice-Rubbed Fried Pork Rinds (Chicharrónes) (page 138) or baked tortilla or pita chips

In a large cast-iron pan, heat the oil over medium heat, add the bacon, and cook, stirring a few times, until golden brown and crispy, about 8 minutes. Using a slotted spoon, remove the bacon to a plate lined with paper towels, let cool slightly, then coarsely chop. Add the chorizo to the pan and cook until golden brown and cooked through, about 10 minutes. Using a slotted spoon, transfer the chorizo to another plate lined with paper towels. Pour off all but 4 tablespoons of the fat from the pan and save for another use (see page 50).

Add the onion to the pan and cook until soft, about 4 minutes. Add the flour and cook, stirring constantly, to form a roux, about 2 minutes. Whisk in the milk and continue whisking until the mixture is smooth, starts to thicken, and the flour taste has cooked out, about 10 minutes.

Whisk in the American, cheddar, and gouda and continue whisking until smooth. Season with the paprika and cayenne and cook for 30 seconds longer. Stir in the chorizo. Remove from the heat and top with the cooked bacon, the jalapeños, and cilantro. Serve in the cast-iron pan with pork rinds on the side.

SERVES 4 TO 6

SPICE-RUBBED FRIED PORK RINDS (AKA CHICHARRÓNES)

MOST COOKS LOOK AT PORK SKIN AS A WASTE PRODUCT. I LOOK AT it and see perfectly golden brown, puffed, crisp chips that put potato chips to shame. I use fried pork skins at BarBacon as an appetizer, either served with a vinegary dipping sauce or in place of tortilla chips for a spinach-bacon dip (page 141) or Bacon Chorizo Fundido (page 137). They're also great paired with bacon. Seasoned with the same rub, it's like a keto diet trail mix.

1 large piece pork skin, about 2 pounds (910 g), trimmed of excess fat (the skin portion should be at least ¼ inch/ 6 mm thick)

6 cups (1.4 L) canola oil

1 recipe BB Rub (page 95)

Put the pork skin in a large pot and cover with water. Weigh it down with a plate the entire time of cooking to keep it submerged. Bring the water to a boil, lower the heat to a simmer, and cook until the skin is soft and pliable but not falling apart and the water is white, 1½ to 2 hours. Add more water as needed to keep the skin well covered.

Using a large spider or slotted spoon, carefully remove the skin and arrange in an even layer, with no folds, on a cooling rack set over a baking sheet. Discard the cooking water. Put the baking sheet in the refrigerator, uncovered, and let cool completely, about 2 hours. When the skin is cold, use a spoon or bench scraper to remove all subcutaneous fat, being careful not to tear the skin.

In a deep-fryer or Dutch oven, heat the oil over medium heat until it reaches 375°F (193°C) on a deep-fry thermometer. Line a baking sheet with several layers of paper towels and place the rub in a bowl.

Cut the skin into strips 2 inches (5 cm) long by 1 inch (2.5 cm) wide. Fry in batches of 3 or 4, prodding the skins with a spider or large slotted metal spatula until they puff up and become lightly golden brown and crispy, about 20 seconds. Remove from the oil, transfer to the prepared baking sheet, and season immediately while hot with some of the rub. Serve hot or at room temperature. Any uncooked strips can be stored in an airtight container in the refrigerator for up to 2 days before frying. The fried pork skins will keep for 2 days stored in an airtight container at room temperature.

MAKES 30 TO 40

BACON AND SPINACH DIP

AT BARBACON, MY VERSION OF THE CLASSIC VEGETARIAN-FRIENDLY dip contains lots of bacon and is served with house-made chicharrónes (page 138), but you can serve yours with chips, toasted bread, crackers, or crudité.

4 cups (960 ml) heavy cream

4 garlic cloves, finely chopped

½ cup (115 g) unsalted butter

8 ounces (225 g) thin-sliced bacon, cut crosswise into thin strips

1 Spanish onion, quartered and thinly sliced

1 teaspoon kosher salt, or more to taste

1 tablespoon all-purpose flour

¼ cup (60 ml) sherry wine

¼ teaspoon freshly ground black pepper

¼ teaspoon grated nutmeg (optional)

1 pound (455 g) frozen spinach, thawed and squeezed dry

¼ cup (25 g) grated Parmesan cheese

1 recipe Spice-Rubbed Fried Pork Rinds (Chicharrónes) (page 138) or baked tortilla chips

In a medium saucepan, combine the cream and garlic. Bring to a boil over high heat, lower the heat to medium, and simmer until thickened and reduced by half, about 10 minutes.

While the cream is reducing, melt the butter in a large sauté pan over medium heat. Add the bacon and cook until the fat begins to render. Remove the bacon with a slotted spoon to a plate lined with paper towels.

Lower the heat to low, add the onion and salt, and continue to cook until the onion is soft and translucent, about 15 minutes.

Add the flour and cook for 1 minute longer, then add the wine and cook for 1 minute more just to kill the alcohol. Whisk in the reduced cream and cook until thickened slightly. Season with salt, pepper, and nutmeg (if using). Fold in the spinach and cook until heated through, about 5 minutes. Transfer the mixture to a 9-inch (23-cm) baking pan and sprinkle the Parmesan evenly over the top.

Preheat the broiler. Place the pan on the highest oven rack and broil until the top is golden brown and bubbly, about 2 minutes. Garnish with the reserved bacon, and serve with the chicharrónes.

SERVES 4 TO 6

KENTUCKY FRIED BACON BITES
with Thai Chile Honey

LISTEN, I LOVE FRIED CHICKEN AS MUCH AS THE NEXT PERSON, BUT chicken has nothing on the pig. Sorry. Starting with slab bacon that has been cooked slowly in its own fat (confit) gives the meat a melt-in-your-mouth texture. Combine that with the light, airy crispness of panko, and you have a bite-size nugget of textural perfection.

6 cups (1.4 L) canola oil

1 cup (125 g) all-purpose flour

3 large eggs, whisked with 2 tablespoons water

2 cups (160 g) panko bread crumbs

3 pounds (1.4 kg) Bacon Confit (page 41), cut into 2-inch (5-cm) squares

1 cup (240 ml) Thai Chile Honey (page 88)

2 tablespoons finely chopped fresh chives, for garnish

In a medium-size deep sauté pan or Dutch oven, heat the oil over medium heat until it reaches 365°F (185°C) on a deep-fry thermometer. Line a baking sheet with paper towels.

While the oil is heating, place the flour, egg mixture, and panko in three separate shallow dishes. Working in batches, dredge the bacon in flour, shaking off any excess, then dip into the egg. Transfer to the panko, covering the bacon completely and pressing lightly to adhere. Fry until golden brown and crispy, about 2 minutes.

Remove the bacon with a slotted spoon to the prepared baking sheet. Serve with the honey on the side or on a platter lightly drizzled with the honey. Garnish with the chives.

SERVES 6 TO 8

SAGE SAUSAGE SPRING ROLLS
with Shrimp and Vietnamese Dipping Sauce

SPRING ROLLS, FRIED ROLLS, OR EGG ROLLS. IT DOESN'T MATTER what you call them. They are the perfect bar food. They are also the perfect vehicle to use ingredients in the kitchen before they go bad. We have a "spring roll of the day" special at BarBacon, and this version with my homemade breakfast bacon sausage scented with earthy sage and fragrant ginger and paired with shrimp is one of my favorite combinations.

12 spring roll wrappers
(made with wheat)

12 ounces (340 g) Ginger-Sage
Breakfast Sausage (page 311)
or your favorite breakfast
sausage, divided into
12 (1-ounce/28-g) portions

4 ounces (115 g) store-bought
matchstick carrots

12 large 16/20 shrimp, peeled,
deveined, and butterflied

24 fresh cilantro leaves,
plus more for garnish

Kosher salt and freshly
ground black pepper

2 large eggs, beaten with
1 tablespoon cold water

4 cups (960 ml) canola oil

Nuoc Mam Cham (page 87)

Place the wrappers on a plate and cover with a clean towel to keep them from drying out while you wrap each spring roll.

Arrange a spring roll wrapper in front of you in a diamond orientation. Place one portion of the sausage in the center in a horizontal line. Top the sausage with some of the carrots, a shrimp, and then 2 cilantro leaves and season with a salt and pepper. Brush the sides of the wrappers with the egg wash. Fold the bottom corner over the filling. Fold the left corner over the filling. Fold the right corner over the filling. Brush the rest of the spring roll wrapper with more of the egg wash, then tuck in the sides of the upper corner of the spring roll wrapper. This is to avoid overhang. Roll the spring roll upward, tightly, until the final remaining corner is wrapped and secured.

(To freeze: After rolling, dredge in cornstarch and tap off excess. Put on a sheet pan lined with parchment paper so that they do not touch each other and tightly cover with plastic wrap. Freeze until firm, then transfer to freezer bags. The rolls will keep, tightly wrapped, in the freezer for up to 2 months. To fry after freezing, go straight from the freezer into the hot oil as described below. Do not thaw first.)

In a medium Dutch oven, heat the oil until it reaches 325°F (165°C) on a deep-fry thermometer. Line a baking sheet with paper towels. Using a ladle or a pair of tongs, gently immerse a spring roll into the hot oil. Be very gentle so that the oil does not splash on you. Fry the spring rolls until they are golden brown and crispy, about 4 minutes. Remove and let drain on the prepared baking sheet. Serve with the Nuoc Mam Cham and garnish with cilantro.

MAKES 12

BACON BAO BUNS

BRAISED PORK BELLY IS THE CLASSIC FILLING OF CHOICE FOR steamed buns, but confit bacon is far and away superior because you get that silky mouthfeel with a good dose of smoky goodness. You will need to find butterflied bao buns, which are readily available in most Asian groceries or online.

1 tablespoon canola oil

8 ounces (225 g) Bacon Confit (page 41), cut crosswise into 8 equal pieces

¼ cup (60 ml) Vietnamese Glaze (page 85)

6 prepared bao buns, fresh or frozen

¼ cup (60 ml) Nuoc Mam Cham (page 87), plus more for dipping

½ carrot, peeled and thinly sliced on a mandoline or with a very sharp chef's knife

½ cucumber, thinly sliced on a mandoline or with a very sharp chef's knife

2 tablespoons chopped fresh cilantro leaves

In a large sauté pan, heat the oil over medium heat until it begins to shimmer. Add the bacon and cook until heated through and golden brown, about 5 minutes. Add the glaze and cook until the glaze has reduced and the bacon is nicely glazed, about 2 minutes.

While the bacon is cooking, steam the buns (see Note): Line your steamer with parchment paper or lettuce leaves and set over a pot with a few inches of boiling water in it. Make sure there is at least 1 inch (2. 5 cm) of space between the buns. Cover and steam the buns until just firm to the touch. Fresh buns will take 12 to 15 minutes and frozen between 3 and 5 minutes. Transfer to a serving plate and set aside.

In a small bowl, combine the Nuoc Mam Cham, carrot, cucumber, and cilantro and toss to coat.

To assemble, place a piece of bacon inside each bun with a small amount of the dressed salad. Serve immediately with more Nuoc Mam Cham on the side for dipping.

NOTE: *You can use a steamer insert that fits into saucepans or purchase an inexpensive bamboo steamer at kitchen supply stores. You can also make your own steamer. To do so, make 3 large, evenly-sized balls of aluminum foil. Place the balls in a large pot and lay a ceramic plate on top to make sure it's fairly level. Remove the plate, then add a few inches of water to the pot, bring to a boil, and lower to a medium simmer. Rub a little sesame oil on the plate, then place as many dumplings as will fit on top without crowding. Gently lower the plate onto the foil balls, then cover pot with a lid.*

MAKES 6

BURNT ENDS

BURNT ENDS ARE TRADITIONALLY MADE WITH BEEF BRISKET AND are beloved and revered by enthusiasts worldwide. Brisket is hard to get right, as the meat is prone to overcooking and drying out. My pork belly version is far more user friendly, because pork belly is fattier than brisket, and therefore harder to dry out. And pork tastes better than beef. Sorry, Texas.

1 recipe BBQ Bacon (page 30), smoked to an internal temperature of 195°F (91°C)

1 recipe BBQ Glaze (page 84)

1 recipe BarBacon BBQ Sauce (page 82) or your favorite store-bought BBQ sauce

If you've already made the BBQ Bacon but did not cook it to an internal temperature of 195°F (91°C), put the bacon on a wire rack set over a baking sheet and bake it in a 225°F (107°C) oven until it reaches an internal temperature of 195°F (91°C), about 2 hours.

Remove the bacon from the oven, let cool to room temperature, then refrigerate on the rack, loosely covered with foil, until cold, at least 8 hours, or up to 24 hours.

Preheat the oven to 300°F (150°C). Cut the bacon into 1½-inch (4-cm) squares and bake on a wire rack set on a baking sheet until heated through, about 30 minutes.

Remove from the oven and liberally brush with the glaze. Return to the oven for 7 minutes. Remove and brush with more of the glaze and return to the oven for another 7 minutes.

Remove from the oven, transfer to a platter, and serve with the BBQ sauce on the side.

NOTE: *If you don't feel like making my BBQ Bacon (page 30), then just buy a 3-pound (1.4-kg) slab of bacon, coat each side with a few tablespoons of my Magic Rub (page 94), and bake it on a wire rack in a 225°F (107°C) oven until it reaches an internal temperature of 195°F (91°C).*

SERVES 6 TO 8

CELERY AND APPLE RÉMOULADE

TURKEY HAS CRANBERRY SAUCE, AND BACON AND PORK HAVE THIS!

3 ribs celery, thinly sliced
   on the bias

1 Granny Smith apple, cut into
   matchstick strips

½ cup (120 ml) Rémoulade
   Sauce (page 75)

1 teaspoon fresh lemon juice

1 tablespoon celery seeds

½ cup (110 g) sliced cooked
   bacon

In a medium bowl, toss the celery, apple, rémoulade sauce, lemon juice, and celery seeds together until combined. Cover and refrigerate for at least 30 minutes, or up to 2 days to allow the flavors to meld. Garnish with the bacon and serve cold.

**MAKES ABOUT
3 CUPS (900 G)**

CONFITED POTATOES

SERVED IN BARBACON'S SPINACH SALAD (PAGE 191) OR AS A SIDE with any meat or fish dish, these potatoes are very decadent and delicious and reminiscent of my days spent on the line at Robuchon. Cooking potatoes in butter and bacon fat gives a melt-in-your-mouth texture that can't be produced by any other method.

1 pound (455 g) unsalted butter

4 ounces (120 ml) rendered bacon fat (see page 50)

1 head garlic, cut in half

2 tablespoons kosher salt

4 sprigs fresh thyme

1½ pounds (680 g) fingerling or very small new potatoes, scrubbed well

2 tablespoons chopped fresh flat-leaf parsley or rosemary sprig, for garnish

In a medium pot, melt the butter and bacon fat. Add the garlic, salt, thyme, and potatoes. The potatoes need to be completely submerged in the fat. If they are not, add enough warm water to just cover. Cook over medium-low heat until the potatoes are just fork-tender, about 20 minutes. Using a slotted spoon, transfer the potatoes to a bowl.

Remove ¼ cup (60 ml) of the fat that the potatoes cooked in, add it to a large sauté pan over medium-high heat, and cook until it just begins to shimmer. Cut the potatoes in half lengthwise and cook, cut-side down, until golden brown, about 5 minutes. Turn the potatoes over and cook for a few minutes longer on the other side.

Serve on a platter, sprinkled with the rosemary or parsley, as a side dish, or use in salads.

SERVES 4 TO 6

BRAISED RED CABBAGE

THIS SORT OF "HEALTHYISH" SIDE, WITH ITS SWEET-AND-SOUR FLA-vor, is the perfect accompaniment to hearty cold-weather braises such as Bacon Braised Pork Shanks (page 247) and any dish that begins or ends with bacon. If I am serving this with a bacon dish, I'll sometimes leave out the bacon. But, if you like bacon in everything, then by all means keep it in.

1 tablespoon canola oil

6 ounces (170 g) thin-sliced bacon, cut crosswise into ½-inch (12-mm) pieces (optional)

1 large red onion, halved and thinly sliced

½ cup (120 ml) plus 2 table-spoons red wine vinegar

2 tablespoons sugar, or more to taste

1 head red cabbage (about 2 pounds/910 g), cored, halved, and cut into slices ¼ inch (6 mm) thick

Kosher salt and freshly ground black pepper

If using bacon, in a large, deep sauté pan over medium heat, combine the oil and bacon and cook, stirring occasionally, until golden brown and the fat has rendered, about 8 minutes. Remove the bacon with a slotted spoon to a plate lined with paper towels. If you're not using bacon, add the oil to a large, deep sauté pan over medium heat.

Add the onion to the pan and cook until soft, about 5 minutes. Stir in ½ cup (120 ml) water, ½ cup (120 ml) of the vinegar, and the sugar and cook until the sugar has dissolved, about 2 minutes. Add the cabbage, season with salt and pepper, and cook until the cabbage just begins to wilt, about 5 minutes.

Cover the pan and cook, stirring occasionally, until the cabbage is tender, about 15 minutes. Remove from the heat and stir in the remaining vinegar. Taste and add more salt or pepper or sugar, if needed. Serve hot. The cabbage will keep, tightly covered, in the refrigerator for up to 3 days. Reheat in a large high-sided sauté pan over low heat, stirring several times, for about 10 minutes.

SERVES 4 TO 6

CARAWAY SAUERKRAUT

THERE ARE FEW THINGS THAT I DON'T LIKE MAKING FROM SCRATCH, but sauerkraut is one of them. Just buy good-quality store-bought (from the refrigerator section, not in a can). Making it takes time and stinks up your fridge and house to all hell. The caraway seeds give some extra crunch and a rye bread–like flavor. I love serving this as a topping for a Reuben sandwich or the Bacon Bratwurst Burger (page 202) and as a side dish with Confited Potatoes (page 151).

2 teaspoons canola oil

12 ounces (340 g) thin-sliced bacon, cut crosswise into matchstick strips

1 teaspoon caraway seeds

2 pounds (910 g) sauerkraut, drained and rinsed and drained again

In a large, deep sauté pan over medium heat, combine the oil and bacon and cook until the bacon is golden brown and crisp and has rendered its fat, about 8 minutes. Remove the bacon to a plate lined with paper towels.

Add the caraway seeds to the bacon fat in the pan and cook, stirring constantly, for 1 minute. Add the sauerkraut and ½ cup (120 ml) water and cook until heated through and slightly softened, about 10 minutes. Stir in the bacon and serve. The sauerkraut will keep, tightly covered in the refrigerator, for up to 5 days.

**MAKES ABOUT
2 POUNDS (910 G)**

GERMAN POTATO SALAD

THERE MUST BE A GERMAN POTATO SALAD IN A BOOK CALLED *the Bacon Bible*. It's required. My version is heavier on the bacon than most—not shocking—and is pretty much just meat and potatoes. Feel free to add a large handful of blanched green beans or sautéed mushrooms, fresh dill or parsley, or even a large dollop of Dijon mustard to the dressing. It would be *wunderbar*.

1 tablespoon canola oil

8 ounces (225 g) thin-sliced bacon, cut into thirds

2 pounds (910 g) small Red Bliss or Yukon gold potatoes, scrubbed but not peeled

Cold water

Kosher salt

2 Spanish onions, halved and thinly sliced

1 cup (240 ml) distilled white vinegar

¼ cup (50 g) sugar

¼ teaspoon freshly ground black pepper

4 green onions, thinly sliced

¼ cup (13 g) chopped fresh dill or flat-leaf parsley leaves (optional)

In a large, deep sauté pan, combine the oil and bacon and cook over medium heat, stirring occasionally, until golden brown and crispy and the fat has rendered, about 10 minutes. Remove the bacon with a slotted spoon to a plate lined with paper towels. Set aside.

While the bacon is cooking, put the potatoes in a large pot, cover with cold water by 2 inches (5 cm), and add 2 tablespoons salt. Bring to a boil over high heat and cook until just tender, about 12 minutes. Drain well and keep warm.

Add the Spanish onions to the pan with the rendered fat and cook over medium heat, stirring occasionally, until lightly golden brown and soft, about 10 minutes. Increase the heat to high, add the vinegar and sugar, and cook until the sugar has dissolved, about 2 minutes. Season with 1 teaspoon salt and the pepper.

Slice the warm potatoes crosswise into ¼-inch (6-mm) slices and put in a large bowl. Add the onion dressing, the bacon, the green onions, and the dill (if using) and gently mix to combine. Serve warm or at room temperature.

SERVES 4 TO 6

BOSTON BAKED BEANS

BOSTON BAKED BEANS ARE CLASSICALLY MADE WITH DRIED NAVY beans and salt pork and cooked low and slow for hours in the oven. I make my version with canned kidney beans, bacon confit, and a bit of heat (courtesy of Tabasco) and cook them on top of the stove. It's quicker, done in a New York minute (not a long, drawn out Bostonian one), and just as delicious in half the time. If you don't love kidney beans, navy or black beans would work just fine, too. Same goes for the bacon confit; good old slab bacon will get the job done.

1 tablespoon canola oil

1 (1-pound/455-g) piece Bacon Confit (page 41) or slab bacon

1 large Spanish onion, diced

1 tablespoon tomato paste

1 cup (240 ml) store-bought ketchup

¾ cup (180 ml) molasses

½ cup (110 g) packed light brown sugar

1 teaspoon mustard powder

1 teaspoon kosher salt

1 teaspoon Tabasco sauce

½ teaspoon freshly ground black pepper

⅛ teaspoon ground cayenne

4 (15½-ounce/439-g) cans kidney beans, drained, rinsed, and drained again

1 teaspoon apple cider vinegar

In a large Dutch oven or saucepan over medium heat, combine the oil and bacon and cook until the fat begins to render and the meat is lightly golden brown on both sides, about 10 minutes. Transfer the bacon to a plate. Increase the heat to high.

Add the onion to the pot and cook until soft, about 5 minutes. Add the tomato paste and cook, stirring constantly, for 2 minutes.

Add 1 cup (240 ml) water and scrape up any bacon bits that may be on the bottom of the pan. Add the ketchup, molasses, brown sugar, mustard powder, salt, Tabasco, black pepper, and cayenne and stir until smooth. Add the beans and the bacon and bring to a boil. Lower the heat to low and simmer, stirring occasionally, for 30 minutes, adding more water if the mixture becomes too thick. Remove the bacon from the pot, shred or cut into bite-size pieces, and return to the pot. Stir in the vinegar and serve. The beans will keep, tightly covered in the refrigerator, for up to 1 day.

SERVES 6 TO 8

CHAPTER 6

SOUPS

**OUPS ARE JUST ABOUT THE LAST THING** people associate with bacon. Sure, they're both satisfying in cold weather, but that's where the overlap usually ends. I took it upon myself to make them work together and found that even a little bit of bacon can add a lot of oomph to any old soup recipe.

For some soups, I stick to a small amount. In the burnt toast and roasted eggplant soup (page 172), bacon adds a salty element that neither of the other main components has and provides the soup with way more depth than you'd expect. It makes you guess where all that flavor is coming from. In other soups, you know exactly what you're getting: My French onion soup has bacon broth rather than beef broth. It's perfect when you want to impress your friends with a bacon-ified classic. Caramelized onions, melted cheese, and smoky meat. Win. Win. Win.

With the recipes in this chapter, you'll learn how to add in that pop of bacon to any soup. Soon enough, you'll be taking your grand-mother's chicken noodle soup and asking, *Where's the bacon?*

PORK STOCK

GREAT STOCK IS MADE WHEN THERE IS A GOOD BALANCE BETWEEN the collagen from the roasted bones and the flavor of the meat. Pork ribs have this ratio built in, but feel free to use a combination of pork bones and pork butt, which is a cheaper option.

5 pounds (2.3 kg) pork ribs

2 tablespoons canola oil

Kosher salt and freshly ground black pepper

4 cups (960 ml) chicken stock or low-sodium chicken broth

8 cups (2 L) cold water

½ head garlic, crushed, unpeeled

1 large Spanish onion, quartered

1 large shallot, halved

8 sprigs fresh parsley

6 sprigs fresh thyme

1 tablespoon black peppercorns

2 bay leaves

Preheat the oven to 450°F (230°C). Toss the pork ribs with the oil and season with salt and pepper. Transfer to a large rimmed sheet pan or roasting pan and roast until golden brown and slightly charred on the ends, 30 to 45 minutes, turning once.

Transfer the ribs to a large stockpot and discard the fat. Add the chicken stock, cold water, garlic, onion, shallot, parsley, thyme, peppercorns, bay leaves, and 1 tablespoon salt, bring to a boil, then lower the heat to a simmer. Cook, uncovered, until the pork falls off the bone and the stock has reduced and is full flavored, about 4 hours. Remove from the heat, cover, and let cool to room temperature.

Strain the stock through a fine-mesh sieve into a large bowl or a container with a tight-fitting lid and cover. Refrigerate until chilled and the fat has risen to the top. Remove the fat layer and discard it. The stock will keep, tightly covered in the refrigerator, for up to 3 days, or in the freezer for 3 months.

MAKES ABOUT 8 CUPS (2 L)

BUTTERNUT SQUASH SOUP
with Apple-Bacon Relish and Toasted Butternut Squash Seeds

BUTTERNUT SQUASH IS DELICIOUS, AND LUCKILY IT PAIRS REALLY well with bacon. For added smoky notes, I use bacon stock at the restaurant, but you can use any of the liquids noted below. I love contrast of texture, and this smooth, velvety soup benefits from butternut squash seeds and croutons that are toasted in butter to add a nice nutty crunch and the relish that adds sweetness and a touch of acid to cut through the rich flavor.

1 butternut squash, about 3½ pounds (1.6 kg), halved lengthwise, seeds scraped out and reserved

5 tablespoons (75 ml) canola oil

Kosher salt

1 large Spanish onion, coarsely chopped

1 head garlic, roasted, cloves removed

4 tablespoons (55 g) unsalted butter

6 cups (1.4 L) Bacon Stock (page 43) or water, vegetable stock, chicken stock, or any combination

6 fresh sage leaves, plus more for garnish

4 sprigs fresh thyme

1 sprig fresh rosemary

2 bay leaves

1 cinnamon stick

Freshly ground black pepper

¼ teaspoon grated nutmeg (optional)

Honey to taste

Apple-Bacon Relish (page 161)

Croutons (optional)

Preheat the oven to 375°F (193°C). Line a baking sheet with parchment paper or aluminum foil. Brush the cut side and top of the squash with 2 tablespoons of the oil and place on the prepared baking sheet, cut-side down. Roast until soft and the flesh is golden brown, about 1 hour. Remove from the oven, let cool, scoop out the flesh and put it in a bowl, and discard the skin. Set aside.

Lower the oven temperature to 300°F (150°C) and line the same baking sheet with a clean sheet of parchment or foil.

Rinse the squash seeds, removing any strings and bits of squash. Pat dry and place in a small bowl. Stir in 2 tablespoons of the oil and 1 teaspoon salt and mix until evenly coated. Spread out in an even layer on the prepared baking sheet and bake, stirring once, until lightly golden brown and seeds begin to pop, about 15 minutes. Let cool on the baking sheet before serving.

Heat the remaining 1 tablespoon oil in a large Dutch oven over high heat, add the onion, and cook until soft and lightly golden brown, about 5 minutes. Stir in the roasted garlic and cook for 1 minute. Add the butter and cook, stirring occasionally, until it begins to turn golden brown,

(continued)

about 3 minutes. Stir in the squash and cook until the squash begins to deepen in color and dry out, about 10 minutes.

Stir in the stock and bring to a boil. Using butcher's twine, stack the sage, thyme, rosemary, bay leaves, and cinnamon on top of one another, tie together, and add to the soup. Lower the heat to low and cook, stirring occasionally, until the soup thickens and the flavors meld, about 30 minutes.

Remove from the heat, discard the herbs, and let cool. Puree the soup in batches in a blender until smooth. Season with salt, pepper, and nutmeg (if using) and honey to taste, if needed. Transfer back to the pot that you cooked it in and bring to a simmer over low heat. Ladle into bowls and top each serving with a large dollop of the relish, the toasted butternut squash seeds, sage, and croutons, if desired. The soup can be made up to 2 days in advance and stored, tightly covered, in the refrigerator. Reheat over low heat before serving.

MAKES ABOUT 8 CUPS (2 L)

APPLE-BACON RELISH

2 teaspoons canola oil

4 ounces (115 g) thin-sliced bacon, diced

½ small red onion, finely diced

1 large Gala or Granny Smith apple, diced

1 tablespoon sugar

¼ cup (60 ml) apple cider vinegar

Pinch of freshly ground black pepper

2 tablespoons finely chopped fresh parsley leaves

In a large sauté pan, heat the oil over medium heat until it begins to shimmer. Add the bacon and cook until golden brown and crisp, about 8 minutes. Using a slotted spoon, remove the bacon to a plate lined with paper towels.

Add the onion and apple to the pan and cook until soft, about 5 minutes. Add the sugar and vinegar and cook until thickened, about 4 minutes. Return the bacon to the pan and cook for 1 minute. Remove from the heat, transfer to a medium bowl, and stir in the pepper and parsley. Let cool to room temperature before serving. The relish will keep, tightly covered in the refrigerator, for up to 2 days. Bring to room temperature before serving.

MAKES ABOUT 1½ CUPS (355 G)

SMOOTH CHILLED TOMATO SOUP

JUST LIKE BUTTERNUT SQUASH SIGNIFIES FALL, CHILLED TOMATO soup screams summer. Overripe, in-season beefsteak or heirloom tomatoes make this simple chilled soup pretty much perfect on its own or as a great accompaniment to a BLT (page 208) or Spinach Salad (page 191).

2 pounds (910 g) very ripe heirloom or beefsteak tomatoes, diced

1 red bell pepper, diced

1 small cucumber, peeled, seeded, and diced

3 garlic cloves, chopped

1 (1-inch/2.5-cm) slice country white bread, crust removed, diced

1½ tablespoons honey, or more to taste

2 teaspoons kosher salt, or more to taste

3 tablespoons extra-virgin olive oil, plus more for garnish

2 teaspoons aged sherry vinegar, or more to taste

Crispy bacon (optional)

Sliced fresh chives (optional)

In a large bowl, combine the tomatoes, bell pepper, cucumber, garlic, bread, honey, salt, oil, and vinegar. Lightly mash using a potato masher, cover, and refrigerate for at least 8 hours, or up to 24 hours.

In a blender, puree the mixture, in batches, until smooth. Pass through a fine chinois, then taste for seasoning, adding more salt, honey, or vinegar if needed. Transfer to a container with a tight-fitting lid and refrigerate until cold, at least 2 hours, or up to 24 hours.

To serve, ladle the soup into bowls and garnish with the bacon, chives, and a drizzle of olive oil, if desired.

MAKES 4 CUPS (960 ML)

BACON ONION SOUP

FRENCH ONION SOUP IS ONE OF THE FIRST THINGS YOU MAKE IN culinary school, and it is really only about two things: the onions and the stock. The key to perfectly caramelized onions is patience; they must be cooked very low and very slow. The bacon stock sets this soup apart from the classic veal stock versions and, dare I say, elevates it to new status. This recipe is close to the one I learned at the French Culinary Institute years ago, except for the addition of bacon, of course.

4 tablespoons (55 g) unsalted butter

4 large Spanish onions, halved and thinly sliced

1 cup (240 ml) dry sherry or madeira wine

6 cups (1.4 L) low-sodium beef or chicken broth or vegetable stock

2 cups (480 ml) Bacon Stock (page 43)

1 tablespoon beef or chicken base (optional; see Note)

5 sprigs fresh thyme

8 slices sourdough or French bread, ½ inch (12 mm) thick

8 ounces (225 g) shredded Gruyère cheese

4 ounces (115 g) thin-sliced bacon, diced and cooked until crisp (see page 44)

2 tablespoons minced fresh chives

In a large Dutch oven or heavy pot over medium-low heat, melt the butter. Add the onions and spread them out in as thin a layer as possible and cook, stirring as needed to keep the onions from sticking, until they are very soft, a deep golden brown, and caramelized, about 1 hour.

Stir in the sherry and cook until completely reduced. Add the beef or chicken broth, bacon stock, base, and thyme and bring to a simmer. Cook, partially covered, for about 30 minutes, to allow the flavors to combine. Remove and discard the thyme sprigs.

Meanwhile, lightly toast the bread under the broiler; set aside. Ladle the hot soup into eight ovenproof bowls.

Arrange the bowls on a baking pan and place 1 slice of toasted bread over each bowl of soup. Divide the cheese over the bread in each bowl and place under the broiler until the cheese is melted and crusty brown around the edges. Watch carefully so the cheese doesn't burn. Garnish with the bacon and chives. Serve immediately.

NOTE: *Beef or chicken bases are made from roast beef or chicken and are concentrated pastes that intensify the flavor of stocks, especially prepared stocks from the grocery store. One of my favorites is Better Than Bouillon, which can be found in most supermarkets and online.*

SERVES 8

BACON RAMEN

I BELIEVE THAT THE FIRST PERSON TO PUT BACON RAMEN ON THE culinary map was David Chang, the powerhouse behind the global Momofuku restaurant empire and one of the best chefs in the world today. My version is a bit simpler but every bit as satisfying, thanks to the dashi made with bacon stock, mirin, and soy sauce. The honey-soy glaze on the bacon is optional, but adds another level of salt and a touch of sweetness, for a balanced bowl of broth. Use the smokiest slab bacon that you can find for this recipe to achieve the most authentic flavor.

8 ounces (225 g) slab bacon, the smokiest you can find (I prefer Benton's; see page 52) or Garlic-Soy Bacon (page 26) smoked to 195°F (91°C) internal temperature

4 cups (960 ml) low-sodium chicken stock or broth

1 (2-inch/5-cm) piece fresh ginger, smashed

1 garlic clove, smashed

3 tablespoons Soy Glaze (page 85; optional)

½ cup (120 ml) mirin

1 tablespoon low-sodium soy sauce

2 shiitake mushrooms, stemmed and thinly sliced

1 head bok choy (about 6 ounces/170 g), stalks sliced crosswise into ½-inch (12-mm) pieces, leaves left whole; or 2 ounces (55 g) baby spinach leaves

2 (3-ounce/85-g) packages dried ramen noodles, or 6 ounces (170 g) fresh ramen noodles

1 Thai bird's eye chile, thinly sliced

2 soft-boiled eggs (see Note)

In a large saucepan, cook the bacon over medium heat until golden brown on both sides and the fat begins to render, about 10 minutes. Drain the fat into a small bowl and set aside.

Add the stock, ginger, and garlic, increase the heat to high, and bring to a boil. Lower the heat to low, cover, and simmer for 15 minutes. Remove from the heat and let sit for 15

minutes. Remove the ginger and garlic and discard.

Preheat the broiler. Remove the bacon from the broth and pat dry with paper towels. Put the bacon on a baking sheet, brush with the reserved rendered bacon fat (or the glaze, if using), and broil until slightly charred on both sides. Let the bacon cool slightly and cut crosswise into ½-inch (12-mm) slices. Set aside.

Add the mirin, soy sauce, and mushrooms to the stock and bring to a boil over high heat. Lower the heat to low, cover, and cook for 15 minutes. Add the bok choy and cook for 5 minutes longer.

Meanwhile, cook the noodles in water according to the package directions, then drain.

Divide the noodles and broth between two large soup bowls and add the bacon and chile. Carefully peel the eggs and cut in half lengthwise. Add two halves to each of the bowls and serve immediately.

NOTE: *To make soft-boiled eggs: Bring a small pot of water to a boil. Gently lower the eggs into the water and cook for 8 minutes. Remove the eggs with a slotted spoon, plunge into ice water, and let sit for at least 5 minutes before peeling.*

SERVES 2

BACON CHILI

WHAT IS BETTER THAN A HEARTY BOWL OF SPICY CHILI CON CARNE that is chock-full of beef, beans, tomatoes, and spices? Well, in my not-so-humble opinion, a chili con carne that includes bacon. Bacon adds that hint of smoke that chili cooked over a campfire has, but without having to actually build a fire yourself. This is a beef-based chili that includes bacon two ways in its foundation. If you count the crispy garnish on top, you are up to three. Serve with Bacon and Bourbon Cornbread (page 301), if desired.

6 ounces (170 g) slab bacon, cut into lardons (see page 48)

6 ounces (170 g) slab bacon, coarsely ground in a food processor

2 pounds (910 g) ground chuck (80/20)

1 tablespoon kosher salt

¼ teaspoon freshly ground black pepper

1 large Spanish onion, finely diced

6 piquillo peppers, seeded and finely diced

6 Fresno chiles, finely diced

3 garlic cloves, finely chopped

2 tablespoons tomato paste

1 (28-ounce/794-g) can plum tomatoes and juices, crushed

1 tablespoon pureed chipotles in adobo

8 ounces (225 g) cooked black beans, drained

8 ounces (225 g) cooked red beans, drained

2 teaspoons ground cumin

2 teaspoons dried oregano

½ cup (55 g) Bacon Bits (page 49)

8 ounces (225 g) shredded cheddar cheese (optional)

8 ounces (240 ml) sour cream (optional)

Pickled jalapeños (optional)

In a large Dutch oven, cook the bacon lardons over medium heat, stirring occasionally, until the fat has rendered and the bacon is crisp, about 8 minutes. Remove the bacon with a slotted spoon to a medium bowl. Increase the heat to high and cook until the rendered fat begins to shimmer.

Add the ground bacon and beef to the pot, season with salt and pepper, and cook, stirring a few times, until golden brown, about 7 minutes. Using a slotted spoon, transfer the meat to the bowl with the bacon lardons. Remove all but ¼ cup (60 ml) of fat from the pan and reserve for another use. Add the onion, piquillo peppers, and chiles and cook

until soft, about 5 minutes. Add the garlic and cook for 1 minute. Stir in the tomato paste and cook for 2 minutes. Increase the heat to high, add the tomatoes, ½ cup (120 ml) water, and the chipotles and bring to a boil.

Return all of the meat to the pot, then add the beans, cumin, and oregano and bring back to a boil. Lower the heat to low and simmer, stirring occasionally, until thickened, about 45 minutes.

Ladle the chili into bowls and top with a sprinkling of bacon bits, cheese, a dollop of sour cream, and a few pickled jalapeños, if desired. The chili will keep, tightly covered, in the refrigerator for 2 days or in the freezer for up to 1 month.

SERVES 8

BACON LOVES CLAM CHOWDER

THERE ARE FEW THINGS AS SATISFYING AS A BIG BOWL OF CREAMY, hearty clam chowder studded with chewy, briny clams and thick pieces of smoky pork. The porchetta, with its fennel, sage, and rosemary, adds an unexpected flavor not normally associated with classic New England clam chowder.

2 tablespoons extra-virgin olive oil

40 littleneck clams, rinsed and scrubbed

6 ounces (180 ml) dry white wine

6 ounces (180 ml) bottled clam juice

2 tablespoons unsalted butter

6 ounces (170 g) Smoked Porchetta (page 38), cut into lardons (see page 48)

1 Spanish onion, diced

2 ribs celery, diced

2 Yukon gold potatoes, peeled and diced

1 teaspoon chopped fresh thyme leaves

1 bay leaf

Kosher salt and freshly ground black pepper

3 tablespoons all-purpose flour

3 cups (720 ml) heavy cream

2 tablespoons minced fresh chives

In a large Dutch oven or stockpot, heat the oil over high heat until it begins to shimmer, about 1 minute. Stir in the clams, then add the wine and half of the clam juice. Cover the pot and cook, shaking the pot a few times, until all the clams open, about 5 minutes.

Using a slotted spoon, transfer the clams to a large bowl, discarding any that do not open, and let cool slightly. Once cool enough to handle, remove all but 6 clams from their shells and coarsely chop. Reserve the clams in their shells for garnish.

In a large bowl, strain the liquid from the stockpot through a fine-mesh sieve lined with cheesecloth and set aside.

Return the pan to medium heat, add the butter, and cook until it has melted. Stir in the porchetta and cook until golden brown and the fat has rendered, about 8 minutes. Remove the porchetta to a plate lined with paper towels.

Remove all but ¼ cup (60 ml) of the rendered fat from the pan and heat until it begins to shimmer. Add the onion, celery, potatoes, thyme, and bay leaf. Season with salt and pepper and cook until the vegetables begin to soften, about 5 minutes. Stir in the flour and continue to cook, stirring constantly, until it turns a pale blond color, about 2 minutes. Whisk in the remaining clam juice and the reserved clam broth and bring to a boil. Lower the heat to medium-low and cook, stirring occasionally, until the soup begins to thicken, the potatoes are tender, and the raw flour taste has cooked out, about 10 minutes.

Add the cream and bring to a simmer. Add the chopped clams, remove from the heat, and allow to sit for 1 minute.

Ladle the soup into bowls and garnish each with a clam in the shell, a few pieces of crisp porchetta, and some chives.

SERVES 4 TO 6

BURNT TOAST AND ROASTED EGGPLANT SOUP
with Curried Crème Fraîche and Bacon Bits

THICKENING SOUPS AND STEWS WITH BREAD IS A COMMON TECH-nique in Mediterranean cooking. I recommend slightly burning the bread, like in this recipe, because it adds an additional smoky flavor. And you know that I am all about that smoke.

3 pounds (1.4 kg) small eggplants, halved lengthwise

½ cup (120 ml) canola oil

Kosher salt and freshly ground black pepper

3 slices stale sourdough bread, 1 inch (2.5 cm) thick

2½ cups (600 ml) Bacon Stock (page 43) or low-sodium chicken broth or vegetable stock

1½ cups (360 ml) whole milk

1 tablespoon Dijon mustard

1 tablespoon aged sherry vinegar

2 teaspoons fresh lemon juice

Curried Crème Fraîche (recipe follows)

1 small green onion, finely diced

½ cup (55 g) Bacon Bits (page 49)

Croutons

Preheat the oven to 400°F (205°C). Brush the eggplant halves with the oil and season with salt and pepper. Place, cut-side down, on a baking sheet and cook until the bottom is lightly golden brown and the eggplant is soft when pierced with a paring knife or skewer, about 30 minutes. Remove to a wire rack and let cool. Once cool enough to handle, remove and discard the skin and place the flesh in a bowl.

While the eggplant is cooling, toast the bread in a toaster or under the broiler until it is deep golden brown and slightly charred around the edges on both sides. Tear into large pieces.

In a large saucepan, combine the stock and milk and bring to a boil over high heat. Add the bread and cook until it begins to soften, about 5 minutes. Stir in the eggplant and cook for 5 minutes. Using an immersion blender, puree the soup. Alternatively, let cool and transfer to a food processor or blender in batches and puree until smooth.

Return the soup to the pot, bring to a boil, then lower the heat to a simmer. Cook for 5 minutes, or until just heated through. Remove from the heat and whisk in the mustard, vinegar, and lemon juice. Season with more salt and pepper, if needed.

Ladle the soup into bowls and top each bowl with a dollop of the crème fraîche and a sprinkling of green onion, bacon bits, and croutons.

SERVES 8

CURRIED CRÈME FRAÎCHE

1 tablespoon canola oil

1 tablespoon best-quality mild curry powder

1 cup (240 ml) crème fraiche or sour cream

½ teaspoon kosher salt

In a small sauté pan, heat the oil over medium heat until it begins to shimmer. Stir in the curry powder and cook, stirring constantly, until fragrant and the color deepens, about 2 minutes. Add ¼ cup (60 ml) water and cook, stirring constantly, until the water evaporates, about 2 minutes longer. Scrape into a bowl and let cool for 5 minutes.

Add the crème fraîche to the bowl and whisk until smooth, then season with the salt. Cover and refrigerate for at least 30 minutes, or up to 8 hours to allow the flavors to meld. The crème fraîche will keep, covered in the refrigerator, for up to 3 days.

MAKES 1 CUP (240 ML)

BACON TORTILLA SOUP

WHEN I MAKE THIS SOUP, I DIP EVERY SANDWICH I'M EATING INTO it—grilled cheese, pulled pork, BLTs. You name the sandwich, I will dip it. It's also great on its own.

2 tablespoons canola oil

2 Spanish onions, chopped

5 garlic cloves, chopped

1 tablespoon tomato paste

½ to 1 chipotle in adobo, depending on how spicy you like it, chopped

2 cups (480 ml) chicken stock or low-sodium chicken broth

2 cups (480 ml) Bacon Stock (page 43)

3 pounds (1.4 kg) very ripe beefsteak or Roma tomatoes, cored, seeded, and chopped (or two 28-ounce/794-g cans plum tomatoes)

2 ounces (55 g) tortilla chips, crushed

Kosher salt and freshly ground black pepper

½ cup to 1 cup (120 ml to 240 ml) tomato juice or water, if needed

Sour cream (optional)

Chopped fresh cilantro (optional)

Bacon Bits (page 49; optional)

In a large Dutch oven, heat the oil over high heat, add the onions, and cook, stirring several times, until soft, about 5 minutes. Add the garlic and cook for 1 minute longer. Add the tomato paste and chipotle and cook, stirring constantly, for 1 minute.

Add the chicken and bacon stocks, bring to a boil, and cook for 5 minutes. Add the tomatoes. If using fresh tomatoes, cook until they soften and completely cook down, about 15 minutes. If using canned tomatoes, crush them with your hands as you put them into the pot and cook until they soften and break down, about 25 minutes. Add the tortilla chips and cook until completely soft, about 10 minutes. Remove from the heat and let cool.

Transfer the soup to a blender and blend, in batches if necessary, until smooth. Return to the same pot, bring to a simmer, and season with salt and pepper. If the soup is too thick, thin with tomato juice or water as needed. If the soup is too thin and does not coat the back of a wooden spoon, then cook a little longer until thickened. (This will depend on how much water the fresh tomatoes give off.)

Ladle the soup into bowls and, if you'd like, garnish each with dollop of sour cream and sprinklings of cilantro and bacon bits.

SERVES 6 TO 8

BACON CHESTNUT SOUP

YES, CHESTNUTS ARE DELICIOUS ROASTED OVER AN OPEN FIRE, BUT they also work surprisingly well pureed into soup. Roasting them brings out their sweet nutty flavor, adding another dimension to this soup. I love eating this hearty, rich soup in the dead of winter—it's great as a first course at Christmas dinner, too.

2 teaspoons canola oil

5 thin slices bacon

1 tablespoon unsalted butter

1 (12- to 15-ounce/340- to 430-g) jar steamed or roasted whole chestnuts (about 2 cups), chopped

2 cups (480 ml) Bacon Stock (page 43)

2 cups (480 ml) chicken stock or low-sodium chicken broth

1 cup (240 ml) cold water

3 sprigs fresh thyme

½ cup (120 ml) heavy cream

Kosher salt and freshly ground black pepper

Fresh sage leaves

In a large sauté pan, heat the oil and bacon over medium heat and cook until golden brown and crispy, turning once, about 8 minutes. Transfer the bacon to a plate lined with paper towels. Let it cool slightly, then coarsely chop and set aside.

Add the butter to the pan with the rendered fat and cook until it has melted. Add the chestnuts and cook, stirring occasionally, for 5 minutes. Add the bacon and chicken stocks, the cold water, and the thyme and increase the heat to high. Bring to a boil, lower the heat to low, and simmer, partially covered, until

the chestnuts have completely softened and the flavors have melded, about 30 minutes. Remove from the heat, discard the thyme sprigs, and let cool, uncovered, for about 20 minutes.

Transfer to a blender, in batches, and blend until smooth. Return the soup to the pot that you cooked it in and bring to a simmer. Add the cream and cook until heated through and thickened, about 5 minutes. Season with salt and pepper to taste.

Ladle into bowls and garnish with the bacon and sage.

SERVES 4 TO 6

CHAPTER 7

SALADS

A S FAR AS I'M CONCERNED, BACON MIGHT be the only reason to eat a salad, and the ones we serve at BarBacon are very popular with our customers. The key is that the bacon is not simply just thrown into the mix. It plays a part in both the flavor and texture of the salad—like in the dressing for the Spinach Salad (page 191) or deep fried and served alongside sweet ripe watermelon in the Crispy Fried Bacon Pork Belly and Watermelon Salad (page 186).

I love the big meaty bacon lardons paired with the chicken, eggs, blue cheese, and cherry tomatoes in the BarBacon Cobb (page 189) just as much as I like the crispy bits of bacon sprinkled over the Wedge Salad (page 183). For those who still crave a smoky flavor with their veggies, I present the Tuna Bacon Niçoise (page 196), a new spin on the French classic.

Salads are also a great place to use your flavored bacons. Black-peppered bacon works on just about every one of the recipes in this chapter, especially the baby kale salad (page 195), and if you're a hothead, jalapeño bacon will add an extra shot of spicy to the Thai noodle salad (page 192) or the calamari salad (page 180).

CALAMARI SALAD
with Soy-Ginger Vinaigrette

I STILL REMEMBER THE FIRST TIME I TRIED MUSTARD GREENS. I was blown away by the bitter, peppery taste. Who knew that a leaf could pack so much flavor? In the South, ham is often served with greens on the side, so bacon just makes sense for this recipe. The salad is topped with fried calamari, one of my favorite bar appetizers.

FOR THE SOY-GINGER VINAIGRETTE

¼ cup (60 ml) low-sodium soy sauce or tamari

1 tablespoon fresh lime juice

1 tablespoon fresh orange juice

2 teaspoons rice vinegar

2 tablespoons finely grated fresh ginger

2 teaspoons sriracha

2 garlic cloves, finely chopped

2 tablespoons vegetable oil

1 teaspoon toasted sesame oil

FOR THE SALAD

1 pound (455 g) calamari, cleaned and cut into rings ½ inch (12 mm) thick

2 cups (480 ml) shaken buttermilk

4 cups (960 ml) vegetable or canola oil

2 cups (360 g) yellow cornmeal

1 cup (125 g) all-purpose flour

Kosher salt and freshly ground black pepper

3 ounces (85 g) mustard greens, torn into bite-size pieces; or baby mustard greens

3 ounces (85 g) baby arugula

1 watermelon radish or 4 red radishes, scrubbed well and thinly sliced

3 pickled hot cherry peppers, patted dry and thinly sliced

12 ounces (340 g) sautéed bacon lardons (see page 48)

1 tablespoon sesame seeds, lightly toasted

Make the vinaigrette: In a medium bowl, whisk together the soy sauce, lime juice, orange juice, vinegar, ginger, sriracha, garlic, vegetable oil, and sesame oil. Cover and let the flavors meld for at least 30 minutes or cover and refrigerate for up to 1 day.

Make the salad: In a medium bowl, combine the calamari rings and buttermilk, cover, and let marinate, stirring once, for at least 4 hours, or up to 24 hours.

Heat the oil in a large Dutch oven over medium heat until it reaches 350°F (175°C) on a deep-fry thermometer. Line a baking sheet with several layers of paper towels.

In a large shallow bowl, mix together the cornmeal and flour and season well with salt and pepper. Working in batches, remove the calamari from the buttermilk using a slotted spoon and let some of the buttermilk run off. Dredge in the seasoned cornmeal and tap off any excess. Fry until golden brown and crisp, 2 to 3 minutes. Drain on the prepared baking sheet and immediately season with salt and pepper.

In a large bowl, combine the mustard greens, arugula, radish, and cherry peppers, add ¼ cup (60 ml) of the vinaigrette, and toss to coat. Transfer to a platter and scatter the calamari and bacon on top, drizzle with more of the vinaigrette, and garnish with sesame seeds. Serve immediately.

SERVES 4 TO 6

WEDGE SALAD

COME SUMMER, MY STAFF DEMANDS MEALS THAT ARE SATISFYING, but still light and refreshing. Basically they want to eat at BarBacon and still wear a bathing suit. No dish delivers better on this than our wedge salad, an old-school creation that is all about simplicity.

12 ounces (340 g) Bacon Confit (page 41), cut into 8 slices 3 inches (7. 5 cm) long by ½ inch (12 mm) thick

2 tablespoons canola oil

1 cup (240 ml) Bacon–Blue Cheese Ranch (page 78)

4 heads Little Gem lettuce (about 4 ounces/115 g each), leaves separated

12 Tomato Confit halves (page 286)

12 ounces (340 g) blue cheese, such as Maytag blue or Cabrales, sliced into 12 wedges

8 ounces (225 g) Fried Shallots (page 271)

Heat a grill pan, cast-iron pan, or nonstick pan over medium heat. Brush the bacon on both sides with the oil and grill or cook until golden brown on both sides and just heated through, about 8 minutes. Place two pieces of the bacon crisscrossed on each of four large dinner plates.

In a large bowl, put ½ cup (120 ml) of the dressing, then add the lettuce leaves a few at a time and toss to coat with the dressing. Divide the lettuce among the plates over the bacon. Arrange the cheese wedges and tomatoes around the outside and place a handful of shallots on top and drizzle with the remaining dressing, if desired. Serve immediately.

SERVES 4

BLT PANZANELLA

PANZANELLA REALLY IS A SUMMER SALAD, TYPICALLY MADE WHEN home gardens and farm stands are overrun with fresh, ripe beefsteak tomatoes. This salad is so popular that we keep it on the menu all year long, and instead of risking mushy out-of-season tomatoes, I just use my tomato confit, which adds a concentrated hit of tomato flavor.

FOR THE BASIL VINAIGRETTE

¼ cup (60 ml) red wine vinegar

¼ cup (10 g) packed basil leaves

1 clove garlic, chopped

¼ teaspoon kosher salt

¼ teaspoon ground black pepper

½ cup (120 ml) extra virgin olive oil

FOR THE SALAD

6 slices day-old ciabatta bread, halved lengthwise

½ cup (120 ml) oil from Tomato Confit (page 286)

Kosher salt and freshly ground black pepper

1 tablespoon canola oil

12 ounces (340 g) slab bacon or Smoked Porchetta (page 38), cut into lardons (see page 48)

12 to 18 Tomato Confit halves (page 286)

4 ounces (115 g) arugula and mustard greens mix

Thyme Tzatziki (page 76)

Make the vinaigrette: Combine the vinegar, basil, garlic, salt, pepper, and a few tablespoons of water in a blender and blend until smooth. With the motor running, slowly add the oil and blend until emulsified. The vinaigrette can be stored, tightly covered, in the refrigerator for up to 1 day.

Make the salad: Preheat a grill to high or heat a grill pan over high heat. Brush both sides of the bread with ¼ cup (60 ml) of the tomato confit oil and season with salt and pepper. Grill on both sides until lightly golden brown, about 1 minute per side. Let cool for 5 minutes. Cut into 1-inch (2.5-cm) squares and place the cubes in a large bowl.

Put the canola oil and bacon in a large pan and cook over medium heat until golden brown and crisp and the fat has rendered, about 8 minutes. Remove to a plate lined with paper towels to drain, then add to the bowl with the bread. Add the tomatoes and the remaining ¼ cup (60 ml) tomato confit oil and toss.

In a second large bowl, toss the greens with ¼ cup (60 ml) of the vinaigrette until well coated. Add the greens to the bread mixture and toss to combine.

Spread the tzatziki on the bottom of a large platter and place the salad on top. Drizzle with more of the vinaigrette. Serve immediately.

SERVES 4 TO 6

CRISPY FRIED BACON PORK BELLY AND WATERMELON SALAD

with Balsamic Soy Glaze

THIS RECIPE IS AN EXAMPLE OF HOW A COMBINATION OF TEXTURES and flavors working together will create a perfect dish every single time—and some wicked alliteration: sweet, salty, smoky, sour, and shattery!

FOR THE PORK BELLY

4 cups (960 ml) canola oil

1 cup (130 g) cornstarch, sifted

1 pound (455 g) Bacon Confit (page 41), chilled and cut into 8 (1½-inch/2.5-cm) cubes

FOR THE WATERMELON SALAD

2 slices watermelon, 1½ inches (4 cm) thick, rind and seeds removed and cut into 12 equal-size squares, very cold

Balsamic Soy Glaze (recipe follows)

2 green onions (dark green and pale green parts only), thinly sliced

1 teaspoon sesame seeds, lightly toasted

Pinch of freshly ground black pepper

Make the pork belly: In a medium saucepan or Dutch oven, heat the oil over medium heat until it reaches 375°F (193°C) on a deep-fry thermometer.

Place the cornstarch in a shallow dish and dredge the pork in the cornstarch, tapping off any excess. Fry in batches until golden brown and crispy, about 5 minutes. Using a slotted spoon, remove the pork belly to a plate lined with paper towels to drain and let rest for 5 minutes.

Make the watermelon salad: Arrange the pork belly and watermelon on a platter, drizzle liberally with the glaze, and sprinkle with the green onions, sesame seeds, and pepper. Serve immediately.

SERVES 4

BALSAMIC SOY GLAZE

2 cups (480 ml) balsamic
vinegar

¾ cup (180 ml) low-sodium
soy sauce

1 (2-inch/5-cm) piece fresh
ginger, peeled and chopped

¾ cup (180 ml) Mae Ploy
sweet chili sauce

In a medium nonreactive saucepan, bring the vinegar to a boil over high heat and cook until reduced by half, about 10 minutes. Add the soy sauce and cook until reduced by half again, 10 minutes longer. Remove from the heat, add the ginger, and let cool for 5 minutes.

Transfer the mixture to a blender, add the chili sauce, and blend until smooth. Transfer to a bowl and let cool to room temperature before using. The sauce will keep, tightly covered in the refrigerator, for up to 2 weeks.

**MAKES ABOUT
3½ CUPS (840 ML)**

WALDORF SALAD
with Spicy Candied Walnuts

THIS IS NOT THE SALAD THAT WAS CREATED MORE THAN A hundred twenty years ago in New York at the Waldorf Astoria. This is the one that was created three years ago in New York at BarBacon. I added ripe pears and candied walnuts for extra sweetness and texture, mustard greens and radicchio for a touch of bitterness, and buttermilk for tang. This salad is like the city it was created in: a melting pot of flavors and textures.

---

2 ounces (55 g)
baby mustard greens

1 head radicchio, leaves
separated and torn

2 Gala apples, diced

2 ripe Bosc pears, diced

2 small ribs celery, with leaves,
thinly sliced crosswise

Tarragon Buttermilk Dressing
(page 77)

12 thin slices bacon, cooked
until crisp (see page 44)
and crumbled

½ recipe Spicy Candied
Walnuts (page 293)

In a large bowl, combine the mustard greens, radicchio, apples, pears, and celery (with the celery leaves). Add about half of the dressing and mix to coat well.

Divide the salad among serving plates and drizzle with more dressing, if desired. Top with the bacon and walnuts and serve immediately.

SERVES 4 TO 6

BARBACON COBB

THIS SALAD IS AN AMERICAN CLASSIC, AND MIGHT BE THE ONLY salad that leaves you full after eating it. I love the bacon lardons here—thick, meaty, salty bites that dominate the flavor of whatever can fit on the fork with them. One of my favorite dressings—tarragon buttermilk—finishes it off. ·

1 tablespoon canola oil

12 ounces (340 g) slab bacon, cut into lardons (see page 48)

2 (8-ounce/225-g) boneless, skinless chicken breasts

Kosher salt and freshly ground black pepper

1 head romaine lettuce, chopped

Tarragon Buttermilk Dressing (page 77)

1 small English cucumber, diced

1 pint (455 g) cherry tomatoes, halved

8 ounces (225 g) blue cheese, crumbled

6 hard-boiled eggs (see Note), peeled, finely chopped

2 ripe Hass avocados, peeled, halved, pitted, and cut length-wise into 6 slices

In a large sauté pan, combine the oil and bacon and cook over medium heat until golden brown and crispy, about 10 minutes. Remove the bacon with a slotted spoon to a plate lined with paper towels and set aside.

Remove all but 2 tablespoons of the rendered bacon fat from the pan and save for another use (see page 50). Increase the heat to high and heat until the rendered bacon fat begins to shimmer. Season the chicken on both sides with salt and pepper and add to the pan. Cook until golden brown on both sides and just cooked through, about 9 minutes total. Remove the chicken to a cutting board, loosely tent with aluminum foil, and let rest for 5 minutes before slicing.

In a large bowl, combine the lettuce and half of the dressing and toss to coat. Add the cucumber, tomatoes, and blue cheese. Mix well and place in a serving dish. Sprinkle the bacon over the salad and arrange the eggs on the sides. Slice the chicken and fan off to one side of the salad. Spoon the remaining dressing over the top and top with the sliced avocado.

NOTE: *To make hard-boiled eggs: Put eggs in a medium saucepan and cover with cold water by 2 inches (5 cm). Bring to a boil and cook for 1 minute. Remove the pan from the heat, cover, and let sit for 17 minutes. Drain and transfer to a bowl filled with ice water for 10 minutes. Drain and use immediately, or refrigerate, covered, for up to 2 days.*

SERVES 4

SPINACH SALAD

THIS IS WHAT SPINACH SALADS WANT TO BE WHEN THEY GROW UP.
Crispy bacon, butter-poached fingerling potatoes, and perfectly poached eggs are paired with a "bit" of spinach, making this more of a dinner entrée than a lunchtime favorite.

FOR THE BACON VINAIGRETTE

2 tablespoons canola oil

2 large shallots, chopped

¼ cup (60 ml) dry sherry

5 ounces (150 ml) Bacon Stock (page 43)

FOR THE SALAD

2 cups (455 g) unsalted butter, cut into pieces

6 garlic cloves, chopped

Kosher salt

6 sprigs fresh thyme

1½ pounds (680 g) fingerling potatoes, scrubbed

3 ounces (85 g) baby spinach

6 thin slices bacon, cooked until crisp (see page 44) and crumbled

4 poached eggs (see Note)

Make the vinaigrette: Heat the oil in a medium saucepan over medium heat. Add the shallots and cook, stirring occasionally, until soft, about 5 minutes. Add the sherry and cook until reduced by half. Transfer the mixture to a blender, add the bacon stock, and puree until smooth. Return to the saucepan and bring to a simmer over low heat. Cover and keep warm.

Make the salad: In a medium pot, melt the butter over medium-low heat and add the garlic, salt, thyme, and potatoes. The potatoes need to be completely submerged in butter. If they are not, add enough warm water to just cover. Cover the pot and cook until the potatoes are just fork-tender, about 20 minutes. Remove the potatoes with a slotted spoon to a bowl.

Remove ¼ cup (60 ml) of the butter that the potatoes cooked in, add it to a large sauté pan over medium-high heat, and cook until it begins to shimmer. Cut the potatoes in half lengthwise and cook in the butter, cut-side down, until golden brown, 2 to 3 minutes.

Turn the potatoes over and cook for 2 minutes more.

In a large bowl, combine the spinach, half of the vinaigrette, and half of the bacon and toss to coat. Divide the spinach among four large dinner plates and arrange the potatoes around the spinach. Top each plate with a poached egg, sprinkle with the remaining bacon, and drizzle with a bit more of the warm dressing.

NOTE: *To make poached eggs: Add enough water to come 2 inches up the side of a 2-quart (2 L) saucier pan. Add 1 teaspoon kosher salt and 2 teaspoons white vinegar and bring to a simmer over medium. Meanwhile, crack 1 cold large egg into a small ramekin. Carefully drop the egg into the center of the pan. Turn off the heat, cover and let cook for 5 minutes. Remove with a slotted spoon and season the top with salt and pepper.*

SERVES 4

THAI NOODLE SALAD

with Bacon, Chiles, and Basil

THIS IS JUST ONE OF THOSE SALADS THAT WORKS AS A SIDE DISH OR as a main entrée topped with grilled chicken, shrimp, or Bacon Confit (page 41). The longer it sits in the refrigerator, the better the flavor. It's great for picnics, too.

½ cup (120 ml) fish sauce

¼ cup (60 ml) low-sodium soy sauce

1½ tablespoons rice vinegar

Kosher salt

12 ounces (340 g) dried pad Thai rice noodles

8 ounces (225 g) thin-sliced bacon, thinly sliced crosswise

1 small red onion, halved and thinly sliced

8 garlic cloves, finely chopped

2 Thai bird's eye chiles, thinly sliced

1 small red bell pepper, halved, seeded, and thinly sliced

¼ cup (10 g) torn fresh basil leaves

8 ounces (225 g) Fried Shallots (page 271)

¼ cup (35 g) chopped salted peanuts (optional)

In a small bowl, whisk together the fish sauce, soy sauce, and vinegar. Set the sauce aside.

Bring 12 cups (2.8 L) water to a boil in a large pot and add 1 tablespoon salt. Add the noodles and stir to separate; cook until barely tender to bite, 2 to 3 minutes, then drain. If not using immediately, rinse well with cold water to keep the noodles from sticking together, and drain again.

While the water is coming to a boil, cook the bacon in a large, deep sauté pan over medium heat until crisp (see page 44) and the fat has rendered, about 8 minutes. Remove the bacon with a slotted spoon to a plate lined with paper towels.

Add the onion to the rendered fat, increase the heat to high, and cook until soft, about 4 minutes. Add the garlic and chiles and cook for 1 minute.

Add the noodles, the bell pepper, and half of the sauce and cook, stirring and separating the noodles, until they are coated in the sauce. Taste and add more sauce if needed. Cover and refrigerate for at least 1 hour, or up to 24 hours. Stir in the basil just before serving and transfer to a large, shallow bowl or platter. Garnish with fried shallots and peanuts, if desired, before serving.

SERVES 4 TO 6

BABY KALE SALAD

with Candied Pecans, Bacon, Goat Cheese, Granny Smith Apples, and Maple-Bacon Vinaigrette

MY UPDATED VERSION OF A FALL SALAD STARS THE SUPER TRENDY, oh-so-hip kale. I use baby kale at BarBacon because it is less chewy and, truth be told, makes for a prettier plate, but you can definitely substitute Tuscan (also known as lacinato) kale when making it at home. I like to wait until apple-picking season before I make the vinaigrette, but nothing should stop you from using the vinaigrette throughout the year, if you please.

FOR THE VINAIGRETTE

¾ cup (180 ml) canola oil

12 ounces (340 g) slab bacon, cut into lardons (page 48)

1 large shallot, finely chopped

1 large Granny Smith apple, peeled and cored

1 (2-inch/5-cm) piece fresh ginger, peeled and grated

½ cup (120 ml) pure maple syrup

¼ cup (60 ml) apple cider vinegar

¼ cup (60 ml) sherry vinegar

¼ cup (60 ml) whole-grain mustard

Kosher salt and freshly ground black pepper

FOR THE SALAD

6 ounces (170 g) baby kale; or 12 ounces (340 g) Tuscan kale, stems removed and coarsely chopped

1 large Granny Smith apple, thinly sliced

¾ cup (90 g) Fried Spiced Candied Pecans (page 294), coarsely chopped

5 ounces (140 g) soft goat cheese

Make the vinaigrette: In a large sauté pan, heat the oil over medium heat. Add the bacon and cook, stirring a few times, until golden brown and crisp, about 10 minutes. Using a slotted spoon, transfer the bacon to a plate lined with paper towels and set aside. Pour the oil and bacon fat into a bowl to cool.

In a blender, puree the shallot, apple, ginger, maple syrup, cider vinegar, sherry vinegar, and mustard until smooth. Reduce the blender speed to low and slowly add the reserved oil and bacon fat in a steady stream. Season with salt and pepper.

Make the salad: In a large bowl, combine the kale and apple slices, add the dressing, and toss to coat. Transfer to a platter and top with the candied pecans, goat cheese, and bacon.

SERVES 6

TUNA BACON NIÇOISE

HAILING FROM THE SOUTH OF FRANCE—NICE, TO BE EXACT—THIS IS truly one of the world's great composed salads. However, I doubt the world has seen one made with "tuna bacon" until now. Sounds like an oxymoron, but it works, and once the rest of the world discovers it . . . look out, France! If you want to keep this salad strictly pork-free, leave out the bacon lardons and skip the step for rolling the Tuna Bacon in cooked bacon—I won't hold it against you!

8 ounces (225 g) marble potatoes (or small new potatoes)

Cold water

Kosher salt

1 cup (240 ml) Basil Vinaigrette (page 184)

Freshly ground black pepper

1 pint (455 g) cherry tomatoes, halved

1 English cucumber, diced

1 small head romaine lettuce, outer leaves removed, coarsely chopped

4 ounces (115 g) baby kale

8 ounces (225 g) slab bacon, cut into lardons and cooked until golden brown and crispy (see page 48)

1 pound (455 g) Tuna Bacon (page 37), cut crosswise into slices ¼ inch (6 mm) thick

1 cup (235 g) Castelvetrano or Picholine olives, pitted and halved

¼ cup (13 g) fresh parsley leaves

Put the potatoes in a medium pot and cover with cold water by 2 inches (5 cm). Add 1 tablespoon salt, bring to a boil, and cook until tender when pierced with a paring knife, about 7 minutes. Drain and let rest until cool enough to handle, about 5 minutes. Cut the potatoes in half, put in a bowl, add 3 tablespoons of the vinaigrette, season with salt and pepper, and gently toss to dress the potatoes. Set aside.

In a small bowl, combine the tomatoes and 2 tablespoons of the dressing and toss to coat. In a separate bowl, toss the cucumber with 2 tablespoons of the dressing.

In a large bowl, combine the romaine and kale. Add ¼ cup (60 ml) of the dressing, toss well to coat, and season with salt and pepper. Transfer the greens to a large platter.

Arrange the potatoes, tomatoes, cucumber, bacon, tuna bacon, and olives on top. Drizzle with more of the dressing and garnish with parsley leaves.

SERVES 4 TO 6

CHAPTER 8

SANDWICHES & TACOS

HEN I TELL PEOPLE ABOUT BARBACON, THEY always ask about our BLT, and I'll admit that it's really fucking good. Before opening the restaurant, I knew I had to nail down the BLT. I do mine the way my wife likes it—because it's delicious and because she'd kill me if I didn't. Instead of mayo, I use a fried egg and avocado. They add both richness and flavor, but the bacon still plays the main role. Once I nailed down *that* BLT, I started looking at all the other bacon I was making, like tuna bacon. Could I turn that into something like a BLT? The answer was yes. I took that tuna bacon, added some mayo, topped it with lettuce and tomato, and created another sandwich I couldn't stop eating.

From there, I got even more creative with the bacon choices in my sandwiches. I took my BBQ bacon and turned it into a play on pulled pork. I took my lamb bacon and added some Middle Eastern flair for a gyro. I went deep into southern tradition and Kentucky-fried some thick-cut pork bacon, only to find out that it was the most delicious heart attack I could imagine—multiple layers of crispness, a rich bacon rémoulade, and a pretzel bun? Done.

I knew I also needed something a little lighter, so when one of the guys in the kitchen made tacos for staff meal one day, I picked his brain. He got me going on all kinds of bacon tacos. My favorite ones have homemade bacon chorizo and loads of fresh pico de gallo. Tacos are also a great place to try all the varieties of flavored bacons. Jalapeño bacon with our bacon chorizo taco (page 236) is unbelievable. Cajun bacon on an oyster po' boy taco (page 241): Who is not going to eat that?

Try some of the recipes I came up with and get your brain working, too. Have fun with it. Once you master a few of these sandwiches and tacos, you'll learn how to start mixing and matching ingredients for your own favorites.

BARBACON BURGER

PRETTY MUCH ANY BURGER WILL TASTE GOOD WITH A PILE OF crispy bacon on top of it, but this burger doesn't aim to be good; it strives to be the best. No store-bought patty will do. I grind the meat fresh and prefer chuck, which has a meat to fat ratio of 80 percent to 20 percent. Yes, I top the burger with bacon, but I also include it finely diced in the burger for extra juiciness. The crowning jewel is a double dose of mustard goodness—on the bacon and in the sauce.

1½ pounds (680 g) ground chuck (80/20)

12 thin slices bacon, finely diced

2 tablespoons BB Rub (page 95)

8 thin slices cheese (American, smoked cheddar, Gruyère, or smoked gouda; optional)

White Wine Grainy Mustard Sauce (page 81)

4 pretzel buns (or your favorite burger buns), halved and lightly toasted

Iceberg lettuce

Sliced beefsteak tomato

Sliced red onion

8 slices Honey Mustard–Glazed Bacon (page 46)

In a medium bowl, combine the beef and bacon, season with ½ teaspoon of the rub, and form into four patties. Season both sides of each with the remaining rub.

Heat a grill to high or heat a grill pan or cast-iron pan over high heat. Cook the burgers on both sides until golden brown and a crust has formed and cooked to your desired doneness:

    6 minutes total for rare

    7 minutes total for medium-rare

    8 minutes total for medium

    9 minutes total for medium-well

During the last 1 minute of cooking, top each patty with 2 slices of cheese, if desired, and close the lid of the grill, or put a lid on your pan, and cook until the cheese melts.

Spread some of the mustard sauce on the top and bottom of each bun. Place the lettuce, then tomato, then onion on the bottom buns. Place the burgers on top of the onion and top each burger with 2 slices of the glazed bacon. Put the bun tops on and serve.

MAKES 4

BACON BRATWURST BURGER

BRATWURST ON ITS OWN DOESN'T HAVE A LOT OF FLAVOR TO IT. IT'S delicious, but definitely just a mild sausage made from pork and veal and cream and sweet spices. It could use a dose of something, and to me, that something is the smoky, salty taste of bacon. My sausage may not be classic, but the way it's served is—with mustard, pretzel, and kraut, just like you would find it in every German beer garden.

4 Bacon Bratwurst patties (page 62)

2 teaspoons canola oil

Freshly ground black pepper

¼ cup (60 ml) Honey Mustard Glaze (page 86)

4 pretzel buns, split and lightly toasted

Caraway Sauerkraut (page 153)

8 pieces Honey Mustard–Glazed Bacon (page 46)

Preheat a grill to medium heat or a grill pan over medium heat. Brush the sausage patties on both sides with the oil, season with pepper, and grill until golden brown and slightly charred on both sides and cooked through, about 5 minutes per side.

Spread some of the honey mustard glaze on the top and bottom of each bun, put a sausage patty on the bottom of the bun, and top with a large spoonful of sauerkraut and 2 slices of glazed bacon. Serve immediately.

MAKES 4

GRILLED PORK TENDERLOIN CUBAN SLIDERS

THIS IS ONE OF MY ALL-TIME FAVORITE SANDWICHES. IF YOU WANT to make this into a full-size sandwich instead of sliders, I recommend adding some sliced ham from the deli. It's one too many ingredients for a slider, but an essential flavor for an authentic Cuban.

½ cup (120 ml) white wine vinegar

1 head garlic, cloves peeled and chopped

2 tablespoons kosher salt

¾ teaspoon freshly ground black pepper

2 teaspoons dried oregano

⅓ cup (75 ml) canola oil

2 pork tenderloins (about 1½ pounds/680 g each)

24 pretzel or potato slider buns, split

¼ cup (60 ml) Dijon mustard

1 tablespoon mayonnaise

8 ounces (225 g) shredded Gruyère cheese

24 Bread and Butter Pickles (page 276)

6 thin slices bacon, cooked until crisp (see page 44), each slice quartered

In a blender, combine the vinegar, garlic, salt, pepper, and oregano and blend until smooth. Add the oil and continue blending until the marinade is emulsified.

Pour the marinade into a gallon-size zip-top bag. Add the pork, seal tightly, and make sure it is evenly covered with the marinade. Refrigerate for 2 days.

Remove the pork from the marinade 30 minutes before cooking and wipe the marinade off with paper towels.

Preheat a grill to high or grill pan over high heat. Grill the pork until golden brown and charred on both sides and an instant-read thermometer inserted into the center registers 140°F (60°C). Remove the pork to a cutting board, loosely tent with aluminum foil, and let it rest for 10 minutes before slicing. Slice the pork crosswise into medallions ¼ inch (6 mm) thick.

Preheat the broiler. Put the bun tops and bottoms, cut-side up, on a baking sheet in an even layer. Mix the mustard and mayonnaise together and spread the mustard mixture on the buns. Divide the cheese among the tops and bottoms. Put under the broiler until the cheese just begins to melt and the rolls are lightly toasted, about 45 seconds.

Place a slice of pork on the bottom rolls and top each with a pickle and 2 pieces of bacon. Top with the bun tops and serve.

MAKES ABOUT 24

SMOKED ROAST BEEF FRENCH DIP

DESPITE THE NAME, THIS SANDWICH IS ALL-AMERICAN AND COM-
pletely unknown in France. In fact, the only thing that is French about it is the bread
and the name of the sauce that it's dipped into (au jus). Classically, this sandwich
is served with beef that is seasoned heavily and roasted in the oven to medium-
rare doneness. I prefer smoking my beef, which adds a touch of bacon-like flavor,
because, well, everything should taste like bacon—or should I say, *le bacon.*

3 pounds (1.4 kg) eye-of-round
beef roast, excess fat trimmed

1 cup (240 ml) low-sodium
soy sauce

1 cup (240 ml)
Worcestershire sauce

¼ cup (24 g) coarsely ground
black pepper

1 tablespoon red chile flakes

2 cups (180 g) soaked and
drained hickory or pecan
wood chips

5 cups (1.2 L) low-sodium
canned beef stock or broth

1 cup (240 ml) Brisket Sauce
(page 84)

½ cup (115 g) unsalted butter,
at room temperature

2 sturdy French baguettes,
cut crosswise into quarters
and split

Romaine lettuce (optional)

Place the beef in a gallon-size
zip-top bag. In a medium
bowl, whisk together the soy
sauce, Worcestershire sauce,
black pepper, and chile flakes.
Pour the marinade over the
beef, seal well, and turn upside
down a few times to make sure
that the roast is completely
covered in the marinade. Place
in a large bowl or on a baking
sheet and refrigerate for at
least 1 day, or up to 3 days
(I marinate it for 3 days at
BarBacon). Remove the beef
from the marinade 30 minutes
before smoking and pat dry
with paper towels.

Prepare your smoker according
to the manufacturer's directions. As to the temperature
to smoke, I keep it fairly low,

at 250°F (120°C). Remember:
Do not raise the lid of the
smoker any more than you
absolutely need to (it reduces
the temperature inside every
time you do).

Place the drip pan over the
chips and fill it with the stock;
place a rack on top of the drip
pan. Place the roast in the
center of the rack and partially
close the smoker lid, leaving it
open only a couple of inches.
Smoke for about 2 hours,
until the internal temperature reaches 125°F (52°C)
for medium-rare (see Note).
Remove from the smoker,
loosely tent with aluminum
foil, and let the beef rest at

(continued)

room temperature for 30 minutes before carving (the meat temperature will rise 5 to 10 degrees after it is removed from the smoker).

Carefully remove the drip pan with the stock in it and strain the liquid through a sieve into a large saucepan. Whisk in the Brisket Sauce and bring to a simmer over medium heat.

Preheat the broiler. Butter the cut side of the bread, place on a baking sheet, and broil until lightly golden brown, about 2 minutes.

Add half of the sliced beef to the stock mixture and cook for 1 minute, just to heat through. Remove from the heat and divide the beef among the bread pieces. Add the lettuce, if desired. Serve with a bowl of the stock mixture as a dipping sauce on the side.

NOTE: *What constitutes rare and medium-rare cooked meat? To satisfy the government, the Beef Council says rare beef means an internal temperature of 140°F (60°C). Well, that is okay if you like well-done and dry meat. If you like moist, rosy meat (like I do), rare begins at 120°F (49°C) and starts to become medium-rare at 125 or 130°F (52 or 54°C). To cook your meat properly, you must purchase and use a good instant-read digital meat thermometer and remember that once your meat is removed from the heat source, it needs to rest before slicing. Resting time can increase the internal temperature another 5 to 10°F (-15°C to -12°C).*

SERVES 8

SMOKED ROAST BEEF SANDWICH

NOT SURE WHY SMOKED ROAST BEEF ISN'T A THING IN EVERY DELI on every corner. Until it is, you'll have to make it yourself. It's made from an inexpensive cut, but feel free to trade up. This sandwich will only get better with quality. After the beef is cooked and rested, ideally you would slice it paper-thin on a deli slicer. If you don't have one (and why would you?), then the next best things to use are an electric knife or a really sharp carving knife: Cut across the grain slowly into thin slices. It takes some practice, but this sandwich is about flavor and not appearance, so no one will know if you mess up.

½ cup (120 ml) Horseradish Bacon Mayonnaise (page 73) or store-bought horseradish mayonnaise

8 slices ciabatta or good-quality white bread, ¼ inch (6 mm) thick, lightly toasted

2 ounces (55 g) baby mustard greens or arugula

8 Tomato Confit halves (page 286), or 4 slices beefsteak tomato

8 thin slices bacon, cooked until crisp (see page 44)

8 ounces (225 g) Smoked Roast Beef French Dip (page 205), thinly sliced, warm

8 slices Gruyère or good-quality Swiss cheese

Spread the mayonnaise on each slice of bread. Divide the mustard greens, tomatoes, bacon, beef, and cheese on top of four of the slices, and top with the remaining slices of bread.

SERVES 4

SHANI BLT

TRYING TO IMPROVE ON THE CLASSIC BLT IS NOT EASY. I MEAN, WHY mess with perfection? And when you're creating it for your wife, you really better be on your game. Adding one of her favorite things on earth, avocado, with its creamy goodness (a healthier alternative to mayonnaise), was the first step . . . Adding a fried egg was the second, because everything tastes good with a fried egg. She loves it, so I succeeded.

3 tablespoons unsalted butter
or vegetable oil

4 large eggs

Kosher salt and freshly
ground black pepper

8 slices ciabatta bread, ¼ inch
(6 mm) thick, lightly toasted

1 large ripe avocado, peeled,
pitted, and cut into 8 slices

Thinly sliced ripe
beefsteak tomato

12 slices bacon, cooked
to chewy perfection
(see page 44)

In a large sauté pan, heat the butter over medium heat until it just begins to sizzle. Carefully crack the eggs into the pan and season with salt and pepper. Cook until the white is set and the yolk is still runny, about 2 minutes.

While the eggs are cooking, put 4 slices of the bread on a flat surface. Top each slice with 2 slices of avocado, a slice of tomato, and 3 slices of the bacon. Place an egg on top of each and top with the remaining 4 slices of bread. Eat immediately!

SERVES 4

BUFFALO CHICKEN BREAST SANDWICH

with Bacon–Blue Cheese Ranch

IF YOU HAVE A BAR, **THEN YOU BETTER HAVE SOMETHING WITH THE** phrase *Buffalo chicken* on the menu. This is mine. Based on the spicy classic from that city in upstate New York, but all combined on a sandwich. Crispy, smoky, spicy, and delicious.

4 boneless, skinless chicken breasts, about 6 ounces (170 g) each, slightly pounded to an even thickness

Kosher salt and freshly ground black pepper

1 cup (125 g) all-purpose flour

3 large eggs, lightly whisked with 2 tablespoons water

2 cups (160 g) panko bread crumbs

½ cup (120 ml) canola oil

½ cup (120 ml) rendered bacon fat (see page 50)

4 tablespoons (55 g) unsalted butter

¼ cup (60 ml) hot sauce, such as Tabasco or Frank's

½ cup (120 ml) Bacon–Blue Cheese Ranch (page 78), plus more for serving

4 soft buns (hamburger, kaiser, or pretzel), split

¼ small head iceberg lettuce, shredded

8 thin slices bacon, cooked until crisp (see page 44)

4 slices pickled hot cherry peppers, each skewered on a 6-inch (15-cm) wooden skewer

Put the chicken on a baking sheet lined with aluminum foil and season both sides with salt and pepper. Put the flour in a small baking dish and season with salt and pepper. Put the eggs in a small baking dish and season with salt and pepper. Put the panko in a small baking dish.

Line another baking sheet with paper towels. Heat the oil and bacon fat in a large, deep sauté pan over medium-high heat until the fat begins to shimmer. While the fat is heating up, dredge the chicken in flour and tap off any excess, then dip in the egg wash and let excess drip off, then dredge in the panko, pressing the crumbs on so they adhere. Fry the chicken until golden brown on both sides and just cooked through, about 5 minutes per side. Transfer the

chicken to the paper towel–lined baking sheet.

Melt the butter in a small saucepan, add the hot sauce, and cook until heated through, about 2 minutes. Liberally brush the chicken on both sides with the hot sauce butter.

Spread 1 tablespoon of the ranch dressing on the bottom of each bun, add a large handful of the lettuce, and place a chicken breast on top. Top the chicken with 2 slices of the bacon, spread the remaining ranch dressing on the tops of the buns, and place on top of the bacon. Skewer each sandwich with a hot cherry pepper on top. Serve more ranch dressing on the side, if desired (and most do).

SERVES 4

GRILLED CHEESE WITH BACON

FOR THIS SANDWICH, I USE SEMOLINA–GOLDEN RAISIN BREAD FROM Amy's Bread in New York City. It's sweet from the raisins and aromatic from the fennel seeds and just works surprisingly well with nutty Gruyère and fontina cheeses. If you can't find it in your town, you can use plain semolina or a high-quality white bread. And to put another spin on the classic grilled cheese and tomato soup, I recommend serving it with a bowl of Smooth Chilled Tomato Soup (page 162) and a side of Bread and Butter Pickles (page 276).

1¼ cups (135 g) shredded Gruyère cheese

1¼ cups (135 g) shredded fontina cheese

½ cup (115 g) soft unsalted butter

8 slices semolina–golden raisin bread, ½ inch (12 mm) thick

8 thin slices bacon, cooked until crisp (see page 44) and kept warm

In a medium bowl, combine both cheeses. Butter 4 slices of the bread on one side, each with 1 tablespoon of the butter. Divide the cheese among the 4 remaining slices of bread and top with the buttered bread, butter-side up.

Preheat a large nonstick sauté pan over medium heat for 2 minutes. Cooking one or two sandwiches at a time, put them in the pan, butter-side down, and cook until the bottom is golden brown, about 3

minutes. Just before turning, spread 1 tablespoon of the butter over the top of each, and using a spatula, flip the sandwiches over and continue cooking until the bottom is golden brown and the cheese is completely melted, about 3 minutes longer.

Lift up the top slice, add 2 slices bacon to each, and return the slice and press down to adhere.

SERVES 4

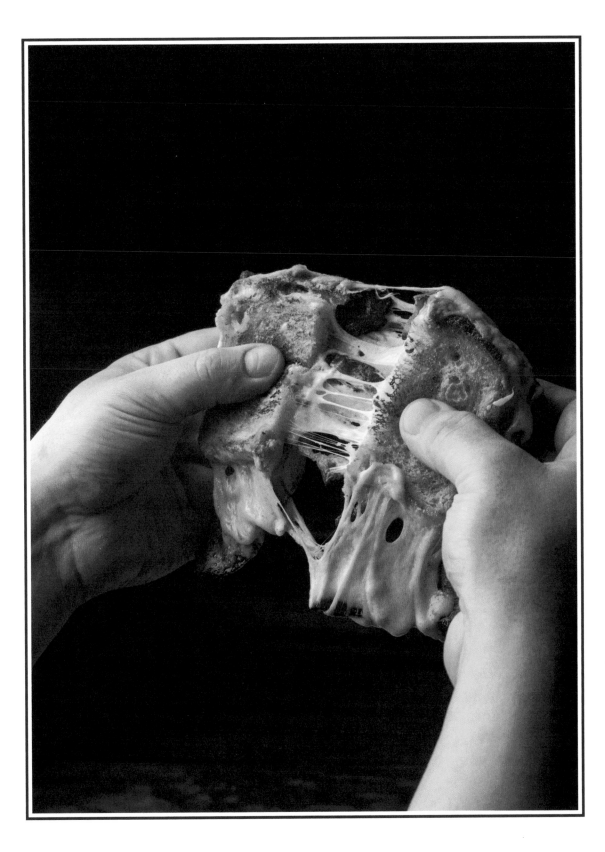

ITALIAN GRILLED CHEESE

ITALIANS WOULD PROBABLY USE PANCETTA IN THIS SANDWICH, which is traditionally unsmoked cured pork belly. Feel free to use it if you'd like, but the homemade smoked porchetta makes a huge difference with its touch of smoke and herbal notes. The pickles in this sandwich also add much-needed acid to the richness of the cheese and bacon.

1¼ cups (135 g) shredded Gruyère cheese

1¼ cups (135 g) shredded fontina cheese

½ cup (115 g) soft unsalted butter

8 slices ciabatta bread, ½ inch (12 mm) thick

½ cup (115 g) coarsely chopped Hot Italian Pickles (Giardiniera; page 281)

8 slices Smoked Porchetta (page 38), cooked until crisp (see page 44) and kept warm

In a medium bowl, combine both the cheeses. Butter 4 slices of the bread on one side, each with 1 tablespoon of the butter. Divide the cheese and the pickles among the 4 remaining slices of bread and top with the buttered bread, butter-side up.

Preheat a large nonstick sauté pan over medium heat for 2 minutes. Cooking the sandwiches one or two at a time, put them into the pan, butter-side down, and cook until the bottom is golden brown, about

3 minutes. Just before turning, spread 1 tablespoon of the butter over the top of each, and using a spatula, flip the sandwiches over and continue cooking until the bottom is golden brown and the cheese is completely melted, about 3 minutes longer.

Lift up the top slice, add 2 slices porchetta to each, and return the slice and press down to adhere.

SERVES 4

LOBSTER ROLL

BACON'S SMOKE AND SALT LEVELS COUNTERBALANCE THE MILD sweetness of lobster in this roll, and bacon's crispness adds another level of texture to lobster's chewiness. If you are squeamish when it comes to cooking your own lobster, then by all means buy cooked lobster meat from your local fishmonger. Just make sure it is the freshest meat that you can find. It will make all the difference in the world. Bacon can do a lot of things, but it can't make imitation or spoiled lobster meat taste good.

Ice

Kosher salt

1 lemon, cut in half

3 (1½-pound/680-g) live lobsters

½ cup (120 ml) Bacon Mayonnaise (page 72) or store-bought mayonnaise

¼ teaspoon celery salt

¼ cup (13 g) coarsely chopped celery leaves

2 tablespoons minced fresh chives

¼ teaspoon freshly ground black pepper

8 ounces (225 g) slab bacon, cut into lardons (page 48) and cooked until crisp (see page 44)

4 brioche buns, split and lightly toasted

½ cup (115 g) unsalted butter, melted

Prepare an ice bath in a large bowl. Bring a large pot of salted water to a boil. Squeeze the juice of the lemon into the water and add the halves.

Plunge the lobsters into the boiling water, head first, and cook for about 11 minutes. Transfer with tongs to the ice bath and let sit until chilled, about 5 minutes. When the lobsters are cool, remove the meat from the claws, joints, and tails. Discard the tomalley (see Note), any roe, and shells (or save for another use). Cut the meat into ½-inch (12-mm) pieces.

In a large bowl, whisk together the mayonnaise, celery salt, celery leaves, chives, and pepper. Fold in the lobster and bacon. (The lobster salad can

be made up to 8 hours in advance and stored, tightly covered, in the refrigerator. Fold the bacon in just before serving.)

Preheat the broiler. Brush the cut sides of the buns liberally with the melted butter. Put on a baking sheet and broil until light golden brown. Mound the lobster salad on the bottom of each bun and top with the bun tops. Serve immediately.

NOTE: *To remove the tomalley, use a small spoon to scoop out the liver (the tomalley)—it will be black if uncooked and green if cooked—along with any coral or eggs, which will be black if uncooked and bright red if cooked. You can reserve and use for sauces or compound butters or discard.*

SERVES 4

KENTUCKY FRIED BACON BANH MI

OUR VARIATION OF THIS STREET FOOD CLASSIC HAS, OF COURSE, thick-cut tender Bacon Confit (page 41) that has been breaded and fried (and it's somewhat healthy thanks to the pickled vegetables and herbs). This recipe calls for Nuoc Cham (page 87), a salty tangy sauce, but for those who prefer a sweet sauce, you can substitute Nuoc Mam Cham (page 87). You can't go wrong either way.

FOR THE PICKLED VEGETABLE SALAD

1 small carrot, peeled and coarsely grated

½ English cucumber, thinly sliced

8 fresh basil leaves, torn

8 fresh mint leaves, torn

¼ cup (10 g) lightly packed fresh cilantro leaves

¼ cup (60 ml) Nuoc Cham (page 87) or Nuoc Mam Cham (page 87)

FOR THE SANDWICHES

8 slices ciabatta bread, ¼ inch (6 mm) thick

½ cup (120 ml) Chipotle Bacon Mayonnaise (page 73), or ½ cup (120 ml) store-bought mayonnaise combined with 1 tablespoon pureed chipotles in adobo

1 recipe Kentucky Fried Bacon (page 42), hot

Make the pickled vegetable salad: In a medium bowl, combine the carrot, cucumber, basil, mint, and cilantro. Add the nuoc cham and mix well. Let sit at room temperature while you prepare the sandwiches.

Make the sandwiches: Put the bread on a flat surface and spread each slice with 1 tablespoon of the mayonnaise. Put 3 slices each of the bacon on 4 slices of the bread. Top the bacon with a large spoonful of the pickled vegetable salad, then top with the remaining slices of bread.

SERVES 4

SONORAN HOT DOG

THIS DEEP-FRIED BACON-WRAPPED HOTDOG REPRESENTS A FUSION of flavors and cultures from the United States and Mexico. Grilled perfectly, atop a buttered bun and slathered with mayonnaise and a spicy relish, this hot dog may convince you to never use mustard or ketchup again!

8 thin slices bacon (I use pecan-smoked at BarBacon)

8 best-quality all-beef hot dogs

4 cups (960 ml) canola oil

½ cup (115 g) soft unsalted butter

8 potato roll hot dog buns, split

½ cup (120 ml) mayonnaise

2 teaspoons rice vinegar

Spicy Relish (page 280)

Chopped fresh cilantro leaves

Wrap a piece of the bacon around each hotdog and hold it in place with toothpicks. Refrigerate while the oil comes to temperature.

Heat the oil in a medium Dutch oven or deep-fryer until it reaches 350°F (175°C) on a deep-fry thermometer. Line a baking sheet with several layers of paper towels.

Fry the hot dogs, in batches, making sure to keep them totally submerged in the oil (using tongs or a spider), until the bacon is golden brown and crispy, about 3 minutes. Remove the hot dogs and let drain on the prepared baking sheet.

Heat a nonstick pan or griddle over medium heat. Butter the cut sides of the buns, place in the pan, butter-side down, and toast until light golden brown, about 30 seconds.

Combine the mayonnaise and vinegar. Spread the bottom of each bun with some of the mixture, then top with a hot dog. Add a dollop of the relish and the cilantro leaves. Serve immediately.

SERVES 4 TO 8

LAMB REUBEN
with Special Sauce

THE REUBEN IS AN AMERICAN HOT GRIDDLED SANDWICH THAT originated in Omaha, Nebraska, of all places. I say that because the Reuben is the quintessential New York City sandwich. Every Jewish deli and Greek diner has one on the menu, and BarBacon is no different. Well, one thing is different. Mine features lamb bacon instead of the classic corned beef. Yes, you can use corned beef in this recipe, but after trying this version, you won't want to.

½ cup (120 ml) Special Sauce (page 80)

8 slices rye bread, ½ inch (12 mm) thick

16 thin slices Swiss cheese

12 ounces (340 g) thinly shaved or sliced Lamb Bacon (page 32)

1 (1-pound/455-g) bag sauerkraut, drained, rinsed well, and drained again; or 1 pound (455 g) Caraway Sauerkraut (page 153)

½ cup (115 g) soft unsalted butter

Spread 1 tablespoon of the Special Sauce each on all 8 slices of the bread. Divide the rest of the ingredients among 4 slices of the bread as follows: cheese, bacon, sauerkraut, and cheese. Top with the remaining bread slices, sauce-side down.

Heat a cast-iron griddle or large cast-iron pan or nonstick pan over medium-low heat. Spread 1 tablespoon of the butter over each top slice of bread. Place two sandwiches, butter-side down, in the skillet. Spread 1 tablespoon butter over each new top slice of bread.

Cook, uncovered, over low heat until the bottoms are golden brown, about 5 minutes. Flip over and cook for about 5 minutes longer, or until the bottoms are golden brown and the cheese is melted. During the last 1 minute of cooking, put a lid on the pan to ensure that the cheese has completely melted. Repeat to make the remaining two sandwiches. Serve immediately.

MAKES 4

OPEN-FACED CHICKEN BLT

THIS ISN'T JUST A BLT WITH CHICKEN. IT IS A DELICIOUS SANDWICH served on buttery brioche toast slathered with a rich, slightly smoky, slightly spicy mayonnaise, topped with lettuce and tomatoes tossed in a light, fresh, tangy basil vinaigrette, and served with housemade pickles on the side. Phew, that was a mouthful, and so is this sandwich, so we serve it open-faced at the restaurant, but feel free to close the sandwich when making it at home.

8 slices brioche bread, ¼ inch (6 mm) thick, crusts removed if desired

1 pound (455 g) boneless, skinless chicken breasts

2 tablespoons canola oil

Kosher salt and freshy ground black pepper

½ cup (120 ml) Chipotle Bacon Mayonnaise (page 73)

4 romaine lettuce leaves, chopped

¼ cup (60 ml) Basil Vinaigrette (page 184)

8 slices beefsteak tomato, ¼ inch (6 mm) thick

8 thin slices bacon, cooked until crisp (see page 44)

Bread and Butter Pickles (page 276)

Heat a grill to high or a grill pan over high heat. Grill the bread until light golden brown on both sides, about 30 seconds per side. Remove the bread to a plate.

Brush the chicken breasts on both sides with the oil and season with salt and pepper. Grill the chicken until golden brown and charred on both sides and just cooked through, about 5 minutes per side. Remove and let rest for 5 minutes. Slice on the diagonal into slices ¼ inch (6 mm) thick.

Spread each bread slice with 1 tablespoon of the mayonnaise. Divide the chicken over the bread.

Toss the lettuce with 2 tablespoons of the vinaigrette and divide the lettuce over the chicken. Top the lettuce on each sandwich with 2 slices tomato and drizzle the remaining vinaigrette on top of the tomatoes. Top each sandwich with 2 slices of the bacon and a few pickles. Serve two halves per person.

MAKES 4

BBQ BACON BLT

THIS IS MY SPIN ON THE BBQ BRISKET SANDWICH FROM TEXAS. BIG, thick slices of bacon on big, thick slices of white bread slathered with homemade BBQ sauce. It's topped with crisp, fruity coleslaw that pairs well with the salty, smoky pork. Sometimes I try to convince myself that the pineapple makes it healthy. It doesn't, but it does add a sweetness that enhances the saltiness of the bacon and BBQ sauce, making it even more delicious.

12 thick slices BBQ Bacon (page 30) smoked to 195°F (91°C)

1¼ cups (300 ml) BarBacon BBQ Sauce (page 82) or your favorite store-bought brand

8 slices good-quality pain de mie or Pullman bread, ½ inch (12 mm) thick

4 slices ripe beefsteak tomato, ½ inch (12 mm) thick

1 tablespoon canola oil

1¼ cups (340 g) Pineapple-Jalapeño Coleslaw (page 272)

Preheat the grill to high, a grill pan over high heat, or the broiler. Grill the bacon until charred on both sides and just cooked through, about 2 minutes per side. Brush with some of the BBQ sauce, and transfer to a plate. If using a broiler, put the bacon on a sheet pan and broil until golden brown on both sides and just cooked through, about 2 minutes per side, then brush with the BBQ sauce.

Grill or broil the bread until light golden brown on both sides, 30 to 45 seconds. Brush the tomatoes with the oil and grill or broil on one side until golden brown and just warmed through, about 45 seconds.

Spread 1 tablespoon of the BBQ sauce on each slice of bread. Top 4 of the slices with the coleslaw, then a tomato slice, then 3 slices bacon, then a few more tablespoons of the sauce. Top with the remaining slices of bread. Serve immediately.

SERVES 4

SMOKED PORCHETTA BLT

IF ITALIANS MADE BLTS, I'M GUESSING THIS IS WHAT THEY WOULD look like and taste like. Customers pull me aside, often, and tell me this is one of the best sandwiches they have ever had. Who am I to argue with them?

FOR THE BASIL AIOLI

½ cup (120 ml) mayonnaise

3 tablespoons Basil Vinaigrette (page 184), or ¼ cup (7 g) fresh basil leaves

¼ teaspoon kosher salt

FOR THE SANDWICHES

2 tablespoons canola oil

12 slices Smoked Porchetta (page 38), ¼ inch (6 mm) thick

8 slices ciabatta bread, ¼ inch (6 mm) thick, lightly toasted

4 romaine lettuce leaves, shredded

1 cup (225 g) Pickled Fennel (page 283), drained

8 slices beefsteak tomatoes, ¼ inch (6 mm) thick

Make the basil aioli: In a small bowl, whisk together the mayonnaise, vinaigrette, and salt until combined. Cover and refrigerate for at least 30 minutes, or up to 24 hours to allow the flavors to meld. (Alternatively, if you don't feel like making the vinaigrette, you can just combine the mayonnaise, basil leaves, and salt in a food processor and process until smooth.) The aioli will keep, tightly covered, in the refrigerator up to 3 days.

Make the sandwiches: Heat 1 tablespoon of the oil in a large sauté pan over high heat until shimmering and sear half of the porchetta on both sides until golden brown and crispy and just heated through, about 2 minutes per side. Repeat with the remaining oil and porchetta.

Spread 1 tablespoon of the aioli on each slice of bread. Top 4 of the slices with some of the lettuce and fennel, then 2 slices tomato, then 3 slices porchetta. Top with the remaining slices of bread. Serve immediately.

MAKES 4

SMOKED TURKEY CLUB

THIS WAS EASILY MY FAVORITE SANDWICH GROWING UP AND IS still a go-to when I'm in a deli for lunch. This version changes little from the original, as classics are classic for a reason. I'm just substituting my home-smoked turkey bacon for the processed lunchmeat.

2 teaspoons canola oil

8 thin slices bacon, preferably maple or black pepper bacon

12 ounces (340 g) sliced Turkey Bacon (page 31)

½ cup (120 ml) Bacon Mayonnaise (page 72) or store-bought mayonnaise

8 slices sandwich bread (white, rye, whole grain, or whole wheat), or 4 soft hoagie rolls, lightly toasted

4 romaine lettuce leaves

4 slices beefsteak tomato

Combine the oil and pork bacon in a large sauté pan and cook over medium heat until golden brown and crispy, about 8 minutes. Remove to a plate lined with paper towels.

Add the turkey bacon to the pan and cook just to heat through, about 2 minutes.

Spread 1 tablespoon of the mayonnaise on each slice of bread. Top 4 of the slices with the lettuce, then tomato, then 2 slices of the pork bacon, then the turkey bacon, then top with the remaining bread slices. Serve immediately.

SERVES 4

LAMB GYRO

SO MAYBE THIS IS NOT THE GYRO THAT YOU WILL SEE IN GREECE OR at the Greek restaurants in Queens, New York, but the flavors are all still Mediterranean and delicious. The spicy merguez sausage is tempered perfectly by the goat cheese and tzatziki. I love serving this with Tabbouleh (page 288) and Thyme Tzatziki (page 76) for a complete meal.

4 (5-ounce/140-g) Bacon and Lamb Merguez patties or links (page 68)

2 tablespoons canola oil

1 cup (225 g) Bacon Hummus (page 127)

4 individual naan breads, lightly toasted on each side

½ small red onion, thinly sliced

8 Tomato Confit halves (page 286)

1 cup (115 g) crumbled soft goat cheese

Romaine lettuce, for garnish (optional)

Thyme Tzatziki (page 76)

Heat a grill to high or a grill pan or griddle over high heat. Brush the sausages with the oil and grill until charred on both sides and just cooked through, about 8 minutes total. Remove and let rest for 5 minutes. If using links, slice on the bias into slices ½ inch (12 mm) thick.

Spread a thin layer of the hummus over the top of each naan and sprinkle with the onion. Top with the sausage, tomatoes, goat cheese, and lettuce, if desired. Serve open-faced with tzatziki on the side. Fold to eat.

SERVES 4

CHIPOTLE BACON TACOS
with Toasted Cumin Slaw and Chipotle-Lime Mayonnaise

I LOVE PAIRING CHIPOTLE (A SMOKED JALAPEÑO) WITH BACON FOR a double dose of smoke and to add a touch of heat against the natural sweetness of pork. The citrusy slaw adds crunch and much-needed freshness and acid, which all smoked meats benefit from. Feel free to use store-bought bacon; just season it with a few sprinkles of the Chipotle Rub (page 94) and bake it according to the directions on page 44. It will still be delicious, I promise.

8 (6-inch/15-cm) flour tortillas

8 slices Chipotle Bacon (page 27) smoked to 195°F (91°C) internal temperature, ½ inch (12 mm) thick

Toasted Cumin Slaw (page 289)

Chipotle-Lime Mayonnaise (page 74)

Lime wedges

Preheat the oven to 300°F (150°C). Wrap the tortillas in aluminum foil and warm in the oven while you grill the bacon.

Heat a grill to high or a grill pan over high heat on your stove. Grill the bacon until golden brown and slightly charred on both sides, about 1 minute per side.

Put the warm tortillas on a flat surface. Put a slice of the grilled bacon in the center, top with a large spoonful of the slaw, a generous drizzle of the mayonnaise, and a squeeze of lime. Roll and eat!

SERVES 4 TO 8

JERK BACON TACOS

with Black Bean–Mango Salsa and Habanero Sauce

WE SERVE THESE TACOS AT BARBACON TO GET A BIT OF ISLAND FLAVOR in the heart of New York City. Spicy habaneros in both the jerk marinade and sauce benefit from the cooling effect of the salsa. If you don't have time to make homemade jerk bacon, just add some store-bought jerk marinade to store-bought bacon and braise in the oven before putting it on the grill. You can also find prepared habanero sauces at the store, so feel free to use one if you don't want to make your own.

8 (6-inch/15-cm) flour tortillas

2 tablespoons canola oil

8 slices Jerk Bacon (page 28), ½ inch (12 mm) thick, smoked to 195°F (91°C) internal temperature

1 recipe Black Bean–Mango Salsa (recipe follows)

¼ cup (60 ml) Habanero Sauce (page 89) or store-bought habanero sauce

2 limes, quartered

Fresh cilantro leaves (optional)

Preheat the oven to 300°F (150°C). Wrap the tortillas in aluminum foil and warm in the oven while you cook the bacon.

In a large nonstick pan, heat the oil over medium heat until it begins to shimmer. Add the bacon and cook until golden brown on both sides, about 2 minutes per side. Remove to a plate lined with paper towels.

Put the warm tortillas on a flat surface and top each with 1 slice of the bacon, a few spoonfuls of the salsa, and a few dashes of the habanero sauce. Squeeze with lime juice, garnish with cilantro, if desired, and serve immediately.

SERVES 4 TO 8

BLACK BEAN–MANGO SALSA

THIS FRUITY, FRESH, FLAVORFUL SALSA IS EXCELLENT WITH tortilla chips, spooned over roasted meat or fish, or as a topping for tacos.

Juice of 1 fresh lime

1 tablespoon agave or honey

½ teaspoon kosher salt

⅛ teaspoon ground black pepper

1 (15.5-ounce/439-g) can black beans, drained, rinsed, and drained again

1 medium mango, peeled, pitted, and finely diced

1 jalapeño, finely diced

¼ cup (35 g) finely diced red onion

¼ cup (10 g) finely chopped fresh cilantro leaves

In a medium bowl, whisk together the lime juice, agave, salt, and pepper. Add the beans, mango, jalapeño, onion, and cilantro and mix until just combined.

Cover and let sit at room temperature for at least 30 minutes before serving. The salsa can be made up to 8 hours in advance and refrigerated, tightly covered, for up to 2 days, and is best served at room temperature.

MAKES 3 CUPS (750 G)

BACON CHORIZO BREAKFAST TACOS

BREAKFAST TACOS OFFER EVERYTHING THAT IS BELOVED ABOUT the taco, with the added bonus of creamy, cheesy scrambled eggs. If you don't feel like making homemade sausage, just use equal parts finely diced thin-sliced bacon and Mexican chorizo (heck, you can even use plain old breakfast sausage and these will still be delicious).

12 (4-inch/10-cm) flour or corn tortillas

1 tablespoon canola oil

12 ounces (340 g) Bacon-Chipotle Chorizo (page 66) or fresh chorizo sausage, casings removed if necessary

1 small red onion, halved and thinly sliced

8 large eggs

1 cup (115 g) shredded Monterey Jack cheese

4 tablespoons (10 g) chopped fresh cilantro

2 green onions (dark green and pale green parts only), thinly sliced

1 large ripe Hass avocado, finely diced

Pico de Gallo (page 273)

Avocado Salsa Verde (page 90; optional)

Lime wedges

Preheat the oven to 300°F (150°C). Wrap the tortillas in aluminum foil and warm in the oven while you prepare the filling.

Heat the oil in a large sauté pan over high heat. Add the sausage and cook, breaking it up into small pieces, until golden brown. Add the onion and continue cooking until soft and the sausage is cooked through, about 5 minutes longer.

Lower the heat to low. Whisk the eggs together in a medium bowl until light and fluffy. Add the eggs to the pan and gently stir the eggs and sausage to form loose curds. Sprinkle the cheese over the eggs and mix until the eggs are scrambled and cooked to your preference. Remove from the heat and fold in 2 tablespoons of the cilantro and the green onions.

Arrange the tortillas on plates and top each with a generous heap of the egg and sausage mixture, a bit of avocado, pico de gallo, and salsa verde (if using), and garnish with a sprinkling of cilantro and a squeeze of lime juice. Serve immediately.

SERVES 6

BAJA FISH TACOS

THE CLASSIC FRIED FISH TACO THAT HAILS FROM CALIFORNIA IS simplicity at its best: pristine, firm white fish fried to golden perfection and simply topped with fresh crunchy cabbage and a cold, creamy, spicy sauce. In my opinion, it is only missing one thing . . . but not anymore.

8 (6-inch/15-cm) flour or corn tortillas

2 cups (480 ml) canola oil

2 (8-ounce/225-g) white fish fillets (such as halibut or cod), each fillet cut lengthwise into 4 equal pieces

Kosher salt and freshly ground black pepper

½ recipe Fish Dredge (page 96)

½ cup (120 ml) Baja Sauce (page 91)

3 tablespoons Habanero Sauce (page 89)

Toasted Cumin Slaw (page 289)

1 cup (110 g) Bacon Bits (page 49)

Preheat the oven to 300°F (150°C). Wrap the tortillas in aluminum foil and warm in the oven while you fry the fish.

Put the oil in a medium-size, deep sauté pan over medium heat and heat until it reaches 350°F (175°C) on a deep-fry thermometer. Line a baking sheet with parchment paper and another one with paper towels.

Season the fish on both sides with salt and pepper. Put the fish dredge in a small baking dish. Dredge the fish pieces in the mixture, pressing it in so that it adheres to all sides. Transfer to the parchment-lined baking sheet. Fry the fish, in batches, until golden brown and just cooked through, about 4 minutes. Remove to the paper towel–lined baking sheet to drain.

Lay the tortillas on a flat surface. Spread 1 tablespoon of the Baja sauce over each one, leaving a 1-inch (2.5-cm) border. Lay a piece of the fish in the center, drizzle with 1 teaspoon of the habanero sauce, top with a large spoonful of the slaw, and sprinkle with some of the bacon bits. Serve immediately.

SERVES 4 TO 8

KENTUCKY FRIED BACON TACOS

I REMEMBER THE FIRST TIME I MADE KENTUCKY FRIED BACON. I liken it to when man discovered fire. I thought I was a culinary genius. Tender pieces of bacon cooked slowly in its own fat, then breaded with light-as-air bread crumbs and fried to golden brown perfection. Here, I serve it encased in warm tortillas and topped with a variety of toppings.

4 (6-inch/15-cm) flour or corn tortillas

4 pieces Kentucky Fried Bacon (page 42), warm

Toppings (suggestions follow)

Preheat the oven to 300°F (150°C). Wrap the tortillas in aluminum foil and warm in the oven for 15 minutes.

Lay the tortillas on a flat surface. Place 1 piece of the bacon in the center of each and top with a few tablespoons of toppings.

Here are a few of my favorites combinations:

Grilled Corn Succotash (page 290) and Habanero Sauce (page 89)

Buffalo sauce (page 211), Bacon–Blue Cheese Ranch (page 78), and Pickled Jalapeño Salad (page 285)

Piperade (page 287) and Avocado Salsa Verde (page 90)

MAKES 4

PICKLED JALAPEÑO CHIMICHURRI TACOS

with Grilled Chicken and Bacon

I'M OBSESSED WITH PICKLED JALAPEÑO SALAD AND TEND TO throw it on everything I eat, except maybe dessert. One day, I had the brilliant idea of tossing it into a food processor with some cilantro, and the next thing you know I had this delicious version of chimichurri (insert emoji with a head exploding, please). Chimichurri is great as it is, with its assortment of fresh herbs and lots of garlic ... but add a bit of acid (for example, pickled jalapeños) and it is a perfect match for chicken and bacon. Here, I serve it with my chicken taco.

½ cup (120 ml) low-sodium soy sauce

½ cup (120 ml) Worcestershire sauce

2 tablespoons ancho chile powder

2 (8-ounce/225-g) boneless, skinless chicken breasts

3 tablespoons canola oil

1 Vidalia onion, cut crosswise into slices ¼ inch (6 mm) thick

Kosher salt and coarsely ground black pepper

8 (6-inch/15-cm) flour or corn tortillas

¾ cup (80 g) Bacon Bits (page 49)

Pickled Jalapeño Chimichurri (page 88)

In a medium bowl, combine the soy sauce, Worcestershire sauce, and chile powder and whisk until smooth. Put the chicken in a large zip-top bag, pour the marinade over, and seal tightly. Place in a bowl and refrigerate for at least 4 hours, or up to 24 hours.

Remove the chicken from the marinade, rinse with cold water, and pat dry with paper towels. Brush with 2 tablespoons of the oil and season each breast with ½ teaspoon salt and ¼ teaspoon black pepper., being careful to coat both sides. Brush the onion slices with the remaining 1 tablespoon oil and season with a pinch of salt and pepper on both sides.

Heat a grill to high or a grill pan over high heat. Grill the chicken on both sides until golden brown and slightly charred and just cooked through, about 5 minutes per side. Remove to a plate and let rest for 5 minutes. Grill the onion until golden brown and charred on both sides and soft, about 4 minutes on both sides.

Grill the tortillas on both sides until slightly marked, about 10 seconds per side. Slice the chicken breasts on the bias into slices ½ inch (12 mm) thick. Coarsely chop the onion.

Put the tortillas on a flat surface and place several slices on the chicken in the center of each. Top with the onion, bacon bits, and a few spoonfuls of chimichurri. Serve immediately.

SERVES 4 TO 6

OYSTER PO' BOY TACOS

TACOS ARE JUST OPEN-FACED WRAP SANDWICHES. ANY TACO CAN BE made into a sandwich, and any sandwich, even an iconic New Orleans version like the oyster po'boy, can be made into a taco. Of course, the original doesn't contain bacon, but we won't hold that against it.

8 (6-inch/15-cm) flour tortillas

2 cups (480 ml) canola oil

½ recipe Fish Dredge (page 96)

24 shucked oysters (do not drain them)

Kosher salt and freshly ground black pepper

1 recipe Celery and Apple Rémoulade (page 149)

Hot sauce, such as Tabasco or Frank's

¾ cup (80 g) Bacon Bits (page 49)

Preheat the oven to 300°F (150°C). Wrap the tortillas in aluminum foil and warm in the oven while you fry the oysters.

In a medium-size, deep sauté pan over medium heat, heat the oil until it reaches 350°F (175°C) on a deep-fry thermometer. Line a baking sheet with paper towels.

While the oil is heating, put the fish dredge in a shallow dish. Season the oysters with salt and pepper and dredge in the fish dredge on both sides.

Fry the oysters in batches until golden brown and crispy, about 4 minutes. Remove with a slotted spoon or tongs to the prepared baking sheet.

Lay the tortillas on a flat surface. Spread a few tablespoons of the rémoulade down the centers and top with 3 fried oysters each. Drizzle with a few dashes of the hot sauce and sprinkle with bacon bits. Roll and eat.

SERVES 4 TO 6

CHAPTER 9

ENTRÉES

ACON, ALWAYS THE BRIDESMAID AND never the bride. At BarBacon, I've been trying to change that. Bacon is no longer the favorite side dish, but rather the dish itself. In the first half of this chapter, we'll explore bacon's layers, its flavors, its textures. We'll use it in traditional recipes to amp up the familiar. We will reintroduce you to your classics, to your go-to comfort foods, like mac and cheese (where I add bacon three ways), adjusted and reinterpreted and made new with bacon as the star. Classics like this should serve as a gateway drug, building your confidence and showing you what you can really do with bacon. Once you know just how awesome it is beyond breakfast, you can start to really experiment like I do.

Once you're ready to take it to a new level, you can start building dishes around bacon, dishes that you would never expect. What about bulgogi for example? It's a dish that usually has meat, so why not swap out the classic beef for bacon? Add in that unctuous fat, a little smoke, and some fun? It's genius.

The more I work with bacon, the more I realize its true potential. You can fry it, boil it, grill it, shave it, play with it in so many different ways. I challenge you this—once you work your way through this chapter and really understand how to use bacon, take any of your favorite meat-based dishes and try to swap out that meat for bacon. You won't be mad you did.

BACON AND LAMB SAUSAGE CASSOULET

ALL CASSOULETS ARE MADE WITH WHITE BEANS, BUT THE OTHER ingredients vary—duck or goose confit, sausages, or additional meat. Here, we substitute bacon for the duck confit and double down with bacon and lamb merguez. This is a hearty dish that is easy enough to pull off. This is great served family-style as is with a large spoon at the table, with some chopped chives or parsley for color.

3 cups (720 ml) chicken stock

2 cups (480 ml) Bacon Stock (page 43)

1 sprig fresh thyme

1 small Spanish onion, halved; plus 1 medium Spanish onion, diced

3 garlic cloves, smashed; plus 3 garlic cloves, chopped

¾ teaspoon dried herbes de Provence

1 teaspoon black peppercorns

12 ounces (340 g) slab bacon, cut into lardons (see page 48)

2 tablespoons rendered bacon fat (see page 50)

10 ounces (280 g) cooked Bacon and Lamb Merguez (page 68), diced

2 ribs celery, diced

1 large carrot, peeled and diced

4 (15.5-ounce/439-g) cans Great Northern beans, rinsed and drained

Finely chopped chives or parsley leaves, for garnish (optional)

In a medium saucepan, combine both stocks, the thyme, halved onion, smashed garlic, herbes de Provence, and peppercorns and bring to a boil. Remove from the heat, cover, and let steep for at least 30 minutes, or up to 2 hours. Strain into a medium bowl, wipe out the pan, and return the strained broth to the saucepan over low heat.

In a 5-quart (5-L) cast-iron pot over medium heat, cook the bacon lardons in the rendered bacon fat until almost crispy, then add the sausage and cook for another 2 minutes to draw out the flavor.

Add the diced onion, chopped garlic, celery, and carrot to the pot and cook until soft but not colored, about 6 minutes.

Add the beans and stock, simmer for 30 minutes, then remove from the heat. Garnish with the chives or parsley, if desired, and serve.

SERVES 4 TO 6

BACON BRAISED PORK SHANKS

CURING, BRAISING, AND FRYING. OKAY, I'M NOT GOING TO LIE, THIS recipe takes time (a good two days) and effort, but the reward is oh, so great! Hind shanks, which come from the back leg of the pig, can be chewy when cooked incorrectly. Is there a simpler way to cook pork shank? Yes. Is it as good as this one? No. I love serving this with Rosemary-Scented Apple Puree (page 270) in the fall, or with Rosemary Mashed Potatoes (page 292), Caraway Sauerkraut (page 153), and White Wine Grainy Mustard Sauce (page 81) for a showstopping holiday dinner.

2 cups (360 g) Diamond Crystal kosher salt

2 cups (400 g) granulated sugar

2 tablespoons black peppercorns, plus freshly ground black pepper to taste

1 tablespoon coriander seeds

¼ cup (20 g) coarsely chopped fresh rosemary

5 bay leaves

4 pork shanks, about 1½ pounds (680 g) each

4 cups (960 ml) rendered bacon fat (see page 50), or a combination of bacon fat and canola oil, enough to cover shanks in pot so they are completely submerged

3 tablespoons canola oil

In a food processor, combine the salt, sugar, peppercorns, coriander, rosemary, and bay leaves and process until coarsely ground.

Put the shanks in a large baking dish and pour the salt mixture over, making sure that each shank is completely coated. Cover and let cure in the refrigerator for at least 2 days, or up to 4 days.

Preheat the oven to 220°F (105°C). Remove the shanks from the refrigerator, rinse well with cold water, and pat dry with paper towels; season both sides of each with pepper.

In a large Dutch oven or pot large enough to fit the shanks with at least 2 inches (5 cm) more height, cook the bacon fat until it just melts. Add the shanks to the pot, cover, and place in the oven. Cook until the meat is tender and the interior registers 195°F (91°C) on an instant-read thermometer, 3 to 4 hours.

Let the shanks cool to room temperature in the fat, then transfer the pot to the refrigerator and let sit, covered, until chilled through, at least 8 hours, or up to 24 hours.

Using tongs or a large spoon, carefully remove the shanks from the fat and transfer to a baking sheet. Return the pot to the stovetop and heat the fat until it registers 365°F (185°C) on a deep-fry thermometer. Fry the shanks, in batches, until golden brown and crispy, about 5 minutes. Transfer to a plate lined with paper towels to drain slightly. Serve immediately.

SERVES 4

BACON LOVES
CLAM CHOWDER GNOCCHI

MY HEAD CHEF, NICK KAROLY, MADE THIS FOR HIS TASTING WHEN he applied for the job. I told him I wanted him to re-create something classic that had bacon in it and what I got was actually two classics: creamy New England clam chowder and *pasta alle vongole* with pillowy potato gnocchi standing in for the spaghetti. It is a soup that eats like a meal.

2 cups (480 ml) Bacon Clam Stock (page 250)

24 littleneck clams, scrubbed

4 tablespoons (55 g) unsalted butter

2 shallots, finely diced

3 garlic cloves, finely diced

½ cup (120 ml) heavy cream

3 tablespoons finely chopped fresh flat-leaf parsley leaves, plus more for garnish

Freshly ground black pepper

2 tablespoons canola oil

8 thin strips bacon, cut into fifths

Gnocchi (page 251)

Finely grated zest of 1 lemon

In a large Dutch oven, bring the stock to a boil. Stir in the clams, cover the pot, and cook, shaking the pot a few times, until all of the clams open, about 5 minutes. Remove the cooked clams to a large bowl (discard any that have not opened). Let cool, then reserve 6 in shell for garnish. Remove the meat from the remaining clams and discard the shells. Strain the clam broth through a fine-mesh sieve lined with cheesecloth into a medium bowl and set aside. Rinse out the pot and return it to medium heat.

Add 2 tablespoons of the butter to the pot and cook until melted. Add the shallots and garlic and cook until soft, about 1 minute. Add the reserved broth, increase the heat to high, and cook until reduced by half. Add the cream and cook until slightly reduced, about 2 minutes. Stir in the parsley and season with ¼ teaspoon pepper. Remove from the heat and stir in the cooked clams. Cover and keep the sauce warm.

While the sauce is reducing, put the oil and bacon in a large, deep sauté pan over medium heat and cook until golden brown and just crispy, about 8 minutes. Remove to a plate lined with paper towels, let cool slightly, and coarsely chop.

You should have about ¼ cup (60 ml) rendered fat in the pan; heat over medium heat, then add the remaining 2 tablespoons butter and cook until melted. Add the gnocchi in two batches and cook until golden brown on each side, about 1 minute per side.

With a slotted spoon, transfer the gnocchi to the sauce and gently stir to coat. Divide among 4 large shallow bowls and garnish with the bacon, parsley, and a bit of lemon zest.

SERVES 4

BACON CLAM STOCK

1 onion, peeled and quartered

1 large carrot, peeled and cut into 4 pieces

2 ribs celery, cut into 4 pieces

5 thin slices bacon, cut in half

2 tablespoons canola oil

1 cup (240 ml) dry white wine

4 cups (960 ml) best-quality clam stock

5 sprigs fresh thyme

In a food processor, combine the onion, carrot, celery, and bacon and pulse until finely chopped.

Heat the oil in a large Dutch oven over high heat until it begins to shimmer. Add the onion mixture and cook, stirring constantly, until soft and fragrant, about 5 minutes. Add the wine and cook until completely reduced.

Add the stock, 1 cup (240 ml) water, and the thyme and bring to a boil over high heat. Lower the heat to low and simmer until reduced to about 4 cups (960 ml) and the flavors have melded, about 30 minutes. Strain into a clean saucepan and keep warm. Or let cool to room temperature, transfer to a container with a tight-fitting lid, and refrigerate for up to 3 days or freeze for up to 1 month.

**MAKES ABOUT
4 CUPS (960 ML)**

GNOCCHI

2 pounds (910 g) Idaho potatoes (about 4), scrubbed well and pricked with a fork

2 large egg yolks, lightly beaten

3 tablespoons minced fresh chives

Kosher salt

1 teaspoon freshly ground black pepper

¾ cup (95 g) to 1½ cups (190 g) all-purpose flour

Preheat the oven to 375°F (193°C). Put the potatoes on a baking sheet and bake until very soft, about 1 to 1½ hours, depending on the size, turning them once. Remove to a wire rack and let sit until cool enough to handle.

Halve the potatoes lengthwise, scoop out the flesh, and discard the skins. Using a food mill or potato ricer, rice the potatoes into a large bowl.

In a small bowl, whisk together the egg yolks, chives, 1½ teaspoon salt, and the pepper until smooth. Add the egg mixture to the potato mixture and mix until completely combined. Begin adding the flour ¼ cup (30 g) at a time and gently fold into the potatoes using a rubber spatula. Add just enough additional flour to make a stiff dough. Knead the dough gently until smooth but still slightly sticky.

Line a baking sheet with parchment paper and dust with flour. Divide the dough into four equal portions.

Gently roll each piece into a rope 12 inches (30.5 cm) long and about 1 inch (2.5 cm) in diameter, flouring as needed to prevent the dough from sticking to the surface. Place dough ropes on the prepared baking sheet and let rest, uncovered, for 30 minutes.

After the dough has rested, place the ropes on a floured surface. Cut each rope into 1-inch (2. 5-cm) pieces with a bench scraper or knife and set aside.

Bring a large pot of salted water to a boil over high heat. Add the gnocchi to the boiling water and cook until they rise to the surface, then cook for 1 minute longer. Drain and, using a large slotted spoon, transfer to a clean baking sheet in a single layer. The gnocchi can be made 1 day in advance and stored on a sheet pan in a single layer and covered with plastic wrap.

MAKES ABOUT 48; SERVES 4

BACON FRIED RICE
with Bacon Spare Ribs

THE BACON SPARE RIB MAKES THIS DISH. I'M A JUNKIE FOR BONE-
less spare rib tips, but they are always inevitably overcooked. These aren't. They are
moist, juicy, and packed with all the umami one can conjure without MSG. The
secret to perfect fried rice is using day-old cold rice. So, if you have the time, make
the rice the night before, spread it on a baking sheet to cool, then transfer to a
container and refrigerate overnight. If you'd like, skip the scrambled eggs and serve
fried sunny-side-up eggs on top of the rice.

FOR THE BACON SPARE RIBS

1½ pounds (680 g) slab bacon, preferably Garlic-Soy Bacon (page 26)

2 tablespoons Chinese five-spice powder

1 cup (240 ml) hoisin sauce

¼ cup (60 ml) pineapple juice

2 tablespoons low-sodium soy sauce

1 heaping tablespoon light brown sugar

1 generous tablespoon clover honey

1 teaspoon garlic powder

2 teaspoons finely grated fresh ginger

1 tablespoon grenadine

1 tablespoon canola oil

FOR THE FRIED RICE

¼ cup (60 ml) low-sodium soy sauce

2 teaspoons oyster sauce

½ teaspoon toasted sesame oil

8 ounces (225 g) thin-sliced bacon, diced

3 large eggs, lightly beaten

1 Spanish onion, diced

2 carrots, peeled and diced

2 cups (260 g) jasmine rice, cooked and chilled (see Note)

½ cup (65 g) frozen peas, thawed

2 large green onions (dark green and pale green parts only), thinly sliced on the bias

Sriracha (optional)

Make the bacon spare ribs: Preheat the oven to 225°F (107°C). Rub both sides of the slab bacon with the five-spice powder, place on a baking sheet lined with parchment paper or aluminum foil, and cook until the bacon reaches an internal temperature of 195°F (91°C), about 2 hours. Let cool to room temperature. Wrap in foil and refrigerate until cold, at least 4 hours, or up to 48 hours.

Combine the hoisin sauce, pineapple juice, soy sauce, brown sugar, honey, garlic power, ginger, and grenadine in a small saucepan and cook over high heat, whisking occasionally, until the sugar

(continued)

has dissolved and the mixture has thickened slightly, about 7 minutes. The sauce can be made up to 2 days in advance and stored, tightly covered, in the refrigerator.

Cut the cooled bacon crosswise into slices ½ inch (12 mm) thick. Heat the oil in a large nonstick pan over medium heat. Add the bacon in batches and cook until golden brown on both sides, about 6 minutes. Remove to a plate lined with paper towels. Drain the fat into a small bowl and save for another use (see page 50).

Return the pan to high heat, add half of the sauce and half of the bacon, and cook until the bacon is glazed on both sides, about 2 minutes per side. Wipe the pan out and add the remaining sauce and bacon and cook 2 minutes per side. Set aside, covered to keep warm.

Make the fried rice: In a small bowl, whisk together the soy sauce, oyster sauce, and sesame oil and set aside.

Cook the bacon in a large nonstick or cast-iron pan over medium heat until golden brown and crispy, about 8 minutes. Remove to a plate lined with paper towels. Remove all but 1 tablespoon of the rendered bacon fat from the pan, put in a small bowl, and set aside.

Add the eggs to the pan and cook, stirring constantly, until fluffy and barely set, about 2 minutes. Transfer to a plate.

Increase the heat to high, add the reserved bacon fat to the pan, and heat until it begins to shimmer. Add the onion and carrots and cook, stirring occasionally, until soft, about 5 minutes. Add the rice, peas, and soy sauce mixture and cook, stirring constantly, until

the rice is coated and heated through. Add the eggs and bacon and cook for 1 minute longer.

Transfer to serving bowls and top each with a bacon spare rib, green onions, and sriracha, if desired.

NOTE: *To cook rice: Put the rice in a colander and rinse well with cold water until the water runs clear. In a medium saucepan with a tight-fitting lid, combine the rice, 3 cups (720 ml) water, and 1 teaspoon salt and bring to a boil. Stir once, cover, and lower the heat to low. Simmer for 18 minutes. (Do not lift the lid or stir!) Remove from the heat and let stand, covered, for 5 minutes; fluff with a fork. Spread onto a baking sheet and let cool for 10 minutes. If you're making fried rice, cover and refrigerate the rice for at least 4 hours, or up to 24 hours.*

SERVES 4

BEEF BACON BULGOGI SKILLET

I LOVE MAKING THIS DISH *AND* SERVING IT IN A CAST-IRON SKILLET. At the restaurant, I use individual cast irons, but feel free to use a 9-inch (23-cm) skillet. Just place it on a trivet at your table and serve it family-style with a large bowl of white rice or some crusty bread for soaking up all of that flavorful marinade.

FOR THE PICKLED VEGETABLES

3 cups (720 ml) cold water

2 tablespoons kosher salt

2 English cucumbers, halved and sliced ¼ inch (6 mm) thick

1¼ cups (300 ml) rice vinegar

½ cup (100 g) sugar

2 tablespoons sambal oelek

1 carrot, peeled and cut into matchstick strips

½ head white or green cabbage, finely shredded

FOR THE BULGOGI

¾ cup (180 ml) low-sodium soy sauce

¾ cup (180 ml) clover honey

6 garlic cloves, chopped

2 tablespoons grated fresh ginger

2 teaspoons sambal oelek

1½ teaspoons toasted sesame oil

2 tablespoons canola oil

16 thin slices Beef Bacon (page 34) cut crosswise into 8 pieces each

Make the pickled vegetables: In a large bowl, combine the cold water and salt and whisk until dissolved. Stir in the cucumbers and let sit in the refrigerator for 2 hours. Drain well.

Combine the vinegar and sugar in a medium nonreactive saucepan and bring to a boil over high heat. Cook until the sugar is dissolved. Remove from the heat, whisk in the sambal, and let cool for 5 minutes. Stir in the drained cucumbers and the carrot and transfer to a container with a tight-fitting lid. Refrigerate for at least 4 hours, or up to 48 hours. Just before serving, transfer the pickled vegetables and the brine to a bowl and stir in the cabbage.

(continued)

Make the bulgogi: In a medium bowl, whisk together the soy sauce, honey, garlic, ginger, sambal, and sesame oil. Let sit at room temperature for at least 30 minutes to allow the flavors to meld. The marinade can be made up to 24 hours before using and stored, covered, in the refrigerator.

Heat the oil in a 9-inch (23-cm) cast-iron pan over high heat until it begins to shimmer. Add the bacon in batches and cook until golden brown and charred on both sides, about 3 minutes per side. Drain off most of the fat into a bowl and save for another use (see page 50).

Add the marinade to the bacon in the pan and cook until the marinade thickens and the bacon becomes lightly glazed, about 5 minutes.

Remove the pan from the heat and top with the pickled vegetable mixture. Serve immediately.

SERVES 4 TO 6

BACON LOVES MAC AND CHEESE

I COULDN'T IMAGINE OPENING A BAR WITHOUT MAC AND CHEESE on the menu, and I couldn't imagine making a mac and cheese without bacon. This recipe gets a triple dose of bacon, starting with the sauce and ending with the bread crumbs, proving yet again that too much of something (umm, bacon, that is) is never enough.

FOR THE BACON LARDONS

1 tablespoon canola oil

1 pound (455 g) slab bacon, cut into lardons (see page 48)

FOR THE BREAD CRUMBS

¼ cup (60 ml) rendered bacon fat, reserved from the lardons

1 tablespoon unsalted butter

1 cup (80 g) panko bread crumbs

FOR THE MACARONI AND CHEESE

1 quart (960 ml) whole milk

2 tablespoons rendered bacon fat, reserved from the lardons

2 tablespoons unsalted butter

¼ cup (30 g) all-purpose flour

2 cups (225 g) shredded American cheese

2 cups (225 g) shredded smoked gouda

Kosher salt and freshly ground black pepper

1 pound (455 g) dried elbow macaroni, cooked in salted water until al dente and drained

¼ cup (11 g) finely chopped fresh chives

Make the bacon lardons: In a large sauté pan over medium heat, combine the oil and bacon and cook, turning a few times, until the bacon is golden brown and crispy and the fat has rendered, about 8 minutes.

Remove the bacon using a slotted spoon to a plate lined with paper towels. Pour ¼ cup plus 2 tablespoons (90 ml) of the fat into a small bowl and set aside for making the bread crumbs. Save the rest for another use (see page 50).

Make the bread crumbs: Heat the reserved bacon fat and the butter in a small sauté pan over high heat until it begins to shimmer. Add the panko and cook, stirring occasionally, until golden brown and crispy, about 5 minutes. Transfer to a plate.

Make the macaroni and cheese: Preheat the oven to 375°F (193°C). Butter a 9 by 13-inch (23 by 33-cm) baking dish or a 12-inch (30.5-cm) cast-iron pan.

In a large pot, bring the milk to a simmer over low heat.

Combine the remaining 2 tablespoons bacon fat and the butter in a medium saucepan over high heat until it begins to shimmer. Add the flour and cook, stirring constantly, for 1 minute. Slowly add the warm milk, whisking until smooth. Lower the heat and cook the béchamel sauce until thickened and the flour taste has cooked out, about 7 minutes. Remove from the heat, add both cheeses, and whisk until smooth. Taste for seasoning, adding salt, if needed, and a good dose of black pepper.

In a large bowl, stir the cheese sauce into the cooked pasta, fold in the bacon, and transfer to the prepared baking dish or pan. Bake until bubbly and lightly golden brown on top, about 20 minutes. Remove from the oven and sprinkle with the bread crumbs and chives. Serve immediately.

SERVES 6 TO 8

SKILLET PASTA CARBONARA

THIS IS KIND OF A CROSS BETWEEN CARBONARA AND THE CREAMI-
est, richest mac and cheese you've ever eaten. The classic Roman dish is made with
cured pork jowl known as guanciale, which is not smoked. You can totally use it in
this recipe, or even bacon for that matter, but I love using the smoked porchetta,
with its fennel and herbal undertones, adding even more flavor to the dish.

1 pound (455 g) dried
gemelli pasta

Kosher salt

1 tablespoon canola oil

12 ounces (340 g) Smoked
Porchetta (page 38),
finely diced

8 large egg yolks

1½ cups (360 ml) heavy cream

½ cup (50 g) freshly grated
Parmigiano-Reggiano cheese,
plus more for serving

12 Tomato Confit halves
(page 286)

Freshly ground black pepper

4 over-easy eggs

Chopped fresh chives

Bring a large pot of water to
a boil over high heat, add the
pasta and 2 tablespoons salt,
and cook until just al dente,
about 8 minutes. Remove
1 cup (240 ml) of the pasta
water and set aside. Drain
the pasta.

While the water is coming
to a boil, combine the oil and
porchetta in a large, deep sauté
pan over medium heat and
cook, stirring occasionally,
until golden brown and crisp,
about 8 minutes. Remove with
a slotted spoon to a plate lined
with paper towels.

While the bacon is cooking,
whisk together the egg yolks,
cream, and Parmesan in a large
bowl until smooth.

Add the hot drained pasta to
the pan that the pancetta was
cooked in and toss for 1 minute over low heat to coat the
pasta in the bacon fat. Remove
the pan from the heat and
pour the egg mixture into the
pasta, whisking quickly until
the eggs thicken, but do not
scramble (this is done off the
heat to ensure the eggs don't
scramble). Stir in the bacon
and the tomato confit.

Thin out the sauce with a bit
of the reserved pasta water,
if needed, until it reaches the
desired consistency. Season
the carbonara with pepper
and taste for salt. Mound the
pasta into warm serving bowls
and garnish each with a fried
egg and chopped chives. Serve
with additional cheese on
the side.

SERVES 4

SMOKED PORCHETTA AND CHICKEN POT PIE

THIS RECIPE IS MEANT TO TAKE ADVANTAGE OF ANY LEFTOVER Smoked Porchetta (page 38), but if you don't have any left because you already ate it all or you didn't feel like making it, of course regular bacon will fill in just perfectly. (It always does.) Feel free to cook your own chicken, but why not take advantage of those delicious rotisserie ones you can pick up at the supermarket?

2 cups (480 ml) heavy cream

5 tablespoons (70 g) unsalted butter

1 Spanish onion, diced

2 large carrots, peeled and diced

1 large rib celery, diced

2 Yukon gold or red potatoes, diced

Kosher salt and freshly ground black pepper

⅓ cup (40 g) all-purpose flour

4 cups (960 ml) low-sodium chicken stock or broth

1 chicken bouillon cube (optional)

1 teaspoon finely chopped fresh thyme leaves

4 cups (780 g) diced or shredded cooked chicken, skin removed, white and dark meat

2 cups (475 g) diced Smoked Porchetta (page 38); or cooked bacon lardons (see page 48)

1 cup (135 g) frozen green peas

¼ cup (13 g) chopped fresh flat-leaf parsley

1 sheet frozen puff pastry, thawed and rolled slightly

1 large egg, beaten with 1 tablespoon water

Crispy bacon, for garnish

Preheat the oven to 400°F (205°C). Butter a 9 by 11-inch (23 by 28-cm) baking dish and place it on a baking sheet lined with aluminum foil.

In a small saucepan, bring the cream to a boil. Lower the heat to a simmer and cook until reduced by half, about 10 minutes. Remove from the heat.

Melt the butter in a large Dutch oven over high heat. Add the onion, carrots, celery, and potatoes, season with salt and pepper, and cook until slightly soft, about 7 minutes.

Add the flour and cook, stirring constantly, until light golden brown, about 3 minutes. Add the stock, bouillon cube, if using, and thyme and

bring to a boil. Cook, stirring often, until the mixture begins to thicken and the flour taste cooks out, about 5 minutes. Add the reduced cream and mix until combined. Add the chicken, porchetta, peas, and parsley and mix until just combined. Season with more salt and pepper, if needed.

Transfer the mixture to the prepared baking dish. Place the pastry over the hot filling, pressing the edges to seal and trimming off any excess. (Use the scraps to cover any exposed filling, if necessary.) Brush the egg wash over the top of the pastry. Using a paring knife, make a few slits in the pastry so the steam can escape. Bake

until the top is golden brown and filling is bubbling, about 45 minutes. Remove from the oven and let cool on a wire rack for 15 minutes before serving. Serve in individual bowls. Garnish with a slice or two of crispy bacon, if desired.

SERVES 6 TO 8

PORK SCHNITZEL
with Bacon-Mushroom Gravy

THE BACON MIGHT APPEAR LIKE THE BRIDESMAID IN THIS DISH, but it's a stunner. Presented smooth in the gravy, it is hard to miss the bacon's presence here. I sometimes serve this alongside my Rosemary Mashed Potatoes (page 292), which include chopped bacon, for an extra dose. And the next day, when the schnitzel no longer has its crispy crust, the bacon gravy (and mashed potatoes) will be what everyone goes for first.

4 boneless pork loin chops (5 to 6 ounces/140 to 170 g each)

1½ cups (190 g) all-purpose flour

Kosher salt and freshly ground black pepper

3 large eggs

4 cups (320 g) panko bread crumbs

4 tablespoons (60 ml) canola oil

4 tablespoons (55 g) unsalted butter

Bacon-Mushroom Gravy (page 93)

Bacon Bits (page 49; optional)

Lemon wedges (optional)

Put each chop between two sheets of plastic wrap or waxed paper and gently pound them out with the flat side of a meat tenderizer until they are an even ⅛ inch (3 mm) thick.

Put the flour in a shallow dish and season with salt and pepper. Whisk the eggs and ¼ cup (60 ml) water together in another shallow dish and season with salt and pepper. Put the panko in a third dish and again season with salt and pepper. Lightly dredge each piece of pork in the flour, then in the egg, and finally into the bread crumbs, pressing the bread crumbs onto the pork gently so they have a nice even coating.

Lay the breaded pork cutlets in a single layer on a plate lined with parchment paper and refrigerate, uncovered, for 10 to 12 minutes to allow the coating to dry out a little and adhere to the pork.

In a large nonstick or cast-iron pan, heat 2 tablespoons of the oil and 2 tablespoons of the butter over high heat until the mixture begins to shimmer. Cook two of the pork cutlets until golden brown on both sides and just cooked through, about 3 minutes per side. Wipe the pan out, add the remaining oil and butter, and repeat with the remaining cutlets. Remove to a sheet pan lined with paper towels and season immediately with a bit more salt.

To serve, ladle some of the gravy onto a large plate and top with a pork schnitzel. Serve with additional gravy on top and garnish with bacon bits and a squeeze of lemon, if desired.

SERVES 4

BACON-WRAPPED PORK TENDERLOIN

PORK TENDERLOIN, UNLIKE PORK BELLY, IS VERY LEAN AND DELI-cately flavored and can use some extra love when preparing. I give it lots and lots of love in the recipe, and while it takes some extra effort the results are so worth it. Brining, confiting, and pan-roasting add flavor, moisture, and texture.

2 pounds (910 g) pork tenderloin

¼ recipe brine for BarBacon Wet Cure (Brined) Bacon (page 23)

4 cups (960 ml) rendered bacon fat (see page 50)

8 thin slices bacon

2 tablespoons canola oil

1 cup (240 ml) BarBacon BBQ Sauce (page 82) or your favorite store-bought (optional)

Put the tenderloin in a gallon-size zip-top bag, add the brine, and seal tightly, pressing out as much air as possible. Put the bag in a large bowl (in case the bag leaks) and cure in the refrigerator for at least 4 hours, or up to 12 hours.

Preheat the oven to 250°F (120°C). Remove the pork from the brine, rinse well with cold water, and pat dry with paper towels.

Cut a piece of plastic wrap into an 18-inch (46-cm) square, put the brined tenderloin on the bottom edge, and roll up halfway tightly. Fold in the edges and finish wrapping tightly until the tenderloin resembles a perfect cylinder. Poke holes with a toothpick through the wrapped tenderloin to allow fat to penetrate the plastic casing.

Put the bacon fat in a medium Dutch oven and heat over medium heat until just warm, about 5 minutes. Add the pork to the pot, making sure that the tenderloin is completely submerged. Cover the pan and cook until the pork reaches an internal temperature of 125°F (52°C), about 2 hours. Remove the pork from the plastic, place on a cutting board, and let cool slightly.

Lay 5 to 7 strips of bacon overlapped on a work surface, wide enough to encompass the length of the tenderloin. Place the unwrapped tenderloin in the center of the bacon, perpendicular to the slices, and roll to cover it with the bacon.

Heat the oil in a large nonstick pan over medium-low heat until it begins to shimmer. Put the bacon-wrapped pork into the pan, seam side down, and cook until the bottom is golden brown, about 5 minutes. Flip the pork over and continue cooking until golden brown and crispy, about 5 minutes longer. Begin brushing the pork with the BBQ sauce (if using) during the last few minutes of cooking. Remove to a cutting board, brush with more sauce, let rest for 5 minutes, and cut into thick slices. Serve immediately.

SERVES 4 TO 6

CHAPTER 10

HOLD THE BACON

I LOVE BACON AS MUCH AS THE NEXT PERSON. IN fact, I love bacon more. I freaking own a restaurant all about bacon. That said, even I need a break sometimes. These breaks are often fresh, bright, and acidic, and they help to cut through all of that delicious fat. While none of these recipes actually have bacon in them, they're all great complements to bacon.

Some of my favorite things to make in the restaurant are pickles. Nobody thinks you can make your own, but once you get the hang of it, they're stupid-easy. They take just a few minutes to put together and they really surprise you with that acid. I love a good bread and butter pickle on a sandwich, for example—the slight sweetness and juicy crispness play the perfect partner to the smoke and salt of an awesome piece of thick-cut bacon. Once you get the technique down for these Bread and Butter Pickles (page 276), you can move on to things like Pickled Fennel (page 283) and pickled jalapeños (page 285) and one of my favorites, Italian giardiniera (page 281). I promise they'll up your sandwich game like crazy.

I'm also a big fan of fresh salads and herbs to go with bacon. When I was working on my lamb bacon, I was trying to come up with fun Middle Eastern–inspired sides. That's how I wrote my tabbouleh recipe (page 288). It's full of couscous, lemon juice, and loads of herbs. It pairs just right with the spices I use and makes the lamb feel like a full meal. The freshness of the cilantro, parsley, and mint really balance out that fattiness and make you crave more. I can't eat one without the other now. No cookbook written by me would be complete without recipes for coleslaw and potato salad. Southern Potato Salad (page 291) is a Sherman family staple at every summer BBQ, and I make it exactly the same way that my mother taught me many (many) years ago. Pineapple-Jalapeño Coleslaw (page 272) is the house slaw at BarBacon and a new classic that I hope to pass on to my children one day.

ROSEMARY-SCENTED APPLE PUREE

PORK AND APPLES ARE A MATCH MADE IN CULINARY HEAVEN. USING a combination of apples gives applesauce a complex flavor. I always use a tart apple such as Granny Smith and pair it with one that's a bit sweeter, like Gala. I've served this apple puree with the Bacon Braised Pork Shanks (page 247) and the tenderloin (page 266). It's also great to eat with pork chops off the grill or even venison, to balance any gaminess.

8 tablespoons (115 g) unsalted butter, cut into pieces

4 sprigs fresh rosemary

3 Granny Smith apples, peeled, cored, and chopped

3 Gala apples, peeled, cored, and chopped

2 tablespoons sugar

Cold water

1 tablespoon fresh lemon juice

¼ teaspoon kosher salt

⅛ teaspoon freshly ground black pepper

In a large sauté pan over medium heat, cook 6 tablespoons of the butter and the rosemary sprigs until the butter begins to turn a golden brown, about 6 minutes. Discard the rosemary and transfer the butter to a blender or food processor.

Add the remaining 2 tablespoons butter to the pan and cook until just melted. Add both types of apples, the sugar, a splash of cold water, the lemon juice, salt, and pepper and cook, stirring occasionally, over medium heat until the apples are soft and light golden brown, about 10 minutes.

Transfer the apple mixture to the blender with the butter and blend until smooth. Serve warm. The apple puree can be made up to 1 day in advance and stored tightly covered in the refrigerator. Reheat over low heat before serving.

MAKES 2 CUPS (480 ML)

FRIED SHALLOTS

CRISPY, SALTY, AND SWEET. THESE TOP MY WEDGE SALAD (PAGE 183) at BarBacon, and I also love them on top of burgers or just as a snack with cocktails. Strain the oil that you use to fry the shallots and use it to cook another dish or to make a vinaigrette. They will keep for a few days at room temperature.

2 cups (480 ml) canola oil

4 large shallots, sliced crosswise into rounds ⅛ inch (3 mm) thick, rings separated

1 cup (240 ml) shaken buttermilk

Kosher salt and freshly ground black pepper

1 cup (125 g) all-purpose flour

In a medium saucepan, heat the oil to 300°F (150°C) on a deep-fry thermometer. Line a baking sheet with several layers of paper towels.

While the oil is heating, put the shallots in a large bowl, add the buttermilk, ½ teaspoon salt, and a pinch of pepper, and stir to make sure each one is coated in the milk. Drain the shallots.

Put the flour in a shallow baking dish and season with ½ teaspoon salt and a pinch of black pepper. Dredge the shallots, working in batches, in the flour and tap off any excess. Fry, in batches, until golden brown, about 2 minutes. Using a spider or slotted spoon, remove and drain on the prepared baking sheet. Season lightly with a bit more salt before serving.

**MAKES ABOUT
2 CUPS (230 G)**

PINEAPPLE-JALAPEÑO COLESLAW

THIS IS A GREAT SWEET AND SPICY SIDE THAT IS SERVED ALONGSIDE many sandwiches at BB. It goes with almost anything while still being light and refreshing. The spiciness of the jalapeños varies considerably from batch to batch, but luckily the pineapple more than makes up for any level of heat coming through. I recommend always having this on hand if you are making any kind of BBQ.

¾ cup (180 ml) mayonnaise

2 tablespoons sugar

2 tablespoons rice vinegar

2 teaspoons kosher salt

½ teaspoon freshly ground black pepper

1 pound (455 g) bag coleslaw mix

2 cups (330 g) finely diced fresh pineapple

1 small jalapeño, halved and thinly sliced crosswise

1 small red onion, halved and thinly sliced

In a large bowl, whisk together the mayonnaise, sugar, vinegar, salt, and pepper until combined.

Add the coleslaw mix, pineapple, jalapeño, and onion and mix until combined. Cover and refrigerate for at least 30 minutes, or up to 8 hours before serving.

SERVES 4 TO 6

PICO DE GALLO

I AM ALWAYS SHOCKED THAT PEOPLE BUY STORE-BOUGHT VERSIONS of pico de gallo when it is so easy to make it at home. The key to a really great relish is using tomatoes that are overripe and flavorful.

2 pounds (910 g) tomatoes (8 plum or 3 large beefsteak), seeded and chopped

1 or 2 jalapeño or serrano chiles, finely chopped

½ white onion, finely chopped

Juice of 1 lime

1 teaspoon kosher salt

¼ teaspoon freshly ground black pepper

¼ cup (10 g) chopped fresh cilantro

In a medium bowl, combine the tomatoes, chile, onion, lime juice, salt, and black pepper. Fold in the cilantro and let sit at room temperature for at least 15 minutes before serving to allow the flavors to meld. The relish will keep, tightly covered in the refrigerator, for up to 3 days.

MAKES ABOUT 4 CUPS (960 G)

BARBACON GUACAMOLE

YES, GUACAMOLE MADE IT INTO THE "HOLD THE BACON" CHAPTER, but that doesn't mean that you can't add bacon to yours. We certainly do at the restaurant. It's sprinkled right on top so it doesn't lose its crunch. I included a BLT variation too!

3 large ripe Hass avocados, peeled and pitted

½ small red onion, finely diced

1 large jalapeño, finely diced

Juice of 2 limes

Kosher salt and freshly ground black pepper

¼ cup (10 g) finely chopped fresh cilantro leaves

Scoop the avocados into a bowl. Add the onion, jalapeño, lime juice, and salt and pepper to taste and coarsely mash with a fork. Fold in the cilantro and serve immediately.

MAKES ABOUT 1 QUART (907 G)

VARIATION

For BLT Guacamole, fold in 1 seeded and diced plum tomato and 4 slices crisp cooked bacon (see page 44), coarsely chopped.

BREAD AND BUTTER PICKLES

BREAD AND BUTTER PICKLES REALLY ARE A HAPPY MARRIAGE OF sweet and tangy flavors thanks to hearty doses of sugar and cider vinegar. I serve these pickles on the side of every sandwich at BarBacon, and they really are one of my favorite things to make and eat.

4½ cups (about 1 pound/ 455 g) thinly sliced (about ¼-inch/6-mm) Kirby cucumbers

1 small sweet onion, halved and thinly sliced

1½ tablespoons kosher salt

12 ice cubes

2 cups (480 ml) apple cider vinegar

1 cup (200 g) sugar

1½ teaspoons mustard seeds

½ teaspoon celery seeds

⅛ teaspoon ground turmeric

In a large bowl, combine the cucumbers, onion, salt, and ice cubes and let sit at room temperature for 2 hours. Transfer the cucumber mixture to a colander and rinse thoroughly under cold water. Drain well and return to the bowl.

Put the vinegar, sugar, mustard seeds, celery seeds, and turmeric in a medium saucepan and bring to a simmer over medium heat, stirring until the sugar dissolves, about 3 minutes. Pour the hot vinegar mixture over cucumber mixture; let stand at room temperature for 1 hour. Cover and refrigerate for 24 hours. The pickles will keep, in an airtight container in the refrigerator, for up to 1 month.

**MAKES ABOUT
1 QUART (1 L)**

BREAD AND BUTTER RELISH

THIS RECIPE IS SO EASY. I JUST TOSS OUR BREAD AND BUTTER PICK-les into a food processor and pulse a few times for a quick pickle relish. Our house-made B&B pickles are great served as slices on a burger or chopped up and slathered on a hot dog.

Bread and Butter Pickles
(page 276)

Drain the pickles, reserving the pickling liquid, and put the pickles in a food processor. Pulse a few times until coarsely chopped. Add a few tablespoons of the liquid and pulse again until you reach the texture of pickle relish.

MAKES ABOUT
3 CUPS (709 G)

FRESNO CHILE JAM

THE FRESNO CHILE IS STILL A RELATIVELY UNSUNG HERO IN THE chile world, but I am hoping to change that. It is similar in color and appearance to the red jalapeño, but the flavor is a bit milder and fruitier. I love using them fresh in soups and stews and pickled in jams and relishes.

1 pound (455 g) Fresno chiles, stems and seeds removed (25 to 30 chiles)

2 cups (480 ml) apple cider vinegar

½ cup (100 g) sugar

2 teaspoons kosher salt

Put the chiles in a food processor and pulse a few times until minced.

Combine the vinegar, sugar, salt, and minced chiles in a small saucepan over high heat and bring to a boil. Lower the heat to medium and continue cooking, stirring occasionally so the bottom does not scorch, until the mixture is reduced by half and has become jam-like, about 30 minutes.

Transfer the jam to a bowl and let cool to room temperature. Cover and refrigerate until cold. The jam will keep, tightly covered in the refrigerator, for up to 2 weeks.

MAKES ABOUT 1 CUP (240 ML)

SPICY RELISH

WHAT HAPPENS WHEN YOU COMBINE BARBACON'S HOMEMADE
Bread and Butter Pickles (page 276) and BarBacon's Fresno Chile Jam (page 279)?
You get this relish, which is great slathered over just about anything, especially the
Sonoran Hot Dog (page 218).

1 recipe Fresno Chile Jam
(page 279)

1 recipe Bread and Butter
Relish (page 278)

In a large bowl, combine the
jam and relish. Cover and
refrigerate for at least 30
minutes to allow the flavors
to meld. The relish will keep,
tightly covered in the refrigerator, for up to 1 month.

**MAKES ABOUT
5 CUPS (1.2 L)**

HOT ITALIAN PICKLES (GIARDINIERA)

I ALWAYS HAVE QUARTS OF GIARDINIERA IN MY REFRIGERATOR AT the restaurant and at home. This ultimate pickled vegetable salad may hail from Chicago, but is very at home at BarBacon on my Italian Grilled Cheese sandwich (page 214).

3 quarts (2.8 L) cold water

½ cup (90 g) Diamond Crystal kosher salt

2 red bell peppers, seeded and diced

2 poblano chiles, seeded and diced

5 jalapeño chiles, halved, seeded, and sliced

1 Spanish onion, diced

2 carrots, peeled and cut into ¼-inch (6-mm) coins

3 ribs celery, cut crosswise into ¼-inch (6-mm) slices

1 small head cauliflower, separated into small florets

1 cup (155 g) sliced green olives

5 cups (1.2 L) distilled white vinegar

4 garlic cloves, finely chopped

2 teaspoons freshly ground black pepper

1 teaspoon dried oregano

1 teaspoon red chile flakes

2 cups (480 ml) olive oil

In a large bowl, whisk together the cold water and salt until the salt dissolves. Add the bell peppers, both chiles, onion, carrots, celery, and cauliflower. Place a plate on top to make sure that the vegetables are submerged. Cover with plastic wrap and refrigerate for at least 8 hours, or up to 24 hours. Drain well. Return to the bowl and stir in the olives.

In a large nonreactive saucepan, combine the vinegar, garlic, black pepper, oregano, and chile flakes and bring to a boil over high heat. Remove from the heat and whisk in the oil. Pour the mixture over the vegetables and let cool to room temperature, then cover and refrigerate for at least 8 hours, or up to 24 hours before serving. The relish will keep, tightly covered in the refrigerator, for up to 2 weeks.

MAKES 2 QUARTS (1.9 L)

PICKLED THAI CHILES

PICKLED CHILES ARE A VERSATILE PANTRY STAPLE, AND THEY CAN be used to add a kick to just about anything: eggs, vinaigrettes, dipping sauces, and one of my favorite recipes in this book, Thai Noodle Salad with Bacon, Chiles, and Basil (page 192). They will keep for weeks, properly stored, in the refrigerator, and they take all of five minutes to make. I remove them from the brine and thinly slice crosswise before serving.

2 cups (480 ml) distilled white vinegar

½ cup (100 g) sugar

2 teaspoons kosher salt

4 ounces (115 g) fresh red Thai chiles (about 35), stems removed, rinsed well in cold water, and patted dry

In a small nonreactive saucepan, combine the vinegar, 1 cup (240 ml) water, the sugar, and salt and bring to a boil over high heat. Cook until the sugar and salt are dissolved, about 3 minutes. Remove from the heat and let cool for 5 minutes.

Put the chiles in a glass jar with a tight-fitting lid or a nonreactive container with a lid. Pour the warm vinegar mixture over them, seal the jar, and refrigerate for at least 1 hour and preferably 24 hours before using. The pickled chiles will keep, in an airtight container in the refrigerator, for up to 3 months.

MAKES ABOUT 35

PICKLED FENNEL

I JUST LOVE THE CRUNCH AND TARTNESS THAT PICKLED FENNEL adds to any pork dish. Anyone that loves spicy Italian sausage should love fennel— it's the crunchy seed that is packing that sausage with so much flavor.

3 cups (720 ml) champagne vinegar

½ cup (100 g) sugar

2 teaspoons kosher salt

1 teaspoon coriander seeds, lightly toasted

1 teaspoon fennel seeds, lightly toasted (see Note)

1 teaspoon red chile flakes

3 small fennel bulbs, trimmed, cored, and cut lengthwise into ¼-inch (6-mm) slices

In a medium-size nonreactive saucepan, combine the vinegar, 1¼ cups (300 ml) water, the sugar, salt, coriander, fennel seeds, and chile flakes and bring to a boil over high heat. Cook until the sugar and salt have dissolved, about 3 minutes.

Put the fennel in a 3-quart (3-L) nonreactive container with a tight-fitting lid and pour the pickling liquid over it, making sure that the fennel is totally submerged. Cover and refrigerate for at least 4 hours before serving. The pickled fennel will keep, tightly covered in the refrigerator, for up to 7 days.

NOTE: *To toast fennel seeds: Put fennel seeds in a small pan over low heat and cook, shaking the pan several times, until the seeds become fragrant, about 5 minutes.*

MAKES ABOUT 1 QUART (1 L)

PICKLED JALAPEÑO SALAD

I LOVE SERVING THIS ON THE SIDE WITH A RICH, FATTY SLAB OF bacon or tossing all the ingredients into a food processor, adding a cup of cilantro leaves, and making a chimichurri that will rock your world.

2 tablespoons extra-virgin olive oil

1 large carrot, peeled and cut into matchstick strips

1 small red onion, halved and thinly sliced

5 large jalapeños, stems removed, halved, and each half sliced lengthwise into 3 pieces

2 garlic cloves, smashed

3 cups (720 ml) distilled white vinegar

1½ tablespoons kosher salt

1 heaping tablespoon sugar

3 sprigs fresh thyme

¼ teaspoon dried oregano

1 bay leaf

In a medium-size nonreactive saucepan, heat the oil over medium heat. Add the carrot, onion, jalapeños, and garlic and cook, stirring occasionally, until soft, about 7 minutes.

Add the vinegar, salt, sugar, thyme, oregano, and bay leaf and bring to a boil. Cook until the sugar and salt have dissolved, about 2 minutes. Remove from the heat and let cool. Transfer to a nonreactive container with a tight-fitting lid and refrigerate for at least 8 hours before eating. The salad will keep, tightly covered in the refrigerator, for up to 5 days.

MAKES 2 CUPS (500 G)

TOMATO CONFIT

I HAVE A LOVE-HATE RELATIONSHIP WITH THESE TOMATOES. I LOVE them because they are just the best tomato you'll ever eat. Concentrated flavor, sweet and a little tart with a hint of thyme . . . so damn good. Too good! Which is why I hate them. They are bit on the labor-intensive side, and even if you make a ton, you still end up going through them quickly because you'll want to put them on everything. Some of my favorite ways to use them are in my Wedge Salad (page 183), Skillet Pasta Carbonara (page 261), and BLT Panzanella (page 184).

Ice water

12 Roma tomatoes

1 cup (240 ml) extra-virgin olive oil, divided

3 garlic cloves, thinly sliced

2 tablespoons fresh thyme leaves

1 tablespoon confectioners' sugar

2 teaspoons kosher salt

Preheat the oven to 200°F (93°C). Line a half sheet pan with a Silpat or parchment paper.

Bring a large pot of water to a boil. Fill a large bowl with ice water. Cut a small X on the bottom of each tomato.

Put the tomatoes in the boiling water and cook until the skin just begins to wrinkle, about 20 seconds. Plunge into the ice water and let sit until cold. Remove the skin from the tomatoes, halve them lengthwise, and remove the seeds. Put on the prepared baking sheet, cut-side up.

In a small bowl, whisk together ⅓ (75 ml) of the oil, the garlic, and thyme and evenly spoon the mixture over the tomato halves. Sift the sugar over the tomatoes and sprinkle with the salt. Bake the tomatoes for about 3 hours, until shriveled and dry but with a little juice left inside. (This could take more or less time depending on the size of your tomatoes. Begin checking after 1½ hours.)

Let the tomatoes cool to room temperature, then transfer to a bowl or jar with a tight-fitting lid. Cover the tomatoes with the remaining olive oil and the oil left from the baking sheet and refrigerate for up to 2 weeks. You can use the tomato oil to cook scrambled eggs or to create a simple tomato vinaigrette with a splash of balsamic, if desired.

MAKES 24

PIPERADE

THIS GARLICKY, PIQUANT SAUCE—OR COOKED RELISH, IF YOU WILL— hails from the Basque region of Spain, where it is served with ham or grilled seafood or other meat. At the restaurant, I stir it into Sweet Potato Hash (page 328).

¼ cup (60 ml) extra-virgin olive oil

10 garlic cloves, thinly sliced

1 Thai chile, thinly sliced

8 roasted red peppers, thinly sliced (see Note)

2 cups (480 ml) tomato juice

Kosher salt

12 fresh basil leaves, coarsely chopped (optional)

1 teaspoon finely chopped fresh oregano leaves (optional)

Heat the oil in a large, deep sauté pan over low heat. Add the garlic and cook, stirring several times, until lightly golden brown, about 5 minutes. Add the chile and cook for 30 seconds.

Increase the heat to high, add the red peppers, and cook, stirring occasionally, until their liquid evaporates, about 10 minutes.

Add the tomato juice and bring to a boil. Lower the heat to medium and cook, stirring occasionally, until the mixture thickens, about 20 minutes. Remove from the heat, season with salt to taste, and add the herbs (if using). Serve hot or at room temperature. The cooled sauce will keep, tightly covered in the refrigerator, for up to 3 days.

NOTE: *You can use prepared roasted red peppers from a jar. If you do, just drain well before using. If making from scratch, preheat the oven to 400°F (205°C). Place the red bell peppers on a baking sheet and drizzle with canola oil and season with salt and pepper. Roast until blistered and soft, turning a few times, about 25 minutes. Remove to a bowl, cover the top of the bowl with plastic wrap, and let the peppers steam for 15 minutes. Remove the skins, stems, and seeds and thinly slice into matchstick strips.*

MAKES 1 QUART (1 L)

TABBOULEH

THIS SUPER-FRESH MIDDLE EASTERN SALAD IS FULL OF CITRUS AND herbaceous goodness. It's the perfect side dish for anything that contains bacon. And for the vegetarians in your life, it is really great just eaten with a fork or wrapped in a lettuce leaf with a few crumbles of feta cheese. This is one of those salads that gets better and better the longer it sits.

½ cup (120 ml) extra-virgin olive oil

½ cup (120 ml) fresh lemon juice (from 3 to 4 lemons)

2 garlic cloves, finely chopped

Kosher salt and freshly ground black pepper

2 cups (100 g) finely chopped fresh flat-leaf parsley

2 cups (80 g) finely chopped fresh cilantro leaves

1 cup (50 g) finely chopped fresh mint leaves

1 small red bell pepper, finely diced

1 small yellow bell pepper, finely diced

1 small green bell pepper, finely diced

1 small rib celery, finely diced

1 small English cucumber, peeled, seeded, and finely diced

1 small red onion, finely diced

3 tablespoons instant couscous

5 lemon segments, finely diced

In a large bowl, whisk together the oil, lemon juice, and garlic and season well with salt and black pepper. Add the parsley, cilantro, mint, three types of bell peppers, celery, cucumber, onion, and couscous and toss well to combine. Cover and refrigerate overnight. The couscous will bloom and become soft from the juices of the vegetables.

Remove from the refrigerator and season with salt and pepper to taste. Stir in the lemon segments right before serving. Enjoy cold or at room temperature.

SERVES 6 TO 8

TOASTED CUMIN SLAW

CUMIN IS USED A LOT IN MIDDLE EASTERN AND MEXICAN COOKING, but I think it is still an underutilized spice in American cooking. I love its earthy flavor in everything from marinades and dressings to spice rubs.

1 tablespoon cumin seeds

1 tablespoon canola oil

2 cups (290 g) fresh corn kernels (from about 3 ears)

Kosher salt and freshly ground black pepper

¾ cup (180 ml) apple cider vinegar

¼ cup (60 ml) light agave nectar or clover honey

1 small head red cabbage (about 2 pounds/910 g), cored and finely shredded

¼ cup (10 g) chopped fresh cilantro leaves

Juice of 2 limes

In a small sauté pan, toast the cumin seeds, stirring occasionally, until fragrant, about 3 minutes. Transfer to a small bowl.

Heat the oil in the same pan over high heat until it begins to shimmer. Add the corn, season with salt and pepper, and cook until lightly toasted and heated through, about 5 minutes. Remove the corn to a plate.

In a large bowl, combine the cumin, vinegar, and agave. Add the cabbage, cilantro, and corn and toss to coat. Taste for seasoning.

Add the lime juice and salt and pepper to taste and toss to combine. Cover and refrigerate for at least 30 minutes, or up to 8 hours to allow the flavors to meld and the cabbage to wilt.

SERVES 4 TO 6

GRILLED CORN SUCCOTASH

WITH OR WITHOUT BACON, THIS SCREAMS SUMMER WITH ITS sweet corn fresh off the cob, tomatoes at their peak of ripeness, and verdant cilantro (you could also use basil or parsley). It is perfect on its own as a light summer salad or eaten alongside any grilled meat or fish. If you are so inclined, add bacon, which makes it even more delicious but is totally optional.

Kosher salt

9 ears fresh corn, shucked and silks removed

6 tablespoons (90 ml) canola oil

Freshly ground black pepper

1 small red onion, peeled and sliced into ¼-inch (6-mm) rounds

1 small red bell pepper, finely diced

2 garlic cloves, finely chopped

1 jalapeño, finely diced

1 large plum or beefsteak tomato, halved, seeded, and finely diced

2 tablespoons soft unsalted butter

¼ cup (10 g) chopped fresh cilantro leaves

6 slices crisp cooked bacon (see page 44), finely diced (optional)

Heat a grill to high or a grill pan over high heat. Bring a large pot of salted water to a boil, add the corn, and blanch for 1 minute. Drain well, brush the cobs with 2 tablespoons of the oil, and season with salt and black pepper. Brush the onion slices on both sides with 2 tablespoons of the oil and season with salt and pepper.

Grill the corn until charred on all sides, about 2 minutes. Let cool slightly, then cut off the kernels and place them in a bowl. Grill the onions until soft and slightly charred on both sides, about 4 minutes per side. Coarsely chop them and add to the bowl with the corn.

In large sauté pan, heat the remaining 2 tablespoons oil, add the bell pepper, and cook until soft, about 4 minutes. Add the garlic and jalapeño and cook for 30 seconds. Add the corn mixture and tomato and cook until warmed through and the tomato softens slightly, about 4 minutes. Stir in the butter and cook until melted. Remove from the heat, add the cilantro and bacon (if using), and taste for seasoning. Serve hot. The succotash can be made 1 day in advance and refrigerated, tightly covered. Reheat over low heat in a sauté pan.

SERVES 4

SOUTHERN POTATO SALAD

A SHERMAN FAMILY FAVORITE THAT I HAVE BEEN EATING AT EVERY summer outdoor celebration and making since I was a kid. Be sure to dress the potatoes while they are still warm so they can absorb the dressing.

1½ pounds (680 g) Red Bliss potatoes (about 6), scrubbed

Cold water

Kosher salt

1 cup (240 ml) mayonnaise

½ cup (120 ml) sour cream

1 tablespoon apple cider vinegar

1 teaspoon sugar

½ teaspoon celery seeds

½ teaspoon mustard powder

¼ teaspoon smoked paprika

¼ teaspoon ground white pepper

1 large rib celery, finely diced

1 small red onion, finely diced

5 hard-boiled eggs (see page 189), peeled and finely chopped

1 teaspoon Magic Rub (page 94)

12 Bread and Butter Pickles (page 276), chopped

In a large saucepan, cover the potatoes with cold water by 2 inches (5 cm). Add 2 tablespoons salt, bring to a boil, and cook until a skewer inserted into the center of a potato meets with no resistance, about 30 minutes. Drain well and let sit until just cool enough to handle (but still warm), about 10 minutes. Cut into 1-inch (2.5-cm) cubes.

While the potatoes are cooling, whisk together the mayonnaise, sour cream, vinegar, 1 teaspoon salt, the sugar, celery seeds, mustard powder, paprika, and white pepper in a large bowl until smooth. Fold in the celery, onion, and eggs.

Fold in the potatoes (while still warm) until incorporated and taste for seasoning, adding more salt or white pepper, if needed. Sprinkle the rub over the top and garnish with chopped pickles. Serve immediately or cover and refrigerate until ready to eat, up to 24 hours.

SERVES 4 TO 6

ROSEMARY MASHED POTATOES

IT IS RARE THAT I SERVE ANY BRAISED MEAT WITHOUT THIS SIDE.
Mashed potatoes, when done well, are hard to beat. I used to make these with rosemary sprigs, but they are really unpalatable. Instead, infusing the cream with rosemary keeps the smooth potato texture intact. I also often add roasted garlic to the mix, but that is totally optional. The real key here is to use far more butter than you might have ever considered before.

7 large Idaho potatoes (about 3½ pounds/1.5 kg), scrubbed

2 cups (480 ml) heavy cream

5 sprigs fresh rosemary

2 cups (455 g) unsalted butter, cut into small cubes

Kosher salt and freshly ground black pepper

Preheat the oven to 425°F (220°C). Using a fork, prick the entire surface of the potatoes, then put them on a baking sheet a few inches apart. Bake until a skewer inserted into the center of a potato meets with no resistance, about 1 hour. Let cool for 10 minutes.

While the potatoes are baking, combine the cream and rosemary in a medium pot. Bring to a boil, remove from the heat, cover, and let sit until the potatoes are done, about 1 hour.

Reheat the cream over low heat until just warm, about 5 minutes. Remove the rosemary stems and discard. Halve the potatoes lengthwise and scoop out the flesh; discard the peels. Pass the potatoes through a ricer (in batches) or a food mill set over a large bowl. Add the warm cream, and mix with a whisk until the cream is incorporated. Begin adding the butter a handful of pieces at a time, whisking until fully incorporated. Season with salt and pepper. Serve immediately, or place the bowl over a large pot filled with a few inches of simmering water to keep warm until ready to serve.

SERVES 4 TO 6

SPICY CANDIED WALNUTS

THIS VERY SIMPLE, BASIC RECIPE FOR CANDIED NUTS CAN BECOME A snack or a topping for a salad in less time than it would take you to drive to the store to buy them. You can substitute pecans, hazelnuts, even peanuts. I call for a pinch of cayenne, which technically is about ⅛ teaspoon, but feel free to add a bit more if you like spicy.

2 tablespoons unsalted butter

½ cup (100 g) sugar

Pinch of ground cayenne

2 cups (240 g) chopped walnuts

Line a baking sheet with a Silpat or parchment paper.

In a medium nonstick sauté pan, combine the butter, sugar, and cayenne and cook over high heat until the butter and sugar have melted, about 3 minutes. Add the walnuts and cook, stirring constantly, until the nuts are coated and slightly caramelized, about 5 minutes.

Transfer the nuts immediately to the prepared baking sheet. Using two forks, quickly separate the nuts. Let cool at room temperature until hardened, about 10 minutes. The candied walnuts will keep, in an airtight container at room temperature, for up to 1 week.

MAKES 2 CUPS (240 G)

FRIED SPICED CANDIED PECANS

ALL AROUND NEW YORK CITY YOU WILL FIND THESE CARTS THAT sell candied nuts that have been deep-fried to crispy perfection. I used to buy bags of them on my way to one of the many kitchen jobs that I had before I owned BarBacon. Now, I make my own, and in addition to snacking on them and washing them down with a cocktail, I use them in salads, main dishes, and desserts.

3½ cups (700 g) plus ¼ cup (50 g) sugar

½ teaspoon ground cayenne

4 cups (400 g) pecan halves

2 teaspoons kosher salt

4 cups (960 ml) canola oil

Line a sheet pan with parchment paper or a Silpat. In a large saucepan, combine 3½ cups (700 g) of the sugar, ¼ teaspoon of the cayenne, and 3 cups (720 ml) water and bring to a boil over high heat. Cook until the sugar has completely disolved, about 5 minutes. Add the pecans and continue cooking over high heat for 5 minutes. Using a slotted spoon, carefully remove the pecans and transfer to the prepared sheet pan in an even layer. Let cool at room temperature for about 20 minutes.

In a large bowl, combine the remaining ¼ cup (50 g) sugar, ¼ teaspoon cayenne, and the salt.

Heat the oil in a large Dutch oven over medium heat until it reaches 325°F (165°C) on a deep-fry thermometer. Line a sheet pan with paper towels.

Fry the pecans, in batches, stirring constantly with a spider or metal slotted spoon, until deep golden brown, not burnt, 3 to 5 minutes. Remove with a slotted spoon to the prepared sheet pan to drain for a few minutes, then while still warm, toss in the sugar mixture. Let cool completely. Store in a container with a tight-fitting lid at room temperature for up to 5 days.

MAKES 4 CUPS (400 G)

CHAPTER 11

BREAKFAST & BRUNCH

HE FIRST THING PEOPLE ASK ABOUT WHEN I tell them about BarBacon is brunch. They ask about basics: bacon and eggs, or bacon, egg, and cheese sandwiches. What they don't know is how versatile bacon is in breakfast and brunch. I've come up with some unique ways to not just eat bacon *with* breakfast and brunch, but to eat bacon in every part of breakfast and brunch.

One of the first things I thought would be cool to play with was bacon fat. I wanted to see if it would work in a cornbread recipe (page 301), so I replaced some of the fat with bourbon bacon fat. It's amazing. It's moist and delicious, and the bacon adds just enough smoke to balance the bourbon. It's not brunch without a little hair of the dog, right?

From there, I wanted to see if I could work it into pancakes. Instead of just adding fat this time, I went all out. I made a bacon granola (!!) and added that to the pancakes (page 303). They're insane. I go into a coma after just a few bites, but I wouldn't have it any other way.

Of course bacon is also perfect for savory dishes, too. After playing around with taco recipes one morning, I had a ton of leftover tortillas hanging around. I decided to fry them up and make myself some huevos rancheros (page 312). How did I add bacon, you ask? I chopped and ground up some bacon, added it to my basic chili recipe . . . and then ladled it over the whole thing. I love a good traditional red salsa with eggs, but that bacon chili just puts these over the top.

Try out some of the recipes in this chapter, and you'll learn just how much you can do with bacon before 2 PM.

BACON GRANOLA

YOU MAY THINK THAT GRANOLA IS HEALTHY, BUT IF YOU REALLY study the label, you will find it is anything but. And, since I am not in the business of healthy eating, I wasn't about to create a healthy version, either. My motto is everything in moderation, but I dare you to just eat a small amount of this. Try adding some to pancakes or simply sprinkling it over yogurt and fruit with mint and a drizzle of honey.

2 teaspoons canola oil

6 thin slices bacon

1 cup (240 ml) clover honey

¼ cup (60 ml) plus 2 table-spoons pure maple syrup

¼ cup (55 g) light brown sugar

½ cup (120 ml) vegetable oil

1½ tablespoons ground cinnamon

1½ tablespoons pure vanilla extract

½ teaspoon kosher salt

4¼ cups (405 g) rolled oats (not quick cooking)

¾ cup (70 g) sliced almonds

¾ cup (90 g) chopped pecans

¼ cup (35 g) hulled sunflower seeds

Preheat the oven to 300°F (150°C). Heat the oil in a large sauté pan over medium heat, add the bacon, and cook until golden brown and crispy on both sides, about 8 minutes. Remove to a plate lined with paper towels to cool slightly, then coarsely chop. Reserve ¼ cup (60 ml) of the rendered bacon fat.

In a medium saucepan over high heat, cook the honey, maple syrup, brown sugar, vegetable oil, reserved bacon fat, and cinnamon, whisking occasionally, until smooth and the sugar has dissolved, about 5 minutes. Remove from the heat and whisk in the vanilla and salt.

Line a half sheet pan with parchment paper or spray with nonstick spray. While the honey mixture is cooking, combine the oats, almonds, pecans, sunflower seeds, and chopped bacon in a large bowl. Pour the honey mixture over and mix well to combine. Spread the mixture onto the prepared baking sheet (or two sheets if needed) in an even layer. Bake for 20 minutes, then stir and bake for another 10 to 15 minutes, until light golden brown. Let cool on a wire rack for about 15 minutes.

Store the granola in containers with tight-fitting lids in a cool, dry place. The granola will keep for up to 1 week.

MAKES 8 CUPS (975 G)

BACON GRANOLA "TREATS" WITH CHOCOLATE CHIPS

THESE ARE MY PICK-ME-UPS WHEN I NEED A BIT OF ENERGY WHILE working the line at BB or after a workout or when I don't have time for a proper breakfast in the morning. These will also be the star of your kid's lunchbox, and you will be the apple of your kid's eye. Pack extra so he/she can sell them and make some money.

3 tablespoons unsalted butter

1 (16-ounce/455-g) bag large marshmallows

4 cups (485 g) Bacon Granola (page 298)

1 cup (175 g) milk chocolate or semisweet chocolate chips

Spray a 9 by 13-inch (23 by 33-cm) baking dish lightly with nonstick spray. Set aside.

Melt the butter in a large pot (nonstick, if possible) over medium heat. Stir in the marshmallows and cook, stirring occasionally, until completely melted, about 7 minutes.

Remove from the heat, fold in the granola and chocolate chips, and mix until completely incorporated. Scrape the mixture into the prepared dish, pressing down slightly until the top is even. Let sit for 15 minutes, then cut into bars. The bars will keep, tightly covered, for up to 3 days.

MAKES 16 SMALL OR 12 LARGE

BACON AND BOURBON CORNBREAD

THIS WAS THE FIRST THING I MADE AFTER MY REVELATION THAT the bacon fat I used to flavor the bourbon for the bar cocktails was also getting flavored with bourbon. I simply replaced the butter in my favorite cornbread recipe with the bourbon bacon fat and was floored by how much bourbon flavor was picked up. Serve with the Blueberry-Bacon Jam on page 319.

1 cup (180 g) fine yellow cornmeal

¾ cup (150 g) sugar

½ cup (65 g) all-purpose flour

¾ teaspoon baking powder

⅛ teaspoon baking soda

½ teaspoon kosher salt

½ cup (120 ml) cold shaken buttermilk

¼ cup (60 ml) bourbon bacon fat (page 100), melted and cooled; or ¼ cup (60 ml) rendered bacon fat plus 1 tablespoon bourbon

1 large egg, separated

1 teaspoon pure vanilla extract

6 thin slices bacon, chopped

Preheat the oven to 350°F (175°C). In a medium bowl, whisk together the cornmeal, sugar, flour, baking powder, baking soda, and salt. Add the buttermilk, bacon fat, egg yolk, and vanilla and whisk to combine.

In a separate bowl, with a clean whisk, whip the egg white until it holds soft peaks. Fold the egg white into the cornmeal mixture until just combined.

Put an 8-inch (20-cm) cast-iron pan over medium heat, add the bacon, and cook until the bacon fat has rendered and the bacon is just starting to pick up color, about 6 minutes. The bacon will continue to cook in the oven. (You want a lot of rendered fat here: The key to a great crispy crust is having a very hot pan and a good amount of fat.)

Scrape the batter into the pan over the bacon and place in the oven. Bake until the top is golden brown and a toothpick inserted into the center comes out with a few moist crumbs attached, 20 to 25 minutes. Let cool on a wire rack for about 10 minutes, then cut into wedges and serve warm.

MAKES 1 (8-INCH/20-CM) ROUND CORNBREAD

BOURBON-BACON-OATMEAL PANCAKES

THE ADDITION OF OATS TO A BASIC PANCAKE RECIPE IS AN EASY WAY to add protein and fiber and start your day off on the right note. The addition of bourbon to the batter? That makes you look forward to the day. For a double infusion of oats and additional texture, I love adding a few handfuls of Bacon Granola (page 298) to the mix on occasion, too (see Variation below). Being healthy never felt so easy.

1¼ cups (155 g) all-purpose flour

⅓ cup (30 g) rolled oats (not quick cooking)

2 teaspoons baking powder

1 teaspoon baking soda

1 teaspoon kosher salt

1 teaspoon ground cinnamon

2 large eggs

¼ cup (60 ml) plus 1 tablespoon bourbon bacon fat (page 100), melted and slightly cooled; or ¼ cup (60 ml) rendered bacon fat plus 1 tablespoon bourbon

¼ cup (55 g) plus 1 tablespoon light brown sugar

2 tablespoons clover honey

1 cup (240 ml) cold shaken buttermilk

Butter, plus more for serving, or nonstick cooking spray

Maple syrup

In a large bowl, whisk together the flour, oats, baking powder, baking soda, salt, and cinnamon.

In a medium bowl, whisk together the eggs, bacon fat, brown sugar, honey, and buttermilk. Add the wet ingredients to the dry ingredients and mix until just combined (lumps are okay). Cover and let the batter sit for 30 minutes.

Preheat the oven to 200°F (93°C). Heat a griddle or cast-iron pan over medium heat and brush with butter or spray with nonstick spray. Working in batches, pour the batter onto the griddle by ¼-cup (60-ml) measures and cook the pancakes until golden brown on both sides, about 2 minutes per side. Repeat with the remaining batter, brushing the griddle with more butter or spraying with more nonstick spray as needed. Transfer the pancakes as they are cooked to a heatproof platter and keep them warm in the oven.

Serve with butter and maple syrup.

VARIATION

To make Bourbon Granola Pancakes: Sprinkle a healthy amount of Bacon Granola (page 298) on each pancake before flipping them on the griddle.

MAKES 12 TO 15

BREAD PUDDING FRENCH TOAST
with Bacon and Rosemary-Orange Maple Syrup

THIS BREAKFAST BREAD PUDDING IS REALLY A PERFECT COMBINA-
tion of savory and sweet. It has all the sweet goodness that sugar and orange and
vanilla bring to any dish with a good dose of savory courtesy of rosemary, fennel,
and bacon. It sounds like a lot going on, and it is, but it all seems to work—and
work very well. If you prefer your French toast made with brioche or challah, feel
free to use either and just add ⅓ cup (35 g) golden raisins and ¼ teaspoon ground
fennel seeds to the egg mixture.

1 loaf semolina–golden
raisin bread, cut into 1-inch
(2.5-cm) cubes

7 large eggs

2 cups (400 g) sugar

2 cups (480 ml) whole milk

2 cups (480 ml) heavy cream

2 teaspoons finely grated
orange zest

2 teaspoons pure vanilla extract

8 thin slices bacon, cooked
until crisp (see page 44),
finely chopped

Rosemary-Orange Maple
Syrup (page 306)

Confectioners' sugar,
for serving (optional)

Preheat the oven to 300°F
(150°C). Spread the bread in a
single layer on a baking sheet
and toast in the oven until a
pale golden blond color, turning once, about 12 minutes.
Remove from the oven and let
cool slightly. Increase the oven
temperature to 350°F (175°C).

Grease a 9 by 13-inch (23
by 33-cm) baking dish with
butter or nonstick spray. In a
large bowl, whisk together the
eggs and sugar. Add the milk,
cream, orange zest, and vanilla
and whisk until smooth. Stir
in the bacon. Add the bread
to the custard mixture and
stir well to combine. Let the
mixture sit, stirring a few more
times, for 20 minutes, or until
the bread has absorbed all of
the liquid.

Transfer the bread mixture to
the prepared pan, cover with
aluminum foil, and bake for 45
minutes. Remove the foil and
continue baking until puffed
and the top is golden brown,
about 30 minutes longer. Cut
into squares and serve with the
rosemary-orange maple syrup
and a sprinkle of confectioners'
sugar.

SERVES 6 TO 8

ROSEMARY-ORANGE MAPLE SYRUP

1 cup (240 ml) pure maple syrup, preferably Grade B

Zest of 1 large navel orange (see Note)

3 sprigs fresh rosemary

In a small saucepan, combine the syrup, zest, and rosemary and bring to a simmer over low heat. Cover, remove from the heat, and let steep for 30 minutes. Remove the zest and rosemary and reheat before serving, if needed.

NOTE: *To zest an orange, use moderate pressure, so as not to remove any pith, and drag a vegetable peeler down the fruit, from top to bottom or around the fruit.*

MAKES 1 CUP (240 ML)

BREAKFAST BREAD PUDDING MUFFINS

THESE SAVORY MUFFINS ARE A NICE ADDITION TO A BREAD BASKET
for breakfast or as the base for eggs Benedict (page 315), and they are the perfect
way to use up day-old bread. You can make this with my Ginger-Sage Breakfast
Sausage (page 311) or substitute your favorite brand or flavor.

8 ounces (225 g) brioche, torn
into bite-size pieces

1 tablespoon extra-virgin
olive oil

6 ounces (170 g) uncooked
Ginger-Sage Breakfast Sausage
(page 311), or store-bought
breakfast sausage, casings
removed if using links

3 green onions (white and light
green parts), thinly sliced

3 large eggs

2 cups (480 ml) whole milk

½ cup (120 ml) heavy cream

¾ teaspoon kosher salt

½ teaspoon freshly ground
black pepper

1 cup (115 g) shredded
cheddar cheese

Preheat the oven to 350°F
(175°C). Spray a 12-cup standard muffin tin liberally with
cooking spray and set aside.

Spread the bread in an even
layer on a large baking sheet
and toast until lightly golden
brown, turning once, about
10 minutes. Remove from the
oven and let cool. Leave the
oven on.

In a medium sauté pan, heat
the oil over high heat until it
begins to shimmer. Add the
sausage and cook, breaking
it up into small pieces with a
wooden spoon, until golden
brown, about 5 minutes. Add
the green onions and cook
until soft, about 2 minutes
longer. Using a slotted spoon,
transfer to a plate and let cool
slightly.

In a large bowl, whisk together
the eggs, milk, cream, salt, and
pepper. Add the bread, sausage
mixture, and cheese and mix
until the bread is completely
coated in the custard mixture.
Let the mixture sit at room
temperature for about 20 minutes, mixing a few more times,
to allow the bread to absorb
the custard.

Divide the bread pudding
among the muffin molds and
bake until the tops are golden
brown and just baked through,
about 20 minutes. Let cool
in the pan on a wire rack for
10 minutes before removing.
Serve warm.

MAKES 12

BACON DUTCH BABY PANCAKES

THESE LIGHT AND AIRY PANCAKES ARE DELICIOUS FOR BREAKFAST or brunch, and the best part is they couldn't be easier: Just dump all the ingredients into a bowl, whisk until smooth, pour into a hot pan, and bake. I serve individual pancakes at BarBacon with Maple Butter (page 310) and Bacon-Blueberry Jam (page 319), but a dusting of confectioners' sugar and a drizzle of pure maple syrup would be just as delicious. Or you can even add more toppings, and make a savory or sweet version. Just don't forget the additional side of bacon.

3 large eggs

1 tablespoon sugar

⅛ teaspoon grated nutmeg

½ cup (65 g) all-purpose flour

½ cup (120 ml) whole milk

4 thick slices bacon

3 tablespoons unsalted butter

Maple Butter (page 310; optional)

Blueberry-Bacon Jam (page 323; optional)

OPTIONAL TOPPINGS

Sunny side-up egg

Maple Bacon and Apple Breakfast Sausage (page 65)

Crispy Bacon (see page 44)

Fresh berries

Confectioners' sugar

Preheat the oven to 425°F (220°C). Line a large plate with paper towels.

In a medium bowl, combine the eggs, sugar, and nutmeg and whisk until smooth. Add the flour and milk and whisk until just combined. It is okay if there are a few lumps. Let stand at room temperature while you prepare the bacon.

Put the bacon strips in a heavy 10-inch (25-cm) cast-iron or nonstick skillet and cook until crisp (see page 44). Transfer the bacon to the paper towel–lined plate. Remove all but 1 tablespoon of the bacon fat and reserve for another use (see page 50). Coarsely chop the bacon and set aside.

Add the butter and place in the oven for 5 minutes. Remove the pan from the oven, pour the batter into the pan, and immediately return it to the oven. Bake until puffed and golden brown, about 20 minutes.

Remove from the oven. Serve immediately, topped with your favorite additions. For savory: Add a sunny side-up egg, bacon sausage, and bacon. For sweet: Fresh berries, maple butter, confectioners' sugar, and of course, bacon.

SERVES 2 TO 4

MAPLE BUTTER

THIS MAPLE BUTTER IS GREAT SPREAD ON MUFFINS, TOAST, AND, OF course, pancakes. If maple syrup is not your thing, you can substitute honey, molasses, or golden cane syrup.

½ cup (120 ml) pure maple syrup

1 cup (225 g) unsalted butter, at room temperature

1 teaspoon kosher salt

½ teaspoon pure vanilla extract

In a small saucepan, bring the maple syrup to a boil over high heat. Cook until it is reduced by half, about 5 minutes. Let cool slightly.

In a medium bowl, combine the syrup, butter, salt, and vanilla and mix until combined. Cover tightly and refrigerate for at least 1 hour, or up to 24 hours to allow the flavors to meld. Remove from the refrigerator 30 minutes before serving. The butter will keep, tightly covered in the refrigerator, for up to 5 days, and in the freezer for up to 1 month.

MAKES 1 CUP (225 G)

GINGER-SAGE BREAKFAST SAUSAGE

SURE, YOU CAN BUY REALLY GREAT SAUSAGE EVERYWHERE TODAY, but making your own at home allows you to control the amount of salt and seasoning. This recipe is so easy to throw together in the morning. Sage is typically the herb that is in breakfast sausage, but if you are not a fan of sage, feel free to substitute cilantro or parsley.

2 pounds (910 g) ground pork shoulder or 80/20 ground pork

1 (3-inch/7. 5-cm) piece fresh ginger, peeled and grated

4 garlic cloves, finely chopped

3 tablespoons finely chopped fresh sage leaves (about 12 leaves)

1¼ tablespoons kosher salt

½ teaspoon freshly ground black pepper

2 tablespoons canola oil

In a large bowl, combine the pork, ginger, garlic, sage, salt, and pepper. Cover and refrigerate for at least 30 minutes, or up to 24 hours. The longer the mixture sits, the better the flavor becomes.

Form the sausage into 8 (4-ounce/115-g) patties. Heat the oil in a large sauté pan over high heat until it begins to shimmer. Cook the patties until golden brown on both sides and just cooked through, about 8 minutes total. Uncooked patties will keep, individually wrapped in plastic wrap then aluminum foil in the freezer, for up to 1 month.

MAKES 8

HUEVOS RANCHEROS

THIS HEARTY BREAKFAST DISH FROM SOUTH OF THE BORDER doesn't typically include bacon. It's also always served with a red chile sauce—not chili con carne—but my cooking is anything but typical.

1½ cups (360 ml) canola oil, plus 1 tablespoon for the bacon

4 (6-inch/15-cm) corn tortillas

2 cups (455 g) Bacon Chili (page 168), heated

2 cups (225 g) shredded sharp cheddar cheese

8 thin slices bacon

4 large eggs

Kosher salt and freshly ground black pepper

1 cup (455 g) BarBacon Guacamole (page 275)

1 cup (240 g) Pico de Gallo (page 273)

Chopped fresh cilantro leaves

Line a sheet pan with paper towels. Heat ¾ cup (180 ml) of the oil in a medium nonstick pan over medium heat until the oil begins to shimmer. Fry the tortillas, one at a time, until just crisp, turning once. Remove with tongs to the prepared baking sheet. Add more oil and allow it to heat, when needed.

Preheat the broiler. Transfer the tortillas to an unlined sheet pan (or just carefully remove the paper towels from the sheet pan they are on). Divide the chili among the tortillas, then top with the cheese. Place under the broiler and broil until the cheese has melted and is lightly golden brown, about 1 minute.

Heat 1 tablespoon oil in a large nonstick pan over medium heat until it begins to shimmer. Add the bacon and cook until crisp (see page 44)

and the fat has rendered, about 8 minutes. Transfer to a plate lined with paper towels.

Break 2 eggs into the pan with the rendered bacon fat and lower the heat to low. Season the eggs with salt and pepper and cook until the whites are completely set and yolks begin to thicken but are not hard. Slide a turner under each egg and carefully flip it over in the pan. Cook the other side to desired doneness; remove to a plate. Repeat with the remaining eggs.

Put one of the chili-cheese tortillas on a plate, top with another chili-cheese tortilla, then add 2 slices of the bacon, an egg, and dollops of guacamole and pico de gallo to each. Garnish with cilantro and serve immediately.

SERVES 4

EGGS BENEDICT
on Breakfast Bread Pudding Muffins with Bacon Hollandaise

I USE MY BREAKFAST BREAD PUDDING MUFFINS IN PLACE OF THE usual English muffins because they add another level of savory flavor to an already savory brunch dish. Obviously, if you don't have any bacon drippings hanging around for the hollandaise, just use all melted butter. It will still be delicious.

1 tablespoon distilled white vinegar

8 large eggs

Kosher salt and freshly ground black pepper

8 Breakfast Bread Pudding Muffins (page 307)

16 thin slices bacon, cooked until crisp (see page 44)

Bacon Hollandaise (recipe follows)

Chopped fresh chives

In a large saucepan or deep skillet, bring 3 inches (7.5 cm) of water to a boil over high heat. Lower the heat to a simmer and add the vinegar.

Break each egg, one at a time, into a custard cup and, holding the cup close to the surface of the water, slip the egg into the water. Cook the egg until the white is completely set and the yolk begins to thicken but is not hard, 3 to 5 minutes. Do not stir. Lift the egg from the water with a slotted spoon.

Drain in the spoon or on paper towels and place on a baking sheet. Trim any rough edges, if desired. Sprinkle with salt and pepper. Repeat with the remaining eggs.

Put a muffin on a plate and top with 2 or 3 slices of bacon. Add a poached egg, then cover all in hollandaise. Garnish with the chives. Serve 1 or 2 portions per person, depending on appetite.

SERVES 4 OR 8

BACON HOLLANDAISE

3 large egg yolks

1 tablespoon fresh lemon juice

Pinch of ground cayenne

½ cup (115 g) unsalted butter, melted and cooled slightly

4 tablespoons (60 ml) rendered bacon fat (see page 50), melted and cooled slightly

In a blender, combine the egg yolks, lemon juice, and cayenne and blend until smooth. With the motor running, slowly add the melted butter, then the bacon fat, and continue blending until emulsified.

MAKES ABOUT 1 CUP (240 ML)

TUNA BACON BAGEL

IN NEW YORK CITY YOU WILL FIND OPEN-FACE BAGEL SANDWICHES at every Jewish and non-Jewish deli, but they will be made with salmon lox or whitefish salad. I love both, and lord knows that being a native New Yorker *and Jewish*, I have eaten a thousand of them. But there's a new version in town, and it contains tuna bacon instead.

1 bagel, split and toasted (my favorite is an everything bagel)

¼ cup (60 g) scallion cream cheese (or you can use plain)

2 (¼-inch/6-mm) slices ripe beefsteak tomato

¼ small red onion, thinly sliced

1 teaspoon capers, drained

Thinly sliced green onion

1 Tuna Bacon steak (page 37), broken into large flakes

Crispy bacon (optional)

Put the bagel on a flat surface, cut-side up. Spread each half with the cream cheese, then add a slice of tomato, some onion, capers, green onions, and tuna bacon to each. If you'd like, add a slice of crispy bacon for good measure. Eat!

SERVES 1 OR 2

MAPLE BACON BARK

THIS IS MY VERSION OF CRACK. MY DRUG OF CHOICE, IF YOU WILL.
Slowly cooked bacon that is glazed over and over with pure maple syrup until it is shatteringly crisp. The key is baking low and slow on a rack and glazing every 4 minutes to create layers of sweet and salty perfection. This is the only thing that gets my kids out of bed, without fail, on the weekend.

12 slices maple bacon, ¼ inch (6 mm) thick

½ cup (120 ml) pure maple syrup

Preheat the oven to 350°F (175°C). Lay the bacon on a rack set on a baking sheet and bake until some of its fat has rendered and the sides have begun to color, 8 to 10 minutes.

Brushing the top of the bacon with maple syrup every 4 minutes, continue to bake until the bacon is cooked through and the top is crispy and caramelized, about 30 minutes longer. The bacon can be prepared up to 3 days ahead, stored between sheets of waxed paper in a zip-top bag, and refrigerated. Let stand at room temperature for at least 30 minutes before serving.

MAKES 12

ALMOND BREAKFAST BUNS

with Blueberry-Bacon Jam and Orange Glaze

THESE BREAKFAST ROLLS CAN BE MADE THE DAY BEFORE—MOLDED, filled, and ready for the oven the next morning. They are sweet and savory, so no matter what mood you wake up in you're covered.

~~~~~~

FOR THE ALMOND-BACON PASTE

7 ounces (200 g) pure almond paste

2 thin slices bacon, cooked until crisp (see page 44) and chopped

¼ cup (50 g) granulated sugar

1 tablespoon light brown sugar

1 large egg

1 tablespoon amaretto, or ¼ teaspoon pure almond extract (optional)

2 teaspoons all-purpose flour

Milk or water if needed

FOR THE DOUGH

1 (7-g) package active dry yeast

¼ cup (60 ml) whole milk, heated to 100 to 110°F (38 to 43°C), plus ¾ cup (180 ml)

¼ cup (50 g) sugar, plus more for yeast

½ cup (115 g) soft unsalted butter, cut into tablespoons, plus more for greasing the bowl

1 tablespoon rendered bacon fat (see page 50)

2 large eggs

5 to 6 cups (675 to 810 g) bread flour

1 teaspoon kosher salt

1½ cups (360 ml) Blueberry-Bacon Jam (page 323)

FOR THE ORANGE GLAZE

1 cup (125 g) confectioners' sugar

½ teaspoon finely grated orange zest

2 to 4 tablespoons fresh orange juice

Make the almond-bacon paste: In a food processor, combine the almond paste, bacon, and granulated sugar and process until coarsely ground. Add the brown sugar, egg, and amaretto (if using) and process until combined. Add the flour and process until smooth. If the mixture is too thick to spread, add milk or water 1 tablespoon at a time until spreadable. Scrape into a bowl. The almond-bacon paste can be made up to 3 days in advance and stored in the refrigerator, tightly sealed. Remove from the refrigerator at least 30 minutes in advance to spread easily.

Make the dough: Lightly butter two 12-cup standard muffin tins (you'll need 16 of the wells).

(continued)

In the bowl of a stand mixer, combine the yeast and the ¼ cup (60 ml) warm milk, add a pinch of sugar, and let sit until bubbly, about 5 minutes. Using the dough hook, add the butter and bacon fat and mix until incorporated. Add the remaining ¾ cup milk, the eggs, and the ¼ cup (50 g) sugar and continue mixing until combined.

Begin adding the flour, 1 cup (135 g) at a time, along with the salt, and continue mixing until a soft dough is formed and the dough is no longer sticky. You may need more or less flour depending on the humidity. Transfer the dough to a lightly floured surface and continue kneading until the dough is smooth and elastic, about 5 minutes, and form into a ball.

Grease a large bowl with softened butter, add the dough, and turn to coat. Cover the top of the bowl tightly with plastic wrap and let the dough rise in a warm place until doubled in volume, about 1 hour.

Preheat the oven to 350°F (175°C). Roll the dough into a 16-inch (40.5-cm) square. Cut into 8 (4-inch/10-cm) squares. Lift each square into a cup in the muffin tin and push all the way down. Divide the almond-bacon paste among the cups, then top each with 1 heaping tablespoon of the jam. Fold the corners over lightly to enclose the filling, but don't push them down. Cover loosely with plastic wrap and let rise in a warm place for 1 hour.

Meanwhile, make the orange glaze: In a small bowl, combine the confectioners' sugar and orange zest, add the orange juice 1 tablespoon at a time, and whisk until smooth and the perfect spreading consistency.

Bake the buns until golden brown, about 25 minutes, reversing the pans halfway through. Remove from the oven and brush generously with the orange glaze while the buns are still hot, then loosen the edges and remove the buns from the tins.

MAKES 16

BLUEBERRY-BACON JAM

YEP, THAT'S RIGHT: I'VE EVEN FIGURED OUT A WAY TO ADD BACON to my fruit jam. Don't knock it until you've tried it. This is super easy and no canning equipment is needed. If you are not a fan of blueberries, blackberries work really well, too. Also, sugar quantities can change depending on the ripeness of your fruit, so taste along the way, increasing the amount of sugar if needed.

14 ounces (400 g) slab bacon, cut into lardons ½ inch (12 mm) long (see page 48)

1 cup (200 g) sugar

¼ cup (60 ml) fresh lemon juice (from about 2 lemons)

3 cups (435 g) blueberries

2 teaspoons cornstarch

Heat a large saucepan over medium heat. Add the bacon and cook until golden brown and crisp, about 8 minutes. Remove the bacon to a large plate lined with paper towels. Pour the fat into a container and save for another use (see page 50). Do not clean the pan; the crispy bits on the bottom will be used in the jam.

In a separate large saucepan over high heat, combine the sugar and ¼ cup (60 ml) water and cook until the sugar has dissolved, stirring once, about 2 minutes. Continue cooking (without stirring) until deep amber in color, about 8 minutes. Lower the heat to low, carefully add the lemon juice (it will spatter), and cook until the mixture is smooth.

Add the blueberries, increase the heat to high, and cook, stirring occasionally, until the blueberries are very soft, about 7 minutes.

Transfer the blueberry mixture to the pan that the bacon was cooked in. In a small bowl, whisk together the cornstarch and 2 teaspoons water, add it to the blueberry mixture, and cook over medium heat, scraping the bottom to release any browned bits from the pan, until the mixture is thickened, about 5 minutes. Stir in the bacon and let cool to room temperature. Transfer to a container with a tight-fitting lid and refrigerate until chilled, at least 4 hours. The jam is best served that day.

MAKES ABOUT 3½ CUPS (840 ML)

LEMON RICOTTA PANCAKES
with Blueberry Syrup

THERE IS THE OCCASIONAL PERSON THAT COMES TO BRUNCH AT BarBacon who just doesn't like bacon. We keep these on the menu for those people—and because they are delicious, light, and lemony. Even the bacon lovers eat them. I like to think of them as palate cleansers between the bacon dishes. Smart.

~~~~~~~~~~~~~~~~~~~~~~~~~~

1 cup (240 ml) pure
maple syrup

1 cup (145 g) blueberries

4 large eggs, separated

1⅓ cups (325 ml) ricotta

6 tablespoons (90 g) unsalted
butter, melted and cooled,
plus more for the griddle

1½ tablespoons grated lemon
zest (from about 2 lemons)

½ cup (65 g) all-purpose flour

1½ tablespoons
granulated sugar

Confectioners' sugar

In a medium saucepan, bring the maple syrup to a boil over high heat. Add the blueberries and cook for 1 minute. Remove from the heat, cover, and let steep while you make the pancakes.

In a medium bowl, combine the egg yolks, ricotta, butter, and lemon zest and whisk until smooth. In a large bowl, stir together the flour and granulated sugar.

In a separate large bowl, with a clean whisk, whip the egg whites until they hold soft peaks.

Add the egg yolk mixture to the flour mixture and whisk until just combined (do not overmix). Fold in the egg whites until just incorporated.

Heat a griddle or cast-iron pan over medium heat and brush with butter or spray with nonstick spray. Working in batches, pour the batter onto the griddle by ¼-cup (60-ml) measures and cook the pancakes for 1 to 2 minutes on each side, or until they are golden, brushing the griddle with more of the melted butter as necessary.

Serve 2 or 3 pancakes per person, ladled with the blueberry syrup and dusted with confectioners' sugar.

~~~~~~~~~~~~~~~~~~~~~~~~~~

MAKES 10 TO 12; SERVES 4

BISCUITS AND SAUSAGE GRAVY

with Kentucky Fried Bacon

HERE I SERVE KENTUCKY FRIED BACON ATOP A BACON FAT–ENRICHED biscuit ladled with creamy rich sausage gravy. Sometimes I add a fried egg, for good measure.

FOR THE BISCUITS

4 cups (500 g) all-purpose flour

4 teaspoons baking powder

1 teaspoon baking soda

1 teaspoon salt

¾ cup (180 ml) chilled rendered bacon fat (see page 50)

1½ cups (360 ml) cold shaken buttermilk

½ cup (120 ml) heavy cream

FOR THE SAUSAGE GRAVY

2 tablespoons vegetable oil

12 ounces (340 g) Maple Bacon and Apple Breakfast Sausage (page 65) or store-bought breakfast sausage, casings removed

3 tablespoons all-purpose flour

1½ cups (360 ml) whole milk

1 cup (240 ml) heavy cream

Kosher salt and freshly ground black pepper

2 tablespoons minced fresh chives, plus more for garnish

FOR SERVING

1 recipe Kentucky Fried Bacon (page 42), warm

Make the biscuits: Preheat the oven to 425°F (220°C). Line a baking sheet with parchment paper.

In a large bowl, combine the flour, baking powder, baking soda, and salt. Using a pastry cutter, stir until the ingredients are incorporated. Cut in the bacon fat using your fingers or the pastry cutter until the mixture resembles coarse meal. Add the buttermilk and gently mix until the mixture just begins to come together.

Scrape the dough onto a lightly floured counter. Pat the dough into a rectangle about ¾ inch (2 cm) thick. Use a 3-inch (7. 5-cm) round cutter to cut out biscuits. Press together the scraps of dough and repeat the process to make 8 biscuits.

Put the biscuits on the prepared baking sheet and brush the tops with the cream. Bake for 12 to 15 minutes, until light golden brown. Let cool on a wire rack.

Make the sausage gravy: Heat the oil in a large sauté pan over high heat, add the sausage, and cook until golden brown, about 8 minutes. Add the flour and cook for 1 minute. Add the milk and cream, bring to a boil, lower the heat to a simmer, and cook until the gravy is thickened to a sauce consistency and the flour taste has been cooked out, about 10 minutes. Remove from the heat, season with salt and pepper, and stir in the chives.

To serve, split the biscuits in half, ladle some of the gravy over each half, and top each with a slice of the bacon. Garnish with more chives.

SERVES 4 TO 6

SWEET POTATO HASH

I CREATED THIS AS A LAST-MINUTE SPECIAL FOR A GUEST WHO showed up at 4:15 PM and still wanted brunch after we threw out all our *mise en place*. I made him this off-menu dish, and he flipped. I'm not sure if you would consider this Mexican or Spanish or American, but it's damn good. If sweet potatoes aren't your thing, you can totally use Russets.

2 large sweet potatoes, cut into 1-inch (2.5-cm) dice

6 thick slices bacon, cut into lardons (see page 50)

4 tablespoons (60 ml) canola oil

Kosher salt and freshly ground black pepper

2 tablespoons unsalted butter

4 poached eggs (see page 191)

½ cup (120 ml) warmed Piperade (page 287)

½ cup (120 ml) Avocado Salsa Verde (page 90)

Fresh cilantro leaves or thinly sliced green onion (optional)

Preheat the oven to 350°F (175°C). Line a baking sheet with parchment paper.

In a large bowl, combine the sweet potatoes and bacon, toss with 2 tablespoons of the oil, and season with salt and pepper. Spread the potatoes and bacon out on the baking sheet in an even layer and bake, stirring once, until the potatoes are soft and the bacon is light brown and slightly crispy, about 35 minutes. Remove from the oven and let cool for 10 minutes. (Or let cool to room temperature, transfer to a baking dish, cover, and refrigerate for up to 2 days.)

Combine 2 tablespoons of the butter and 2 tablespoons oil in a medium cast-iron or nonstick skillet over high heat until it begins to shimmer. Add the potatoes and bacon and cook, stirring until the potatoes and bacon on the bottom become golden brown, about 6 minutes. Turn over, add the ramaining butter and oil, and continue cooking 5 to 6 minutess longer. Remove from the heat and let stand for 5 minutes.

Divide the hash among 4 plates or shallow bowls. Top each with a poached egg, the piperade, and a few tablespoons of the salsa verde; garnish with cilantro, if desired, and serve immediately.

SERVES 4

CHAPTER 12

DESSERTS

**ESSERTS AREN'T SOMETHING THAT I EVER** expected to be making. I've always focused on savory, on the meal itself. That said, desserts have come to be an important part of my repertoire. They're another way for me to explore all of bacon's nuances. In the same way that bacon amps up classic dishes like burgers and lobster rolls, it also amps up delicious desserts like brittles, blondies, cookies, and pies.

The most interesting part of working with bacon in desserts is the way it can be used to infuse the dishes with flavor. Some of these desserts don't even have slabs of bacon in them—rather, only the rendered fat or the flavor that's brought out through gentle poaching.

So, instead of joining the butter-versus-shortening piecrust debate, use rendered bacon fat. It creates fabulously flaky dough with a burst of flavor. It's slightly smoky and a little salty—a great balance to so many different fillings, such as maple-bacon pecan pie (page 354). Infusing cream with bacon has a similar effect. Think of your favorite ice cream, then imagine that with just a touch of salt and an even smoother mouthfeel. Tempting, right?

And, of course, we can't forget about the bacon itself. Simply dipped in dark chocolate (page 345), it shines and plays off the chocolate's sweetness. It's also irresistible crumbled and caramelized in a brittle (page 332) or as a coating for perfectly fried churros (page 337). While it may not seem obvious right off the bat, dessert is yet another area that bacon simply works in.

BOURBON-BACON PEANUT BRITTLE

THIS IS NOT YOUR GRANDMOTHER'S PEANUT BRITTLE. SWEET, salty, and smoky is the way I like my desserts, and this recipe hits all of those notes and then some. Peanuts make it perfect and classic, but you could use cashews or almonds, if you'd like.

10 slices thin-sliced bacon

¼ cup (60 ml) plus 2 tablespoons bacon-infused bourbon (page 100) or plain bourbon

¼ cup (55 g) packed light brown sugar

1½ cups (300 g) granulated sugar

1 cup (240 ml) light corn syrup

1 cup (150 g) Spanish peanuts, skins removed

2 tablespoons unsalted butter

1½ teaspoons pure vanilla extract

1½ teaspoons baking soda

Sea salt or smoked sea salt for sprinkling

Preheat the oven to 400°F (205°C). Line a baking sheet with aluminum foil. Spray another baking sheet liberally with nonstick spray or line with a Silpat.

Lay the bacon in a single layer on the foil-lined baking sheet. Brush the bacon with ¼ cup (60 ml) of the bourbon and sprinkle the brown sugar on both sides. Bake the bacon until it caramelizes and becomes crisp, 13 to 15 minutes. Using tongs, remove the bacon to a cutting board and let cool completely, about 10 minutes. Once the bacon has cooled, chop it with a knife into small pieces. Set aside.

In a medium saucepan, combine the granulated sugar, corn syrup, and ¼ cup (60 ml) water over high heat and bring to a boil, stirring only until the sugar has melted. Continue cooking, without stirring, until the mixture reaches 300°F (150°C) on an instant-read thermometer. Once it has reached 300°F (150°C), stir in the peanuts and continue

cooking until the temperature reaches 310°F (154°C).

As soon as it reaches 310°F (154°C), remove the pan from the heat and carefully stir in the remaining 2 tablespoons bourbon, the candied bacon, the butter, vanilla, and baking soda and wait for the foaming to stop. Once the foaming has stopped, carefully and immediately pour the brittle onto the prepared greased baking sheet and spread it out as much as possible with a greased heatproof spatula. Be careful not to touch the mixture or get it on you—it is very hot and dangerous. Sprinkle with the sea salt. Let cool completely, then break into pieces or coarsely or finely chop. The brittle can be stored in an airtight container at room temperature for up to 1 week.

SERVES ABOUT 24

SMOKED CHOCOLATE TART
with Hazelnut Crust and Chocolate Glaze

YOU CAN'T ACTUALLY SEE PIECES OF BACON IN THIS DESSERT, BUT one bite and you'll know it's there. It lends its salty bite and crunch to the crust, and its rendered fat adds smokiness to the rich, creamy chocolate filling.

FOR THE TART

¾ cup (100 g) skin-on hazelnuts

5 thin slices crisp cooked bacon (see page 44), finely chopped

2 tablespoons granulated sugar

¾ teaspoon kosher salt

1 cup (125 g) all-purpose flour

½ cup (115 g) unsalted butter, slightly softened

1¼ cups (300 ml) Bacon Heavy Cream (page 349)

1⅓ cups (225 g) bittersweet chocolate, chopped (not more than 65% cacao)

2 large eggs

1 teaspoon pure vanilla extract

FOR THE CHOCOLATE GLAZE

2 ounces (55 g) bittersweet chocolate, finely chopped

¼ cup (60 ml) Bacon Heavy Cream (page 349)

1 teaspoon light corn syrup

OPTIONAL TOPPINGS

Chopped toasted hazelnuts

Whipped cream

Make the tart: In a food processor, combine the hazelnuts, bacon, sugar, and ½ teaspoon of the salt and pulse a few times to coarsely chop. Add the flour and pulse until the nuts and bacon are finely ground. Add the butter and pulse until the dough just comes together. Lightly butter a 9-inch (23-cm) tart pan or three 4-inch (10-cm) mini tart pans with a removable bottom or spray with nonstick spray. Press the dough evenly into the bottom and up the sides and refrigerate until chilled, about 30 minutes.

Preheat the oven to 350°F (175°C). Cover the dough in the tart pan with parchment paper and fill with ceramic baking beans or dried pulses. Put the tart pan on a baking sheet and bake for about 15 minutes, until the pastry is firm, then remove the weights

and parchment and cook for about 5 minutes more, until golden brown. Let cool on a wire rack for 15 minutes. Leave the oven on.

In a small saucepan, bring the cream to a simmer over low heat. Put the chocolate in a medium bowl, add the hot cream, and let sit for 20 seconds. Whisk until smooth. Let cool for 5 minutes. Add the eggs, vanilla, and the remaining ¼ teaspoon salt and whisk until smooth. Pour the mixture into the prepared tart shell and bake until the edges are set but the center is still a bit wobbly, about 12 minutes. The filling will continue to set as it cools. Let cool to room temperature, then refrigerate until chilled, about 2 hours.

(continued)

Meanwhile, make the chocolate glaze: In a small saucepan over low heat, combine the chocolate, cream, 1 tablespoon water, and the corn syrup and cook, stirring constantly, until the chocolate is melted and the mixture is smooth, about 3 minutes.

Remove the tart from the refrigerator, pour the glaze over the top, and spread evenly with an offset spatula. Let sit at room temperature until the chocolate is set, about 30 minutes, or refrigerate for 10 minutes. Garnish with the hazelnuts and whipped cream, if desired. Slice and serve. The tart will keep in the refrigerator, tightly covered, for up to 1 week.

MAKES 1 (9-INCH/23-CM) TART OR 3 (4-INCH/10-CM) MINI TARTS

BACON CHURROS
with Chocolate-Orange Dipping Sauce

CHURROS ARE FRIED PATE A CHOUX DOUGH (YOU KNOW, THE STUFF cream puffs are made of) with a crispy, sugary exterior and an almost custard-like interior. They're always served with a chocolate sauce for dipping, so I chose chocolate and orange because it is one of my favorite flavor combinations. I add Grand Marnier to the chocolate sauce, but feel free to just zest a small orange instead to keep this alcohol-free. Hickory powder adds an extra hint of smoky goodness and can be found online. It's optional, but you really don't want to miss out on it.

FOR THE HICKORY CINNAMON SUGAR

1 cup (200 g) sugar

2 teaspoons ground cinnamon

1 teaspoon hickory powder

¼ teaspoon kosher salt

FOR THE CHURROS

6 tablespoons (90 g) unsalted butter

2 tablespoons rendered bacon fat (see page 50)

⅛ teaspoon fine sea salt

1 teaspoon finely grated orange zest

1 cup (125 g) all-purpose flour

3 large eggs, beaten

4 thin strips crisp cooked bacon (see page 44), finely chopped

Vegetable oil for deep-frying

FOR THE CHOCOLATE-ORANGE SAUCE

1 cup (240 ml) heavy cream

1 tablespoon Grand Mariner, or finely grated zest of 1 small orange

1¼ cups (220 g) semisweet chocolate chips

Make the hickory cinnamon sugar: In a large bowl, mix together the sugar, cinnamon, hickory powder, and salt. If not using immediately, transfer to a container with a tight-fitting lid for up to 1 month.

Make the churros: In a medium saucepan, combine 1 cup (240 ml) water, the butter, bacon fat, salt, and orange zest and bring to a boil over high heat. Using a wooden spoon, stir in the flour. Lower the heat to low and stir vigorously until the mixture forms a ball, about 1 minute.

Remove from the heat and immediately transfer the dough to a stand mixer fitted

(continued)

with a paddle. Beat the dough for 1 minute to allow some of the steam to escape. Add the eggs and bacon and mix until fully incorporated and the batter is smooth. Transfer the dough to a pastry bag fitted with a large plain tip.

Heat 2 inches (5 cm) of oil in a deep, heavy pot until it reaches 360°F (180°C) on a deep-fry thermometer. Line a baking sheet with several layers of paper towels. Squeeze a 4-inch (10-cm) strip of dough into the hot oil. Repeat, frying 3 or 4 strips of dough at a time. Fry the churros, turning them once, until golden brown, about 2 minutes per side. Transfer the cooked churros to the prepared baking sheet to drain, then immediately toss in the cinnamon sugar.

Make the chocolate-orange sauce: In a small saucepan, combine the cream and Grand Marnier and bring to a simmer over medium heat.

Put the chocolate chips in a medium bowl and pour the warm cream over the chocolate. Let sit for 1 minute. Slowly whisk until smooth. Serve warm with the churros.

MAKES ABOUT 12

BARBACON CARAMEL POPCORN

WE SERVE BOWLS OF THIS GRATIS AT THE BAR AT BARBACON. SALTY and sweet. Customers don't know what to make of it, so they just keep eating— and thus, keep drinking. Mission accomplished.

1 tablespoon canola oil, plus more for popping the corn

6 thick slices bacon, cut crosswise into ¼-inch (6-mm) pieces

¾ cup (170 g) popcorn kernels

1½ teaspoons kosher salt

½ cup (115 g) unsalted butter, cut into pieces

1 cup (220 g) dark brown sugar

½ cup (120 ml) light corn syrup

1½ teaspoons baking soda

2 teaspoons pure vanilla extract

½ teaspoon coarsely ground black pepper

Preheat the oven to 250°F (120°C). Line a sheet pan with parchment paper. Put the oil and bacon in large Dutch oven and cook over medium heat, turning once, until golden brown and crisp and the fat has rendered, about 8 minutes. Remove the bacon with a slotted spoon to a plate lined with paper towels and transfer the rendered fat to a small bowl.

Measure the rendered fat back into the pot; add additional canola oil as needed to make 7 tablespoons fat total. Pour the popcorn kernels in an even layer in the bottom of the pan and sprinkle 1 teaspoon salt over the top.

Turn the heat to medium-high and cook until a few of the kernels begin to pop. Once the kernels begin to pop, cover the pot. Once the popcorn begins to pop at a rapid rate, start shaking the pan back and forth over the burner. Once the popping slows to several seconds between pops, remove the pan from the heat, remove the lid, and immediately dump the popcorn into a wide bowl.

Melt the butter in a medium saucepan over high heat. Add the brown sugar and corn syrup and cook, whisking constantly, until the sugar has melted and the mixture is smooth. Remove from the heat and whisk in the baking soda, vanilla, and pepper until smooth.

Pour the caramel over the popcorn and gently stir until coated.

Spread the caramel popcorn on the prepared sheet pan in an even layer and bake for 1 hour, stirring once after 30 minutes.

Transfer to a large bowl and add the bacon. The popcorn will keep, tightly covered in a cool, dark place, for up to 3 days.

MAKES ABOUT 12 CUPS (132 G)

CANDIED BACON CHOCOLATE CHIP COOKIES

SOME PEOPLE PREFER NUTS IN THEIR CHOCOLATE CHIP COOKIES. I prefer candied bacon. This was the very first dessert I came up with when I opened BarBacon. These cookies remain on the menu to this day and continue to be extremely popular. In the summer, we serve them sandwiched with bacon ice cream (page 361).

2¼ cups (280 g) all-purpose flour

½ teaspoon baking soda

⅛ teaspoon fine sea salt

¾ cup (170 g) unsalted butter, at room temperature

½ cup (100 g) granulated sugar

1 cup (220 g) brown sugar

1 large whole egg

1 large egg yolk

2 teaspoons pure vanilla extract

1 cup (170 g) good-quality semisweet chocolate, coarsely chopped, or semisweet chocolate chips

12 slices Bourbon Candied Bacon (page 359), coarsely chopped

Confectioners' sugar

Preheat the oven to 325°F (165°C). Line two baking sheets with parchment paper or Silpats.

In a small bowl, sift the flour, baking soda, and salt together and set aside.

In a large bowl, combine the butter and both sugars and, using a handheld mixer, mix until light and fluffy. Add the whole egg, egg yolk, and vanilla and mix until light and creamy, about 2 minutes. Add the flour mixture and mix until just combined. Fold in the chocolate and bacon.

Using a medium ice cream scoop (about 1½ tablespoons), spoon the dough onto the prepared baking sheets, leaving at least 2 inches (5 cm) between the cookies, and bake on the middle rack of the oven until the cookies are light golden brown and still soft in the middle, about 11 minutes. Let the cookies rest for 2 minutes on the baking sheets before removing them to a wire rack with a wide metal spatula. Repeat with the remaining dough.

Once the cookies are cool, dust with confectioners' sugar. Store in a container with a tight-fitting lid for up to 3 days.

MAKES 2 DOZEN

CHOCOLATE-COVERED BACON

WE EAT CHOCOLATE-COVERED STRAWBERRIES, RAISINS, PRETZELS, and potato chips (they're all delicious) . . . but you really haven't lived until you've experienced the salty, smoky, sweet combination of chocolate-covered bacon. Serve it as a dessert on its own; add some texture to it by sprinkling it with smoked sea salt, finely chopped nuts, or crushed pink peppercorns; or eat it any time you feel like rewarding yourself for just being you.

1 pound (455 g) bittersweet, semisweet, milk, or white chocolate, coarsely chopped

2 teaspoons vegetable oil

1 pound (455 g) thick-sliced bacon, cooked until crisp (see page 44)

Crushed pink peppercorns (optional)

Smoked sea salt (optional)

Prepare a double boiler by heating a large saucepan filled with water over high heat until boiling. Lower the heat to a simmer. Set a heatproof bowl over but not touching the simmering water. Add the chocolate to the bowl and stir occasionally with a rubber spatula until smooth and completely melted. Remove the bowl from the pan, stir in the oil, and set aside.

Line a sheet pan with parchment paper. Using tongs, carefully dip half the bacon into the melted chocolate, turning to coat all sides in chocolate (see Note). Transfer to the prepared sheet pan and sprinkle with pink peppercorns and smoked salt, if desired. Repeat with the remaining slices of bacon. Let the chocolate set at room temperature or refrigerate until hard. Once hard, you can store in the refrigerator in a single layer on top of parchment paper in a container with a tight-fitting lid for up to 3 days.

NOTE: *Alternatively, you can use a fork and drizzle the chocolate back and forth over the slices of bacon, or use a combination of white and dark chocolate and/or caramel.*

MAKES ABOUT 1 POUND (455 G)

DULCE DE LECHE BARS

with Bacon-Pecan Shortbread Crust

THIS RICH AND DECADENT BAR COOKIE IS SO FULL OF SWEET, creamy goodness courtesy of dulce de leche. It could put you in a sugar coma on its own, but have no fear, bacon is here to help balance that sweetness with a nice pop of bittersweet chocolate, salt, and smoke. Don't thank me, thank the bacon. If you prefer a less intense chocolate flavor, substitute semisweet or milk chocolate for the bittersweet.

¾ cup (170 g) plus 1 tablespoon soft unsalted butter

6 thin slices bacon, finely diced

¼ cup (50 g) plus 2 tablespoons granulated sugar

1 tablespoon light brown sugar

¼ cup (30 g) finely chopped pecans, plus ½ cup (60 g) toasted chopped pecans

1 large egg yolk

1 teaspoon pure vanilla extract

1½ cups (190 g) all-purpose flour

1 (13-ounce/369-g) jar dulce de leche

1 (14-ounce/397 g) can sweetened condensed milk

7 ounces (200 g) sweetened shredded coconut (about 2⅓ cups)

12 ounces (340 g) bittersweet, semisweet, or milk chocolate, chopped into small pieces

Preheat the oven to 350°F (175°C). Line a 9 by 13-inch (23 by 33-cm) metal baking pan with parchment paper, leaving 1 inch (2.5 cm) of overhang. Spray the paper with vegetable oil spray. Line a baking sheet with parchment paper and set aside.

Melt 1 tablespoon of the butter in a medium nonstick pan over medium heat. Add the bacon and cook until the fat begins to render and the bacon turns a light golden brown, about 4 minutes. Add 2 tablespoons of the granulated sugar and the brown sugar and continue cooking until the sugar melts. Add the ¼ cup (30 g) finely chopped pecans and cook until the bacon and pecans are caramelized, about 3 minutes.

Using a slotted spoon, transfer the mixture to the prepared baking sheet and let cool for 10 minutes.

Put the remaining ¾ cup (170 g) butter and ¼ cup (50 g) granulated sugar in a bowl and, using a handheld mixer, mix until soft and creamy, about 2 minutes. Add the egg yolk and vanilla and mix until combined. Fold in the caramelized bacon and pecan mixture, then fold in the flour until moist crumbs form.

Press the crumbs into the prepared baking pan and bake on the middle rack in the oven until the crust is set and lightly browned, about 25 minutes.

While the crust is baking, whisk together the dulce de leche and sweetened condensed milk in a medium bowl until combined. Fold in the coconut, chocolate, and ½ cup toasted pecans and pour the mixture over the crust, spreading it evenly. Return to the oven and bake until the top is light golden brown, about 35 minutes. Let cool completely on a wire rack before cutting into squares or rectangles. The bars will keep, in a single layer in an airtight container, for up to 3 days at room temperature or up to 2 weeks in the freezer.

MAKES 16 LARGE OR 24 SMALL

BACON-HAZELNUT HOT CHOCOLATE
with Sugared Bacon and Smoked Marshmallows

OKAY, ADMITTEDLY, I HAVE GONE A LITTLE BACON CRAZY WITH this one, and yes, you could just use one of these bacon preparations and still have a mighty fine cup of hot chocolate. But, if you are up for it, give the full recipe a try, just once. You will never go back to the hot chocolate of your childhood.

FOR THE SUGARED BACON

2 teaspoons canola oil

4 thin slices bacon

¼ cup (50 g) raw sugar

FOR THE HOT CHOCOLATE

1 quart (1 L) Bacon Milk (recipe follows) or whole milk

¾ cup (180 ml) chocolate-hazelnut spread, such as Nutella

8 Smoked Marshmallows (page 350)

Make the sugared bacon: Combine the oil and bacon in a small sauté pan over medium heat and cook until the bacon is golden brown and crispy, about 8 minutes. Remove to a plate lined with paper towels and let cool for about 5 minutes. Save the rendered bacon fat for another use (see page 50).

In a mini-prep or food processor, combine the bacon and sugar and process until finely ground. Spread evenly on a large plate and set aside.

Make the hot chocolate: Reserve ¼ cup (60 ml) of the bacon milk and set aside. Pour the remaining milk into a large saucepan and bring to a simmer over low heat. Whisk in the chocolate-hazelnut spread and continue whisking until smooth and the mixture becomes frothy, about 2 minutes.

To coat the rims of the mugs, put the reserved milk on a medium plate. Hold a mug upside down and dip the rim into the milk, letting the excess drip off. Then dip the rim into the bacon sugar mixture until lightly coated. Repeat with the remaining mugs.

Ladle the hot chocolate into the mugs and top each mug with 2 marshmallows. Serve immediately.

SERVES 4

BACON MILK OR BACON HEAVY CREAM

THIS IS THE PERFECT BASE FOR BACON HOT CHOCOLATE OR A BACON milkshake (page 353) or for our wildly popular Bacon Whipped Cream (page 353). Remember, if the bacon fat is too cold when you add it to the milk or cream, it won't separate nicely overnight and you will yield far less after straining. Be sure to warm it beforehand.

1 cup (240 ml) rendered bacon fat (see page 50)

1 quart (1 L) whole milk or heavy cream

In a small saucepan, heat the bacon fat over low heat until it reaches 200°F (93°C) on an instant-read thermometer. Put the milk or cream in a large nonreactive bowl.

Add the bacon fat to the milk or cream and whisk until combined. Cover tightly with plastic wrap and chill for at least 8 hours, or up to 24 hours, until the fat solidifies and separates from the milk or cream.

Carefully skim off the fat and discard. Strain the milk or cream through a cheesecloth-lined fine-mesh sieve into a container with a tight-fitting lid and refrigerate until ready to use. The cream will keep for up to 3 days in the refrigerator.

MAKES 1 QUART (1 L)

SMOKED MARSHMALLOWS

MAKING HOMEMADE MARSHMALLOWS IS SO INCREDIBLY EASY AND delicious that you will never go back to the store-bought kind again. You could totally cold-smoke these marshmallows, but with all the great-quality liquid smoke on the market today, there is no need to. These are delicious served on top of hot chocolate, in between graham crackers for s'mores, or just eating on their own.

~~~~~~

3 (7-g) envelopes
unflavored gelatin

Cold water

1 teaspoon applewood
liquid smoke

1½ cups (300 g) granulated
sugar

1 cup (240 ml) light corn syrup

¼ teaspoon kosher salt

1 tablespoon pure
vanilla extract

1 cup (125 g) confectioners'
sugar

Spray the bottom and sides of a 9 by 13-inch (23 by 33-cm) glass baking dish with nonstick spray and line with parchment, allowing a 2-inch (5-cm) overhang on the long sides. Spray the parchment with nonstick spray and set aside.

Put the gelatin in the bowl of an electric mixer fitted with the whisk attachment. In a medium bowl, stir together ½ cup (120 ml) cold water and ½ teaspoon of the liquid smoke and add it to the gelatin. Let the mixture sit until the gelatin softens, about 5 minutes.

While the gelatin softens, combine the granulated sugar, corn syrup, salt, ½ cup (120 ml) cold water, and the remaining ½ teaspoon liquid

smoke in a medium saucepan and cook over high heat until the sugar dissolves. Attach a candy thermometer to the side of the pan, making sure that the bottom of the thermometer does not touch the bottom of the pan, and cook the mixture, without stirring, until it reaches the soft ball stage, 240°F (116°C) on the thermometer.

Slowly and carefully pour the hot syrup into the bowl with the gelatin and, using a hand-held mixer, mix on low speed for 30 seconds. Slowly increase the speed to high and continue whipping until the mixture is thick and glossy and holds stiff peaks, about 10 minutes. Add the vanilla, mix for 30 seconds longer, then scrape the mixture into the prepared pan

and smooth the top with an offset spatula. Let sit at room temperature until firm, about 3 hours.

Dust the top of the marshmallows liberally with half of the confectioners' sugar. Turn the marshmallows out of the pan, confectioners' sugar down, and peel away the parchment from the bottom. Sift the remaining confectioners' sugar over the bottom. Cut into 12 or 16 equal squares.

Store them in an airtight container at room temperature, sprinkled with a bit more confectioners' sugar, for up to 3 weeks.

MAKES 12 LARGE OR 16 SMALL

BOURBON BACON FLOATER MAPLE MILKSHAKE

THIS IS NOT YOUR ICE CREAM SHOP'S RUN-OF-THE-MILL MILKSHAKE.
Candied bacon, maple syrup, and smoky bacon-infused bourbon take plain vanilla
ice cream and turn it into an adults-only libation that is not for the faint of heart.
Add a chocolate-covered slice for extra indulgence.

¼ cup (60 ml) whole milk

¼ cup (60 ml) pure maple syrup

Pinch of grated nutmeg

4 slices Bourbon Candied Bacon (page 359), coarsely chopped

11 ounces (310 g) vanilla bean ice cream

1 shot bacon-infused bourbon (page 100)

Sweetened whipped cream (see Note) or Bacon Whipped Cream (recipe follows)

In a blender, combine the milk, maple syrup, nutmeg, and 3 slices of the bacon and blend until smooth, about 10 seconds.

Add the ice cream and blend until smooth and thick. Transfer to a tall glass, float the bourbon on top, and add a dollop of whipped cream. Garnish with the remaining chopped bacon.

NOTE: *To make sweetened whipped cream: Combine ½ cup (120 ml) very cold heavy cream, 2 tablespoons granulated sugar or confectioners' sugar, and ½ teaspoon pure vanilla extract and whip using a handheld mixer or large balloon whisk until soft peaks form. Store leftover cream in a bowl, tightly covered, for up to 1 day. Lightly whip before using.*

SERVES 1

BACON WHIPPED CREAM

2 cups (240 ml)) very cold Bacon Heavy Cream (page 349)

3 tablespoons confectioners' sugar

1 teaspoon pure vanilla extract

In the bowl of a stand mixer or a large bowl, combine the cream, sugar, and vanilla and whip, either with the whip attachment or a large balloon whisk, until soft peaks form.

The whipped cream can be made up to 4 hours in advance. Store in an airtight container in the refrigerator before serving. Lightly whip before using.

MAKES 1 QUART

MAPLE-BACON PECAN PIE
with Bacon-Scented Crust

I THINK WE HAVE ALREADY ESTABLISHED THE AFFINITY THAT bacon, maple syrup, and bourbon have for each other and how bacon fat can create a piecrust as flaky as lard can, but with a slightly smoky flavor. The proof is in the pudding—or in this case, the pie. A new holiday favorite, for sure. Serve with sweetened whipped cream (see Note, page 353) or vanilla bean ice cream, if you're feeling especially decadent.

FOR THE CRUST

2½ cups (315 g) all-purpose flour

2 teaspoons granulated sugar

4 ounces (115 g) very cold rendered bacon fat (see page 50), cut into pieces

½ cup (115 g) cold unsalted butter, cut into tablespoons, plus more for greasing

¼ to ½ cup (60 to 120 ml) ice-cold water

FOR THE FILLING

3 large eggs

1 cup (220 g) packed light brown sugar

½ cup (100 g) granulated sugar

½ cup (120 ml) maple syrup, Grade B

½ cup (115 g) unsalted butter, melted

3 tablespoons bacon-infused bourbon (page 100) or regular bourbon

1 teaspoon pure vanilla extract

⅛ teaspoon fine sea salt

1½ cups (180 g) coarsely chopped pecans

5 thin slices bacon, cooked until crisp (see page 44) and crumbled

Make the crust: Combine the flour and sugar in the bowl of a food processor fitted with a metal blade and pulse to combine, two or three 1-second pulses. Scatter the bacon fat and butter over the flour and pulse until the mixture resembles cornmeal mixed with pieces of fat no larger than a pea.

Drizzle in 3 tablespoons of the ice-cold water. Pulse twice. Check to see if the dough is holding together by squeezing a bit in your hand. If it holds together, it's ready. If it breaks apart very easily, add 1 tablespoon of the remaining water, pulse just to combine, and test the dough again. Pulse in more liquid as needed.

Turn the dough out onto a clean work surface. Divide into two equal pieces, and place on two separate sheets of plastic wrap. Flatten and form two disks. Wrap and refrigerate for at least 1 hour, or up to 3 days.

Coat a 9-inch (23-cm) pie plate with nonstick baking spray or brush with softened butter. Dust a work surface and rolling pin liberally with flour. Unwrap one disk of dough and place it on the flour. Working from the middle of the dough outward, roll the dough into a 12- to 13-inch (30. 5- to 33-cm) round.

Lay your rolling pin on one edge of the dough round and gently roll the dough up around the rolling pin. Set the rolling pin gently on the edge of the pie plate and unroll the dough carefully into the pan, easing it into the corners and up the sides of the pan and tucking it in well to form the crust. Trim all but 1 to 2 inches (2. 5 to 5 cm) of the dough from around the edge. Crimp the edges. Refrigerate uncovered for at least 30 minutes, or up to 24 hours.

Make the filling: Preheat the oven to 350°F (175°C). In a medium bowl, whisk together the eggs, brown and granulated sugars, maple syrup, butter, bourbon, vanilla, and salt until smooth. Stir in the pecans and bacon and pour the mixture into the prepared piecrust.

Bake until the filling is set but jiggles slightly in the center when gently shaken, 50 to 60 minutes.

Let the pie cool completely, at least 2 hours. Slice and serve.

MAKES 1 (9-INCH/23-CM) PIE; SERVES 6 TO 8

PEANUT BUTTER AND BACON BARS

THIS IS PRETTY MUCH TWO OF AMERICA'S FAVORITE INGREDIENTS and flavors combined to make one creamy, nutty, buttery, salty bar that your friends will go hog wild over. Note: Make sure you have room in your freezer before beginning; you'll need to use it several times during the making of this bar.

FOR THE DOUGH

1¼ cups (280 g) unsalted butter, at room temperature

¼ cup (60 ml) rendered bacon fat (see page 50), at room temperature

¾ cup (150 g) sugar

1½ teaspoons pure vanilla extract

3 cups (375 g) all-purpose flour

FOR THE FILLING

4 tablespoons (55 g) unsalted butter

1 cup (200 g) sugar

½ cup (120 ml) evaporated milk or heavy cream

1 cup (240 ml) smooth peanut butter

1 (7½-ounce/213-g) tub marshmallow cream

1 teaspoon pure vanilla extract

1 (13.4-ounce/380-g) can dulce de leche

2 cups (300 g) salted peanuts

1 cup (110 g) Bacon Bits (page 49)

2 cups (350 g) semisweet chocolate chips

Preheat the oven to 350°F (175°C). Line a 9 by 13-inch (23 by 33-cm) metal or glass baking pan with parchment paper, leaving an overhang on the two long sides. Spray the parchment and sides of the pan lightly with nonstick spray.

Make the dough: Combine the butter, bacon fat, and sugar in the bowl of a stand mixer fitted with the paddle attachment and beat on high until light and fluffy, about 3 minutes. Add the vanilla and beat for 10 seconds.

Reduce the mixer speed to low and gradually add the flour, mixing until just incorporated. Press or spread the mixture into the bottom of the prepared pan. Bake until lightly golden brown, 25 to

(continued)

30 minutes. Remove from the oven and let cool on a wire rack for 15 minutes while you prepare the filling.

Make the filling: Put the butter in a medium saucepan over high heat and cook until melted. Whisk in the sugar and evaporated milk and bring to a boil over medium-high heat. Continue to boil, whisking occasionally, for 5 minutes. Remove from the heat and whisk in ¼ cup (60 ml) of the peanut butter, the marshmallow cream, and the vanilla until smooth. Pour the mixture evenly over the prepared crust, transfer to the freezer, and chill until firm and cold, about 15 minutes.

Meanwhile, put the dulce de leche in another medium saucepan over low heat and cook until it begins to melt. Stir in the peanuts and cook for 2 minutes. Remove from the heat and fold in the bacon bits. Remove the pan from the freezer and pour the dulce de leche over the peanut butter layer. Return to the freezer until firm and cold, about 15 minutes.

While the dulce de leche layer is setting, pour 1 inch (2.5 cm) of water into a medium saucepan or pot and bring to a simmer over low heat. Place a heat-safe bowl on top of the pot so that the bottom of the bowl is not touching the water.

Add the chocolate to the bowl and stir occasionally with a spatula until smooth and melted. Whisk in the remaining ¾ cup (180 ml) peanut butter until smooth. Remove the pan from the freezer again and pour the chocolate mixture evenly over the top. Return to the freezer until chilled, about 20 minutes.

Cut into bars while cold and refrigerate any leftovers, tightly sealed in a container, for up to 3 days.

MAKES 16 SMALL OR 12 LARGE

BOURBON CANDIED BACON

I INCLUDED THIS IN THE DESSERT CHAPTER, BUT IT COULD EASILY find a home with the brunch or appetizer recipes. It's a sweet way to end a meal. Pair it with a cocktail or serve alongside waffles and eggs for breakfast.

12 thick slices bacon

3 tablespoons bacon-infused bourbon (page 100) or plain bourbon

¼ cup (55 g) packed light brown sugar

Preheat the oven to 400°F (205°C). Line a rimmed sheet pan with a Silpat or aluminum foil.

Lay the bacon strips on the prepared sheet pan. Brush each slice of bacon with bourbon and sprinkle with brown sugar on both sides. Bake for 13 to 15 minutes, until the bacon starts to caramelize and becomes crispy. Remove from the oven and let cool completely. Coarsely chop to use in brittle or cookies (or leave in strips to eat on its own). The bacon can be prepared up to 3 days ahead, stored between sheets of waxed paper in a zip-top bag in the refrigerator. Let stand at room temperature for 30 minutes before serving.

MAKES 12

BACON ICE CREAM COOKIE SANDWICH

DEFINITELY NOT THE SAME ICE CREAM SANDWICH YOU BOUGHT from the man in the musical truck when you were a kid. Folding crispy bacon bits into ice cream is one of the best examples of a savory sweet dessert—a more grown-up flavor, if you will. The bacon-bit ice cream is a delicious treat on its own, but why not take it a step further and serve it squished between two golden brown, buttery chocolate chip cookies studded with more bacon and then roll it in candied pecans and . . . you guessed it: more bacon.

2 quarts (2 L) premium-brand vanilla ice cream

2 cups (220 g) Bacon Bits (page 49)

1 cup (100 g) Fried Spiced Candied Pecans (page 294)

12 Candied Bacon Chocolate Chip Cookies (page 342)

Take the ice cream out of the freezer and let it sit on the counter to soften for 10 minutes. Transfer to a bowl and fold in half of the bacon bits.

Line a 9 by 13-inch (23 by 33-cm) pan with parchment paper, allowing the paper to hang over the sides. Press the mixed ice cream into the pan and smooth the top. Freeze until solid again, at least 1 hour.

In a food processor, pulse the pecans until crumbled. Add the remaining bacon bits and pulse once to incorporate. Transfer the mixture to a rimmed plate and set aside.

Remove the ice cream from the freezer and, using a circle cutter the size of your cookies, press out 6 disks of ice cream and put on top of 6 of the cookies. Alternatively, you can let the ice cream soften slightly and use a #8 ice cream scoop. Top with the remaining cookies and press down gently.

Roll the sides of each ice cream sandwich in the pecan-bacon mixture to fully coat. Freeze on a parchment-lined baking sheet again until firm, about 30 minutes, then serve immediately, or wrap each sandwich individually in waxed paper or parchment paper and keep in the freezer for up to 3 days.

MAKES 6

ACKNOWLEDGMENTS

This book, quite sincerely, would not have been possible without substantial help from many people to whom I am eternally grateful.

To my collaborator, Stephanie Banyas, who saw a book before anyone else could. She took random, often wildly inappropriate ideas with recipes in grams and wove a golden web, crafting a book far beyond anything I could have imagined.

To my photographer, Carol Lee, who surprises me every day with another talent she seemingly picked up on the way to work. I am in awe of her and grateful for her belief in the BarBacon project and her desire to continue on the journey.

To our publisher, Abrams, who literally made this book possible.

To Isobella Jade, whose encouragement and help pushed me to believe writing a cookbook would be every bit worth the heartache . . . the minute it was over.

To my parents, whose love and guidance are with me in whatever I pursue. And, finally, to my wife and kids, who continue to push me to follow my passion and to fulfill my dreams. They are and will forever be my greatest accomplishments.

INDEX

Chipotle-Lime Mayonnaise, 74, 133, 233

Horseradish Bacon Mayonnaise, 73

Maple Bacon Mayonnaise, 73–74

meatballs, *124*, 125

meat doneness, 206

Midnight in Molasses, 103

milkshake, *352*, 353

muffins, 307, 315

mushrooms, 93, 265

mustard

Bacon and Mustard Sausage, 60, *61*

Honey Mustard Glaze, 46, 86

Honey Mustard-Glazed Bacon, 46, 55, 62

White Wine Grainy Mustard Sauce, 81, 247

N

Nodine's Smokehouse, 52–53

Nueske's, 53

Nuoc Cham, 87, 217

Nuoc Mam Cham, 87, 133, 145

nuts

Almond-Bacon Paste, 319

Almond Breakfast Buns, 319, *320–21*, 322

Bacon Chestnut Soup, 176, *177*

Bacon-Hazelnut Hot Chocolate, 348–51, *351*

Bacon-Pecan Shortbread Crust, 346–47, *347*

Bourbon-Bacon Peanut Brittle, 332, *333*

Fried Spiced Candied Pecans, 294, *295*, 361

Hazelnut Crust, 335

Maple-Bacon Nuts, 118

Maple-Bacon Pecan Pie, 354–55

Peanut Butter and Bacon Bars, 356, *357*, 358

Spicy Candied Walnuts, 188, 293

O

Old Fashioned, 104, *105*

onions, *164*, 165

Open-Faced Chicken BLT, 222, *223*

oranges

Chocolate-Orange Sauce, 337–38

Orange Glaze, 319, 322

Rosemary-Orange Maple Syrup, 304, 306

oven-roasted bacon, 45

Oyster Po'Boy Taco, 199, 241

P

pancakes

Bacon Dutch Baby Pancakes, *308*, 309

Bourbon-Bacon-Oatmeal Pancakes, *302*, 303

Lemon Ricotta Pancakes, 324, *325*

pan-fried bacon, 44–45

pantry essentials, 13

panzanella, 184, *185*

pasta

macaroni and cheese, 258–59, *259*

Port Wine-Bacon Marinara for, 92, *124*, 125

Skillet Pasta Carbonara, *260*, 261

peaches, 83

Peameal Bacon, 40

Peanut Butter and Bacon Bars, 356, *357*, 358

pecan pie, 354–55

peppers. *See also* chipotle

Bacon-Cheddar-Jalapeño Sausage, 63

Cherry Pepper Sausage, 67

Fresno Chile Jam, 279

Habanero Margarita, 99, *110*, 111

Habanero Sauce, 89, 234

Habanero Syrup, 111

Pickled Jalapeño Chimichurri, 88, 240

Pickled Jalapeño Salad, 88, *284*, 285

Pickled Thai Chiles, 282

Pineapple-Jalapeño Coleslaw, 225, 272

Piperade, 122, 287

Thai Chile Honey, 88, 142

Perfect Lardons, 48

phosphates, 13

pickled vegetables

Banh Mi, 42, *216*, 217

Bread and Butter Pickles, 68, 212, 222, 276, *277*, 278

Hot Italian Pickles (Giardiniera), 281

Pickled Fennel, 38, 226, 283

Pickled Jalapeño Chimichurri, 88, 240

Pickled Jalapeño Salad, 88, *284*, 285

Pickled Thai Chiles, 282

Pickled Vegetables, 255

sauerkraut, 153, 221, 247

Pico De Gallo, 273, 312

Pineapple-Jalapeño Coleslaw, 225, 272

Piperade, 122, 287

poached eggs, 191

popcorn, *340*, 341

porchetta

Smoked Porchetta, 38–39, *39*

Smoked Porchetta and Chicken Pot Pie, 38, 262–63, *263*

Smoked Porchetta BLT, 226, *227*

pork belly, 15–19

Crispy Fried Bacon Pork Belly and Watermelon Salad, 179, 186, *187*

Pork Brine, 97

pork rinds, 138, *139*

Pork Schnitzel, *264*, 265

pork shanks, 246, *247*, 270

Pork Stock, 158

pork tenderloin, 203, 266, *267*, 270

Port Wine-Bacon Marinara, 92, *124*, 125

potatoes

Bacon and Potato Raclette, *128*, 129

Confited Potatoes, 129, *150*, 151, 153

German Potato Salad, 154

gnocchi, 248, *249*, 251

Loaded Potato Spring Rolls, 120–21, *121*

Loaded Tater Tots, 134, *135*

Rosemary Mashed Potatoes, 247, 292

Editor: Sarah Massey
Designer: Danielle Youngsmith
Production Manager: Kathleen Gaffney

Library of Congress Control Number: 2018936265

ISBN: 978-1-4197-3461-8
eISBN: 978-1-68335-505-2

Printed and bound in USA
10 9 8 7 6 5 4 3 2 1

Abrams books are available at special discounts when purchased in quantity for premiums
and promotions as well as fundraising or educational use. Special editions can also be created
to specification. For details, contact specialsales@abramsbooks.com or the address below.

Abrams® is a registered trademark of Harry N. Abrams, Inc.

ABRAMS The Art of Books
195 Broadway, New York, NY 10007
abramsbooks.com